VALUES AND VALUING

VALUES AND VALUING

*Speculations on the Ethical
Life of Persons*

GRAHAM NERLICH

CLARENDON PRESS · OXFORD
1989

Oxford University Press, Walton Street, Oxford OX2 6DP
Oxford New York Toronto
Delhi Bombay Calcutta Madras Karachi
Petaling Jaya Singapore Hong Kong Tokyo
Nairobi Dar es Salaam Cape Town
Melbourne Auckland
and associated companies in
Berlin Ibadan

Oxford is a trade mark of Oxford University Press

Published in the United States
by Oxford University Press, New York

British Library Cataloguing in Publication Data
Nerlich, Graham
Values and valuing: speculations on the ethical life
of persons.
1. Values. Philosophical perspectives
I. Title
121'.8
ISBN 0–19–824847–4

Cataloging in Publication Data
Data available

Set by Hope Services, Abingdon, Oxon.
Printed in Great Britain by
Biddles Ltd, Guildford & King's Lynn

For Susan

Acknowledgements

I HAVE benefited from the advice of a number of people at one or other stage of writing this book. They have made the product better for their careful criticisms, but of course are not responsible for the ways in which I have or have not taken up what they put to me. My warm thanks are due to the following: Donald Brook, John Chandler, Peter Forrest, Alan Gibbard, John Gill, Philip Pettit, Jack Smart, Stephen Stich, and Michael Stocker. I am indebted to anonymous referees and to several classes of students and, most especially among them, to James Beattie.

G.N.

Contents

1. Valuing in the Life of a Person   1

2. Of Science and Reason   35

3. On the State of Being a Person   61

4. Persons and their Desires   77

5. The Dialectic of Desire and Value   116

6. Emotions and Feelings   138

7. Authentic and Objective Values   166

8. The Meaning and the Goodness of Life   189

References   207

Index   213

1
Valuing in the Life of a Person

1.1 Introduction and aims

1.1.1 A good way of understanding values is to naturalize them. One portrays the good life as that in which human nature flourishes; this takes more than a leaf from the splendid book of Aristotle (ed. 1941). It prompts one to look for the core ideas of ethics in the good life and in *leading* that life—in pursuing value through excellence and virtue in those more or less global projects in which a person cultivates her humanity and aims to make it flourish.

1.1.2 The commoner ideas of morals—duties, rights, permissions, obligations, guilt—barely get a ride on our trip, and then only in the back seat. What follows is mainly concerned with explicating the idea of valuing, something that people do which is connected with, but not the same as, their desiring. To say that someone values something and that it is a value for him or for his culture is not to value it oneself. People's values can damn them; we often speak of the poverty or shabbiness, or worse, of the values of people we know. That sense of valuing and having values is what I try to shed light on in the first six chapters. Only in the last two is an attempt made to explain what it is for values to be correct. Even that leaves us far short of an account of morals.

1.1.3 Naturalizing value means learning about the aspirations and challenges proper to a human life by seeing what people are, and are by nature. Of course, people are far from what they ought to be, so that finding what they are *by nature* must come to more than mere report on how they just happen to turn out. Presumably, the 'more' it comes to must be something normative—but modestly, perhaps, as when we say that a human face ought to have a nose. It is natural for humans to live socially, to learn a conceptually articulate language and begin self-consciously to excel what they unselfconsciously are. That is how a human being ought (in a modest sense) to be. My naturalizing of values does not try to reduce ethical ideas to causal ones. I assume now, but argue lightly later, that pursuit of virtue and excellence comes to more than the unfolding of a life whose profile is determined by a nature, though it might express it.

1.1.4 Culture, like language, is a natural ambience for human life, and what we think of as distinctively human is not achieved outside it. So much is obvious, but to characterize more narrowly what language and culture are and what they do to human life will give us both the compass and the climbing-ropes with which to grope a way. The idiosyncrasies of cultures must find some place in a scheme which does not debilitate the objectivity of value. Nevertheless, I do not use culture as an analytic, systematic idea. The identity and individuation of cultures will not concern us, for a person always aims to transcend a local culture which he understands himself as within. A person's culture is, simply but roughly, the aggregate of all those social influences upon him or her which he or she can be expected to have some access to and some power to describe. I argue later that it is the aggregate of ways in which someone changes her human nature in the forging of a personal character and the pursuing of values. But it will not matter if the idea is understood rather naïvely for the moment.

1.1.5 The core of what I have to say about human nature and its flourishing in the moral life can be summed up in one sentence: it is the nature of humans to become persons. The idea of a person is not the idea of a nature, or of a state of being a person, but is in part the idea of an ideal or a task, something towards which we naturally aspire, all of us with some success, though never complete. These aspirations are something for which our human natures equip us, but nature alone cannot guarantee our success. To be a person, in the most minimal sense, is just to be in a natural-cultural *state*. But being in the state means *being in touch* with the ideals and aspirations, with the task. The idea of being in touch can be helpful, but needs to be more precise. Someone is in the state of being a person who is, to some not quite trivial degree, a rational thinker, who communicates with other persons, who is both conscious and, more importantly, self-conscious. Anyone in that state will under-stand and even take some part in (be in touch with) evaluating and transforming himself—excelling what he presently is. These are the tasks of being a person. By means of this, he is to some degree a free, deliberating agent. These last qualities are not natural ones, but cultural, social ones. The nature of human beings, then, is to become cultured, and cultured in certain ways, towards certain styles and enterprises of life. It is these styles of life, rather than bare life itself, which are the basis of ethical values. I hope to explain how.

1.1.6 I follow a familiar path in claiming that not every human is a person and, perhaps, not every person a human. Though each embryo and foetus is a being, hence a human being, it is not (yet) a person, so not (yet) a full member of the moral family. Similarly, humans in irreversible coma or the darker recesses of idiocy are not persons, though they may once have been persons. Conversely, alien persons are possible—from other galaxies, for instance. Non-human persons are fantasies—so far—but useful ones. I shall often use the pronoun 'it' for persons to remind us that the idea of a person, as these fantasies show, is neither speciesist, racist, nor sexist. In law, some persons are not human beings, though they are not aliens either. Any entity competent to acquire rights and duties is a person. Corporations may be persons. So may states. The persons I want to consider are all individual subjects of experience, which I assume corporations cannot be. I will not try to fit non-individuals into the theory I am about to advance, nor consider why it might or might not be relevant to do so. Though I mention the possibility of non-human persons in passing, from time to time, I have no further systematic reflections to offer about them.

1.1.7 Human nature goes unfulfilled unless humans become persons in at least one basic dimension, the dimension of language-learning. More generally, to be a person is a human need. There is no matching need in persons to be human. Alien persons need not be. But, I shall argue, no person can be just a person; indeed, the idea is hardly intelligible. There can be no personal life without a form of perception and forms of desire, though these need not be the forms of human vision, human pain, or human passion. So there are general needs for persons which can be met only in specific, concrete, causally effective ways which are contingent relative to what persons are. This fact makes for conflicts in personal life—which turns out to be, centrally, the life of reflective, including self-reflective, valuing. The conflicts can usefully be seen as dialectical ones (1.4). To be a person, a being has to alienate many of the concrete, person-contingent features of the particular form of embodiment without which it can have no life. Yet it must often turn out that personal life cannot be furthered at all without fully exploring its natural perceptual and passional powers. It will not seldom be the case that it must return to and regain, in some changed form, the very features of its embodiment which it alienated before. The cyclic struggle of estrangement, differentiation, and recapture is the engine of much of the culture in which human persons live. I develop this idea of a dialectic in personal life both in broadly structural terms and in the more concrete examples; out of such conflicts and resolutions the good life emerges as a flourishing, as the flowering of a self-chosen nature in cultural projects.

1.1.8 A main aim in this work is to fill a gap in existing moral theories. We can see the gap in Rawls (1971) theory of justice. There is a gap, too, in Utilitarianism; it makes no odds whether we consider the hedonistic or preferential versions. It is much the same gap in each case: the content of desire lacks ethical relevance. Thus, no content can make one desire more *reasonable* than another, nor link any of them more closely to the good life (Rawls 1980; Hare 1963: ch. 10). The focus on pleasure and satisfaction in Hedonistic Utilitarianism arises from seeing them as the only factors, in the field of human doings, which relate action to non-moral good. Only pleasure or satisfaction seem able to give us an entry for every action in the calculus of utility while placing no requirement at all on the content of the desires which power action. Preference-utility, more clearly still, despairs of singling out some desires as morally relevant in content. All preferences get an entry at some value in the calculus and, at least for the most part, only those features which neglect content, such as intensity of desire, earn a weighting in value. The gap is there because these theories defer to Hume's claim that reason is, and ought to be, only the slave of the passions. A different orientation in this book might link it to Joseph Butler's view of human nature as essentially turned towards good rather than evil (Butler 1895). Butler's injunction to follow nature, however, looks either empty or pernicious, as Mill complained. The present work aims to show that valuing is something that arises in human populations that achieve a normal environmental development; further, that we can find constraints which make valuing authentic and objective and thus yield values which are correct. Of course, it would still be logically open to someone to say that we *ought* to transcend these values, whatever they are. But if our naturalistic account of valuing is adequate, then such an appeal to duty will lack any alternative ground which is itself plausible and adequate. That is because an adequate theory along the lines I envisage will already encompass all we naturally desire and all that the fuller development of culture and society inclines us towards.

1.1.9 I use the idea of a person to build some structure into desires that tie them to the good life; that is, to the global pursuit of virtue and excellence. But these structures tell us about content, too: for instance, sexual desire naturally leads to a personal drama with a characteristic plot which catches it up into one or another ethical theme (5.1–4). Though sexual desire, at bottom, is utterly contingent to personhood, the structure of values and virtues makes dialectical theatre of it for which a philosopher is a proper audience and critic. Perhaps an insight into the concrete dialectic to which this so readily attaches itself might shed light on how to fill the gap in our best theories of oughts (1.1.8) without competing with them. To fill the gap successfully would be to produce a theory of the deepest human interest, for it would tell us about what can make human life meaningful and rewarding. What follows is spade-work aimed at this.

1.1.10 No one can be a person unless he recognizes others as persons and applies to them the properties in the stratum of person-concepts. He also recognizes that these others will, in turn, recognize him as rational (or as a target for rational appraisal). Persons use *social* concepts (Van de Vate 1971)—those which you can instantiate only if you know how to apply them to others. Having reciprocal personal attitudes lies deep in the state of being a person.

1.1.11 It is an old belief that persons are conscious of themselves. This has always meant more than the ability to see that it is I who now hold the baby, or that the reflection in the mirror is mine. I must have the 'reciprocal attitude' to myself. I need higher-order self-attitudes; my beliefs, desires, and emotions will sometimes have other beliefs, desires, or emotions of mine as their objects. But more is meant than that, too. I must be a critical appraiser of myself, a reflective self-evaluator. It is normative self-attitudes that pick persons out, or so I shall argue. It is only when higher-order attitudes are so well developed that a thing or its action is an object of *value* for itself that it is properly a person. This means that the only kinds of persons we know of are human kinds, but it still leaves personhood as a moral, not a biological, concept.

1.1.12 'Person' is a sortal term—persons are objects of some sort. But the properties which pick out persons among objects are not further sortal terms in the way in which sortal properties (quadruped, feline-shaped) help to pick out cats among animals. That feature allows that a wide range of things other than humans might be candidates for being persons, and it allows that some humans might not be persons. Many of these defining properties admit of degrees, suggesting that some things count as persons in a more fully developed way than others. To be in the *state* of being a person (I shall say) is to be at a low point on a continuum which begins to have deeper interest only some way up. The interest lies in the ideals and the tasks of making oneself a person. I shall argue that this deeper interest begins where persons become things that pursue virtues, and so become objects of value in that they *make* values. They recognize, pursue, and create them in ways yet to be described. So those minimum conditions are not enough for all I mean by a person.

1.2 A cultured life is natural

1.2.1 The massive, complex, human brain is the most striking anatomical fact about a normal human being. It is clear what this fits humans for—which survival-trait the complex brain underwrites: it is the capacity for language, for conceptual thought, for communication in a group whose members recognize each other as fellow communicators, the capacity for consciousness, including self-consciousness—in short, for being persons in the basic sense, the state of personhood. Thus, a language-community is a normal human environment in a very biological sense. The claim that it is the nature of humans to be persons can be defended if we can find at least the rudiments of the state of personhood in what is required for language use (Chapter 3). To say that humans are persons is like the claim that gibbons are arboreal. It ascribes to the animal a feature which it has in virtue of its normal context. Gibbons born captive may never climb a tree and mutant offspring may never be able to. Yet gibbons are tree-dwellers by nature, and that is no less because most gibbons do live in trees than because that is what they are fitted for by their anatomy. So it is on anatomical, genetic, and evolutionary grounds that we find culture as our normal context and, correlatively, that humans are naturally persons.

1.2.2 This might suggest a familiar conclusion that humans are thinking animals by nature and that the natural study is a *mental* one, tying our study to a general philosophy of mind. But it is rather the norms and institutions of *cultural* practices (of which the use of language is a central one) in which the ideology we want is grounded. To claim that culture and language are natural opens a route for explanations of action which skirt most of the philosophical problems current in cognitive studies. So the study will somehow be a cultural one. Of course it is a central observation on human nature that man is a thinking animal. But other animals think; for example, they process perceptual information in very sophisticated ways. They are curious, solve problems, and so on. But without language there are significant ways (which I won't yet try to define) in which they do not and cannot think. It is those deep qualitative differences, rather than any merely quantitative advantages we may have in processing information as animals do, that make us natural candidates for a moral life. What marks us off from other animals is not simply that we are brighter creatures with bigger brains, but that our native intelligence permits a culture and a language. Thus, the issues do not turn on questions of the metaphysics of mind.

1.2.3 We take to language as ducks take to water. Just so, we feel that human beings do not attain a fully human nature without articulate, structured thought, in which we make ourselves the objects of evaluative reflection. So appraisal of self, though cultured, is natural too. If self-appraisal is a part of linguistic competence, as I later argue it is, then the intuition that it is natural is right. Three arguments suggest, further, that in language we find a crucial point which links, just as much as it divides, nature and culture.

1.2.4 First, there is evidence of the great gap that separates human isolates—either feral children or those severely deprived of socio-linguistic contacts in early life, such as the deaf before the eighteenth century—from normal persons. Not many modern cases of this tragic sort are known to us, for rather obvious reasons. Our knowledge of many isolates is quite anecdotal, though Itard's study of the wild child Victor of Aveyron (Itard and Malson 1972) and Curtiss's study of the dreadfully deprived Genie (1977) are careful, methodical, and objective. Those who do not learn language early are condemned to a functional idiocy. Genetically endowed cerebral capacity is necessary, but by no means sufficient, for the profound gap between encultured humans and other animals. Whatever capacities for processing information people share with the remarkable skills of animals, it is in the articulated processes provided by language that the crucial difference lies. (Paul Churchland (1979) and Patricia Churchland (1980) offer opposing views.)

1.2.5 Secondly, no society of genetically normal humans has ever failed to be a community of communicators. Every actual society of people, if not too small or remote for survival, has its language, recognizes speakers and listeners reciprocally, explains what is said by justifying it, and is, however crudely, a society of persons. So humans do not simply happen to develop language: it is in their natures to develop it.

1.2.6 Thirdly, and less directly, thought can only rise to its paradigm instances by expressing itself through the medium of language. Structured conceptual thought needs the usages of a syntactically developed language, even though language gains its structure only as the product, the more or less dimly intended end, of intelligent linguistic activity. Further, if a thinker wants to reflect on what her natural, characteristic activity of articulate thinking is, she must make use of thought's product, language, to do so. Only in its product, language, can thought (can thinkers) find the conceptual tools to understand what articulate, syntactic thinking is. Only in some such degree of self-consciousness can thought become what it most characteristically is, and people take on what we think of as a fully developed human nature. It is in just such processes that they begin to forge as well as understand a nature for themselves as self-conscious animals. Language is not the door which lets out imprisoned thought, but the stuff thought is made of.

1.2.7 This brings us up against a later theme (1.6): that persons express their natures. Language could not have been begun as a deliberate cultural policy to forge a means of communication, since no such policy could be formulated, even inwardly, by individuals. Only an already full-blown language could provide the conceptual structures to articulate the policy. Language began, then, rather as a blind, natural venture within animal groups developing along with their cultures. Yet without acculturation and, especially, language-learning, human animals do not take on a central property of human nature; that is, having the capacity, in a strong sense, to think. So the thinking of persons, which is so natural to them, is not the simple deterministic unfolding of a genetic nature but rather an expression of it.

1.2.8 It would be a narrow view of the function of the human brain to see its role for personhood only in language. Language is just one, though a quite crucial, form of culture, and it is scarcely conceivable that language should develop save in the context of social structures which are recognizable as a culture. Just as language must surely be seen as developing within a culture, so we can scarcely imagine much development for culture unless through language. Most evolutionary growths suggest a kind of dialectic, as this does, not so much of opposition as of presupposition. A growing language presupposes a culture but a growing culture presupposes a language.

1.3   Self-consciousness

1.3.1 I now want to sketch a structure that might constitute the idea of a self-consciousness rich enough to yield an adequate idea of freedom and of evaluation of self. I start with a picture of self-awareness in which I freely draw upon phenomenological sources.

1.3.2 First, states of consciousness have both an object and a subject. Thus states of consciousness are always (propositional) attitudes: I believe that the earth is round, fear that the ghost will come again, intend to take a photograph, and so on. Further, anyone in a state of consciousness is implicitly aware that the subject is distinct from the object: what believes that the earth is round is not that proposition, nor is it the event of judging or entertaining the proposition. Secondly, any state, event, or process of consciousness may be the object of another state (etc.) of consciousness: I may wonder why I believe that the earth is round, be anxious whether it is neurotic to wonder why I believe that, and so on. Thus there are higher-order emotions and desires about beliefs, emotions, and desires; there are also higher-order beliefs about them. (Such desires and emotions come under the microscope later.) These are states in which one is conscious of oneself as a believer, desirer, and so on.

1.3.3 Thirdly, the subject of consciousness can be characterized only by the propositional attitudes that it has—hence, always relative to the contents of its consciousness. (See Hume (ed. 1888) on the elusiveness to introspection of the self; see also Ryle (1949).) Sartre (1956: 21–45) expresses this principle somewhat mysteriously by saying that we can characterize the subject of consciousness only negatively: as that which *is not* the object in a state of consciousness. That looks plainly false: I can be either amused or fearful at the thought that there is a hippo in the drawing room. The object is the same, the consciousness is not. There is indeed a problem how to describe, or, perhaps, to analyse the properties of consciousness apart from specifying its contents (which I look at later in discussing psychic feelings and Sartre's (1962) theory of emotion (6.2; 6.4)).

1.3.4 Fourthly, there is a sense in which the subject may often be weakly conscious of its own conscious states and acts in those states and acts themselves. This weak sense is to be distinguished from the higher-order consciousness we spoke of in stating the second principle. In this weak sense, even though I have no specific thought about these thoughts, wants, and feelings, I could have attended to them. But I do not make them the objects of another thought or feeling. So there is explicit and implicit consciousness of self. In explicit self-consciousness I take an attitude towards some state or process of my conscious life; but in implicit self-consciousness, though I am not ignorant of what state of consciousness I am in, I do not attend to it or make it the object of another event or process of consciousness.

1.3.5 If we suppose that our explicit knowledge of ourselves as we are at some particular time is complete at that time, we may find ourselves caught in paradoxes of self-reference (Popper 1950; MacKay 1960). Perhaps if higher-order feedback on one's total mental state modified the state continuously, then one could approach a self-predictable state in the limit (Goldman 1970: ch. 6; Simon 1957). But there is little to suggest that the actual feedback processes by means of which we adjust our decisions are anything but discrete. Perfect self-knowledge in terms of discrete phrasable beliefs which become objects of one's explicit reflection does look impossible on logical grounds.

1.3.6 Consider an example. A futuristic neurophysiological and computer scientist knows the general laws that determine brain behaviour and she has a super-computer programmed not only with these laws, but also with the precise neuronal structures of someone—Cantankerous. Cantankerous spends a day in our super-scientist's lab under the guise of having his sensory inputs monitored (all of which are, indeed, transmitted to the computer, together with all the subject's relevant physiological states). The computer is set to foretell Cantankerous's behaviour and outputs its predictions a few seconds before he acts.

1.3.7 We can suppose that the predictions work. That is entailed by deterministic assumptions about Cantankerous. Now the scientist decides to raise the game a little by getting the computer to flash its predictions on an electronic print-out board clearly visible to the subject. Unbeknownst to her, but not, of course, to the computer, Cantankerous is counter-suggestible. He has a tiny causal neurosis: he never does what it is suggested to him that he will do. So what will happen? Cantankerous will begin to falsify the predictions made about him. This will not take the computer by surprise, nor would it stagger our scientist, if she knew of the neurosis. The computer can always tell what he will do, for it can easily take into account, in another prediction that it makes, what he will do when shown the public prediction. But it cannot predict what Cantankerous will do in a prediction which he will see. This is no limitation on determinism. It is something about self-reference and prediction. The machine cannot give a well-grounded prediction of what Cantankerous will do when he sees *that* prediction.

1.3.8 The role of Cantankerous's neurosis is simply to make plain the following fact. Not even determinism can guarantee such a prediction the power to take account of the consequences of its own intrusion among the conditions of some causal system, though another prediction may certainly do so. Suppose, now, someone who has an analogue of the predicting computer in his own cortex. His self-knowledge will be remarkably complete. He always knows exactly what he would have done had he not taken that knowledge into predictive account. Nevertheless, unless his resources are infinite, there always will be some knowledge which he does not take into predictive account. He will stop the hierarchy of prediction somewhere. But however (finitely) often and in however (finitely) hierarchical a way he may predict what he will do, given an explicit prediction of what he would do, we may suppose that, theoretically, there is still a further process of deliberation open to him before he acts. He certainly *can* always think again in the light of the fact that he has predicted what he will do, and we need not suppose him to be as fractious as Cantankerous in order to envisage that he might change his mind. These facts about hierarchical acts of self-prediction extend, plainly enough, to other higher-order acts of self-evaluation. They show our behaviour to be always open, in principle, to modification by further self-appraisal.

1.3.9 This has two important consequences for our idea of ourselves as free agents. First, it suggests that we never decide on grounds all of which we explicitly understand, though this is not to say that we are ignorant of them. This ties in with the idea of action as expressing a nature, which is the topic of 1.6. It also gives us a natural point of entry for a discussion of fundamental decisions about values. Sartre pictures radical value-dilemmas as resolvable only by an act of decision which is not merely imperfectly scrutinized, but ultimately arbitrary. More plausibly, radical choices spring from commitments to values which lie too deep to articulate in statable principles (4.6; and Taylor 1977). Whether these are the values of ethics or reason, I argue that it is the practical life of pursuing the good or truth which proves the basis of value. The practice of this life is not to be exhausted in doctrine and principle, though these may guide it. (See 3.4.)

1.3.10 Second, the idea shows us the way out of one nightmare of Hard Determinism—that we find ourselves in the predicament whereby someone tells us what we are about to do and we find ourselves helpless to do other than act this prediction out in all its detail. But quite clearly determinism, even in its strongest defensible form, implies nothing of the sort. To be sure, someone might find himself in that nightmarish predicament, but only if he were in a quite particular, crippling causal state. He would certainly be unfree, but his compulsion would not be a consequence of mere determinism, but of the determinism of some quite rare and special pathology.

1.3.11 Clearly, such an idea concerns not just our understanding of freedom in terms of self-knowledge, self-possession, and self-direction (more will be made of all this when we deal with higher-order desire): it has a great deal to do with the idea of freedom as self-expression, self-construction, and self-realization. Every action is the issuing in concrete, material form of some element of what we are, in a way that we ourselves did not predict, and do not fully understand, however readily others may predict it and however clear and unsurprised about it we ourselves may be after the event. So expressivism, in this perhaps somewhat weakened form, appears as a basic structure of consciousness.

1.4   The dialectical concept of a person

1.4.1 The concepts of action and agency, like that of a person, spring from something like an attitude or commitment to a style of explanation or a mode of understanding. Just what this means is the topic of Chapter 2. The style of explanation has, somehow, to do with ideals of rationality. Persons somehow believe what they ought to believe and, in the view of some, desire what they ought to desire. Dennett calls this the intentional attitude and sees it as an essentially instrumentalist approach to explaining action by rationalizing it. In an interesting passage (Dennett 1978: 284–5) he suggests that moral evil arises from a failure in the target of the intentional stance to display the rationality which we need in order to make the style of explanation work. So, just where we want to place ethical weight on the idea of a person, it fails because the ideals it depends on fail at the same place.

1.4.2 This picture of moral failure is one of human lapses from personal ideals of rationality. But it is not plausible to find the root of evil in mere blunders, obstinacy, carelessness, or stupidity. Dennett might invoke the failure of second-order desires to take effect—wantonness—as another factor. That is no doubt correct, but Dennett has a problem here of which he seems unaware. A person's desires are supposed close to ideal—it wants what it ought to want, just as it believes and reasons as it ought to believe and reason. But, if its first-order desires are as they ought to be, how can we give a crucial role to second-order desires?—for these will naturally be desires to change the (already ideal) first-order desires. Can something be a person in respect of its higher-order wants only if it begins to fail to be a person in respect of its first-order wants? Desires call for much more careful discussion than Dennett ever gives them. How are they unlike beliefs? This is discussed in Chapter 4, but a preliminary skirmish will help to orientate us now.

1.4.3 Almost everyone, from time to time, holds some beliefs that are inconsistent with each other. They may be first-order beliefs. They may conflict across orders, as when I think I have no view on the diet of armadillos yet think that they are carnivores. To hold conflicting beliefs is to fall a little short of the ideals of personhood. To be *aware* of holding conflicting beliefs, without seriously doubting at least one of them, is to fall far short.

1.4.4 Desires are not like that. Almost everyone, from time to time, wants something inconsistent with something else he wants. He cannot satisfy both desires simultaneously. They may be first-order desires. They may conflict across orders, as when I want to have no fleshly lusts, but hunger after caramel gâteau. But I need not fall short of personhood when this occurs. To become aware of conflicting desires and to have each persist as vehemently as before is no sign of failing personhood. It signals, rather, a refractory world. Why this difference?

1.4.5 The *paradigm object* of desire is change. What cannot conceivably be changed can be enjoyed or regretted, but can involve no desire. I can desire the continuance of an existing state of affairs, so long as I see its possibly not so continuing. But these analytic points go only a step towards defining the paradigm object. In the paradigm case I want what is so to cease to be so. I want real change. This is, first, the common case, and were it not in fact the commonest, the concept of desire would hardly be as it is. This makes it a paradigm. So if persons are distinguished by their higher-order desires, they wish—in the commonest case—to *change* their lower-order desires. Thus the paradigm case of a person is one in whom desires *conflict*; it is of special concern to us that desires *of different orders* do. That desire is desire for change means that desires can hardly meet an ideal parallel to the ideal of harmony among beliefs. It means that persons will characteristically be beings in conflict, engaged in struggle, bent on evolving their own inner structures. Of course, the desires of persons might meet an ideal of consistency in respect of their highest-order desires. But it is not clear what this highest order is or, indeed, whether there is one. I shall propose a different ideal shortly. Here, I focus on conflict as the paradigm state of a being whose natural desires—those without which it fails to reach a fully human nature—include higher-order ones.

1.4.6 Higher-order desires can have no proper content of their own: they derive their content from the nature of their target desires. The idea of a person is, therefore, somewhat vacant or formal without recourse to the human or alien nature in which it is made concrete. We can see persons concretely as agents only in the context of desires which are *person-contingent* and which pose the set of problems which it is the life of persons to contend with. Having person-contingent desires must be the paradigm (standard, commonest) case. Now we can see the possibility of moral failure as the normal state of personal beings and actual failure as, presumably, not infrequent. Thus it looks like a serious misunderstanding to see moral lapses as failures to be a person. Of course, we can easily imagine a personal life where higher-order desires are always made effective without much struggle, and even a personal life where higher-order desires never conflict with lower-order ones. Persons could be forever self-satisfied. This is perfectly consistent. But it could hardly be these phenomena which lead us to frame the concept of a person as we do. Once we tie the concept to second-order desires, it implies a struggle in personal life and the possibility of failure. It implies a capacity for evil. But the concrete nature of evil will be contingent on what persons are in just the same way as first-order desires are.

1.4.7 I said a moment ago that the idea of a person is rather abstract. Even so, we can characterize the desires of persons—that is, the ones essential to being a person—in a general, if rather formal, way, and do it by presenting an ideal. A person wants to be free in its person-contingent nature. As we saw, a person cannot be free *of* its person-contingent nature on pain of the emptiness of its desires and its consequent failure to be an agent. In the paradigm case of personal life, a person must change its nature without losing it. Very roughly, a person is free *in* its nature if the reasons why it acts are acceptable to it; that is, if its behaviour-controlling beliefs are what they ought to be, and if the desires expressed in its actions accord with its higher-order desires—or with those it *would, on reflective self-evaluation*, formulate. Nevertheless, the content of these desires remains contingent on its nature.

1.4.8 A human being's first-order desires are, to a large extent, part of its nature (see also 4.3 and 7.1). A human has a character, a persisting pattern of first-order desires. We have just seen that human persons cannot simply rid themselves of human desires, for they would then cease to be agents at all. It is a contingent fact that the human character resists change, that it presents to higher-order desires a problem rather constant in its content. So personal life may take the form of monitoring first-order desires (but see 4.6); the stuff of virtuous, excellent life does not consist of discrete *acts*, but of a continuous *activity*, of shaping, balancing, pruning, or enlarging a human character. The ground-floor problems of value for persons do not lie in which acts to perform but in which life to lead; the basic practical question is not what one shall *do* but what one shall *be*. It calls for sustained observation, reflection, learning, and practice in the growth and refinement of moral skills and strategies. This idea plainly calls for closer inspection, but I want to draw from it now only the following point. It is a paradigm enterprise of persons to *alienate* something of their human nature in pursuit of personal values. That is one side of the dialectical conflict which characterizes personal life.

1.4.9 The rather abstract nature of second-order desires makes it plain that there must be another side. It must be in its human nature that a person finds its freedom. It must largely base its life on desires with a content independent of its being a person if it is to live a concrete life at all. Thus, a person must return to the first-order character it alienates: it must encounter it on a new level, absorb it in a sublimated form, catch it up, new-wrought, into the structure of its personal life. It must forge for itself a *second* nature. Thus, there is a tangible basis, in the formal conditions of personhood, for viewing persons as paradigmatically engaged in an internal dialectical conflict. Let us remind ourselves that a person's subjective values may be tawdry and debased, that they may arise out of imitation of tinsel models of gentility, fashion, toughness, or stoicism. But, whether for good or ill, reflective self-evaluation almost inevitably begins a process of alienation. One tries to put outside or beyond oneself something that one is or has been, so as to become other than it. Or one tries to incorporate, into what one is, something other than that familiar being. This is the path towards excellence—exelling oneself.

1.4.10 Alienation is of at least two kinds. The first-order desire may be repudiated entirely in that one rejects its goal, either because it is the singular desire to do this particular act here and now (or there and then), or because a person repudiates the disposition, the character-trait which constitutes the desire; altern-atively, the desire is tied not to a goal, an end-state, but to a style, a manner of acting, either in that the activity is 'an end in itself', as swimming (often) is, or because the 'end' (see 4.3) is the way the process unfolds, not its final state. For example, one must eat yet one does not gorge and wallow; rather, one eats at table with cutlery, napkins, and conversation in a mannered and sociable way.

1.4.11 Let us say that the set of principles under which desires are alienated and regained—the principles of the dialectic of desire—are (a large) part of culture. This is stipulation: it says what I mean (in large part) by a culture, and what it is to be a cultured person. So far, what makes appeal to culture seem apt is the role of the social concepts (1.1.10) which underlie these principles, and the role of language in providing the apparatus of self-evaluation. As I shall speak of it, a culture is something learned, but also something formed, transcended, and re-formed by persons in the culture; it is something social but also conceptual, so that the groups of non-human primates who have a quite complex social life will, nevertheless, not count as cultured, or only very marginally so; it will also constitute a (possibly quite rough) theory about the world and ourselves so that cultural practices will be seen roughly as (more or less successful) engineering techniques for the production of fulfilling lives. But it remains as natural for humans to produce a culture as for gibbons to thrive in trees.

1.4.12 Against this background, then, I offer a preliminary account of valuing and values. *Subjective* values are the products of a dialectical transformation of lower-order desires under the pressure of higher-order ones, an evolution which goes on in the light of (though not necessarily in conformity with) the meanings of actions, understood through the usages and institutions of a culture. The dialectical process is what makes us valuers and, as it turns out, objects of value. The process gives us our subjective values. But values proper are objective and not merely the objects of somebody's transformed desires. *Objective* values are related to a culture, understood as an engineering programme for producing persons. We may appraise a culture as a programme to develop personhood in humans (or aliens) in as many individuals, in as many dimensions of personhood, and to as high a degree of articulation and expression as is possible. The tasks of being a person are articulated and expressed in low and high culture (though 'high' should mean more articulated), both artistic and scientific, in leisures and pleasures, pursuits and games and interests. Success in the tasks finds expression in the harmonies of individual personalities, of social relations, of our products individually and collectively, the harmonies of persons with the world of nature and of their natures with their personalities.

1.4.13 Whether a culture does all this is no more a matter of subjective feeling or opinion than whether a fitness programme leads to stronger, more flexible, or more agile bodies. Whatever we like to think, capitalist cultures tend to corrupt social relationships, for example. Very different cultures may yield equally good results; some cultures will do the job far better than others. Some will be incommensurable with others because of the differing dimensions of personhood which they excel in developing. But there is neither subjectivism nor cultural relativism in this picture of values. Personhood is the measure of cultures, though the subjective feelings and opinions of people measure nothing objective at all.

1.4.14 The virtues of a person, then, are essentially its strengths and skills: it must be able to pursue and understand its own life as a person, having the capacities and insights to make objective values concrete, or at least pursuing its subjective values in the belief that they are objectively valuable. A more explicit account of this must wait for the development of other arguments.

1.5   Values and desires

1.5.1 I assume that the view of Hard Determinism—that it follows from determinism that no one ever acts freely—is mistaken. I take *formal freedom* as an established idea; that is, it is formally consistent with determinism that some person could have acted otherwise on some occasion of her acting. It is simply a matter of relating the possibility of acting otherwise to her abilities and opportunities, in the ordinary senses of these ideas, other causal conditions simply being irrelevant to our interest in the action. (See Austin 1962; Nowell-Smith 1966; Slote 1982; and Dennett 1978 and 1984.)

1.5.2 Formal freedom gives us a picture of freedom as doing what you please. Yet we all know, from cases of kleptomania and drug addiction, that this is not enough. In less pathological cases, also, someone may act from a desire, and so do what he wants, and yet feel the desire alien and hostile. Freedom, we feel, is something which persons but not animals have. Yet surely animals do what they want often enough. We can give substance to these shadowy thoughts if we can make clear a distinction between what we want and what we value. The kind of distinction needed might be clearer if we see it as falling between what we want and what we *most* want (where the latter does not refer to our strongest desires), or between what we want for now, and what we want in the long term or globally (Watson 1982*b*). So how may we begin to distinguish between desire and value?

1.5.3 Hume (see 4.1) makes any such distinction among desires difficult by the way he distinguishes them from beliefs, seeing reason as subordinate to passion in voluntary action. We shall find reason to query much of Hume's theory: reason and desire complement each other in voluntary action in a way not usefully characterized by metaphors of subservience. It is a main contention of Hume's, however, that in having a certain desire or preference one makes no mistake. It is not contrary to reason if I prefer the destruction of all I notice to the scratching of my finger. One can cry 'False' to my utterance of 'I want . . .', but that merely claims that it is false that I want it, not that the desire itself is false. Any account of desire and value must find room to accommodate that aspect of the logic of desire.

1.5.4 Hume's account of the role of the passions in action thus conflicts sharply with Plato's—as was undoubtedly Hume's intention. To see belief and desire as co-operative in action suggests that Plato's way of expressing the relation between reason and desire might be rescuable, after all. In Plato's myth, each of us is three people. The first is a brutish wanton; the second (arguably) a keen competitor, forever bent on winning (prizes, honours, notoriety, etc.); the last is the reasoner, the philosopher. He (she) has desires, quite certainly: for truth, for goodness, for scrupulous clarity and careful deliberation. It is the function of the last to curb the lusts of the first and keep the second out of the wrong games.

1.5.5 Among the things worth saving from this to set in more realistic contexts is that reason may provide us with motives for action by means of an understanding of what is good. We can interpret this as a matter of judgement about what is of value. This will be a judgement *on* desires; not, as Hume sought to persuade us must always be the case, a judgement *for the sake of* desires, as to ways in which the jostling community of them might best be satisfied. Thus, values will be not just desires to act in this or that way, but *reasons* for action.

1.5.6 The conflict between Hume and Plato can be resolved, I argue, by appeal to higher-order attitudes as basic to values; then we can also capture the idea that freedom comes to more than doing what one likes (or wants). Freedom that goes beyond formal freedom lies in a relationship between a person's system of values and his system of desires and motives. One is most clearly free when motivated to bring some state of affairs about only if one values it or, at least, does not disvalue it. This ideal of harmony between the two systems overlooks the fact that one can act freely in conflict—and, indeed, that one does so rather often. The conflict may be among first-order desires, in which case it will be the intransigence of nature or logic which confines freedom: one can't have one's cake and eat it, highly desirable though each state of affairs may be; one can't (let us say) both play chess in tonight's competition and go to Ashkenazy's one-night-only concert tonight; one can't protest against the government's actions and stay out of jail. It is an inflexible world. This picture of limitations of freedom as a disharmony among desires induced by a confining world is, of course, of the utmost significance. But one's full freedom—in a sense quite central to our interests—is perfectly compatible with disharmony among one's motivational and valuational systems. Indeed, it is mainly in the conflict between the systems, and in the continuing victories of our values, that our true autonomy lies. Conflict is not a peripheral or (causally) dispensable process in the acquiring and forging of anyone's personal freedom. Indeed, it is hardly intelligible without it. A structure of higher-order attitudes (assuming that this is the basis of values) makes no functional or evolutionary sense save in terms of conflict. We must not forget that the values of a free agent may be corrupt.

1.5.7 Let us say, then, that the idea of a system of values is part of the idea of a person. It will prove to be the *social* gift of reflective, evaluative self-consciousness which provides the conceptual foothold for higher-order desires and, at least to begin with, it will be largely the responses of others to oneself that provide the occasions for one's own processes of self-appraisal.

1.6 The expression of human nature

1.6.1 We may say that human nature is *expressed* in the cultural life of persons. There are three aspects of this: one concerns the kinds of causal processes needed to produce a human phenotype whose instances are rich enough in their behaviours (their actions) to count as normal animals; another lies in an analogy between the way in which articulate thought is related to competence in a language and the way that self-excelling is related to practice in an ambient culture; the third concerns the relation of determinism to free action. The first aspect was mentioned in 1.2.6 and 1.2.7. Culture, like language, is something learned. Without it there can be no rich expression of human nature, just as without language there can be no rich conceptual thought. Conceptual thought and human flourishing have only a cultural existence, therefore: they exist only where a learned culture and language sustain them. Yet language is not thought, but only a condition of it, just as culture is not nature, but only the condition necessary for its full expression. In the normal human agent, the impact of the environment is mediated by the cultural institutions of the group.

1.6.2 Second, no other animals known to us express their natures in their lives, as we express our thoughts, deliberately, in language: they merely manifest them. Expressing a nature is uniquely human. We construct our thoughts out of language, using its institutions and ideals (2.4, 3.3, 3.4), as well as its vocabulary and grammar, to make the inchoate concrete and articulate. Yet we do not find our thoughts already there in familiar, pre-existing sentences. Similarly, we use the traditions and ideals of the social world in which we find ourselves to construct a personality which becomes concrete and articulate by reference to our culture, but none finds the type of his character already there, so that he may avoid the perils and the labour of forging it. It is every person's task to construct a nature in the light of traditions and meanings in culture, which, nevertheless, do not provide a personality as a cultural gift (3.5).

1.6.3 It is in their nature for humans to *produce* their lives. Life, including communal life, is led, not merely suffered. The young Marx (ed. 1959) described people as producing their material life, which includes individual lives as well as the life of community, in planned constructions out of the material world, which is thus humanized, reflecting, for the producers, their natures in their products. So one's moral nature, at least, is a product, which is in the end a life one leads. Even so, what one's product really is and what one was in producing it becomes clear to us only after it is produced and its meaning understood in the light of where it fits in our culture (as later chapters spell out). Marx tells us that he got these thoughts from Hegel. As far as I can see into the grand and gloomy arches of the forest of Hegel's thought (Hegel, ed. 1977), he did indeed have such ideas, which he tried to work out on a vast, literally a cosmic, scale.

1.6.4 Now this means something *practical*, as both Aristotle and Hegel stressed in rather different ways. A fully developed human nature is acquired or forged in the process of a person producing its life. Aristotle tells us that to be virtuous is to acquire the habits of virtue, and this includes, no doubt, its skills, techniques, and know-how. The appeal to habit is not the happiest of thoughts, perhaps, though it stresses that virtues characteristically are acquired dispositions. But virtues, unlike some standard habits, are not hard to break, and gain no hold over our spontaneity of choice. They do not in general come from nowhere, but neither are they in general simply there waiting to be exercised or manifested before they have been made products. So not only is temperance, for example, not to be described, for moral purposes, as a causal disposition. It is not so encountered in practical life, as if it were a causal disposition which one has in the way that to grow weary is a disposition one has. At least, that is so for many of us, and for many virtues. A person must venture temperance, find it in the ventured experiment, and build on what she finds of herself in it. She must construct it out of the self-knowledge gained in temperate acts as a new disposition. This feature of self-construction, as one might call it, is not intended to apply only to virtues but to any aspect of character. An adequate idea of a human nature refers us to each individual's pursuit, construction, and discovery of his own nature in a social context; this reflects the existence of real practical problems in the leading of life and in describing what people are.

1.6.5 This last aspect of the idea of expression, together with the feature that intelligence is native to people, suggests that appraisal, especially self-appraisal, will be part of expression. Not, in Hegel's view, a necessarily very conscious appraisal, nor a verbally articulate one (6.7). In the passages (Hegel, ed. 1977: 111–19) which introduce the famous discussion of the dialectic of the master-and-slave relation, Hegel sees as a crucial step in the history of producing and realizing human nature that people began to risk their lives (sometimes, to lose them) in combat, not over food or territory, but over points of honour and the like. He does not see this as an articulate thought. But it is certainly a practical assertion that one is not confined by the limitations of animal life, for one transcends them to move towards peculiarly personal reasons and motives for action. But this does not require one to shed one's identity with an animal life. This identity is seen in the vividly perceived risk of death. Here dumb self-appraisal projected into practical action forges a habit, even a social norm, which becomes recognized and established. Thus, the man of honour literally forces from others in combat a recognition of his transcendence of the animal, while keeping his identity with it. He has thus constructed his not-purely-animal nature out of what he is, and he can go on to appraise it as his objective product which was made real and concrete in the combat and is still attested to by the chained bondsman concretely before him.

1.6.6 The analogy here between constructing one's character in all its natural richness and wrestling to put one's inchoate thought into words, discovering only then what it is one really wanted to say, needs no further elaboration.

1.6.7 Life as expression means that human nature is not a determining essence; or rather, the relevant description of human nature is not such a description. Formal freedom shows that worries about whether determinism is inconsistent with the possibility of acting otherwise are needless. But that remark falls short of much that concerns us in the question of our freedom of action. Sartre was at least right in seeing that it is simply self-delusion to suppose that we can understand ourselves as determined; our inexorable practical problems as agents are quite as often those of choice as they are of causal limitations on our actions. No deterministic theory can be cast in the stratum of concepts in which we understand ourselves as agents. If we learn another vocabulary in which we see ourselves as wholly causal creatures, it is not in such terms that we can face the problems of what to do in our lives. To suppose so will be to act in bad faith, to make excuses for ourselves that do not exculpate. The practical dilemmas of how to act and respond to action cannot be framed in a causal language. I shall discuss this further in the next section.

1.7   In defence of description

1.7.1 What I shall argue in this book is, in two ways, more descriptive than prescriptive. First, I am not directly concerned with 'oughts' and 'mays', but with what it is to be a person, to have values and, by making them, to be, oneself, valuable. Almost all the book is about valuing, whether or not the resulting values are proper, corrupt, or absurd. Problems of the nature of valuing lie deeper than those of duty, obligation, permission, or guilt; value questions are quite intimidating enough without accepting the burden of explaining normative judgements as well. Second, we need to defend and exploit an ideology that fits moral questions, and this might tempt us towards dualism. But dualism is fatal to a unified understanding of nature and values. It would be strange not to hope that my conclusions about valuing fit comfortably with the present world-view of science, without themselves constituting a scientific view. However, it would be folly to constrain what I wish to say about value by the requirement of making sure of this. No prescriptive ontology is adopted here.

1.7.2 A plain reason for not pushing one's ontology in the direction of dualism is that a dualist's strategy is to keep a certain group of ideas autonomous by obscuring what they apply to. The obscurity lies in positing entities which resist inclusion in a unified understanding of the mind. The resistance and the obscuring are one. It is a requirement on the aim of a unified understanding that one eschews dualism. Nevertheless, the autonomy of action-theoretic ideas, their independent life in our deepest understanding of where we fit in the world, which I defend in Chapters 2 and 3, lies at the heart of any sound theory of values. So one has to hang onto these ideas in some way that does not oblige us to forgo all hope of an integrated picture of human life.

1.7.3 What, then, is the relation of action-concepts to the concepts of, say, physics? The former may supervene on the latter. This, or something rather like it, seems plausible. If they do supervene, then it will be hard to stray into dualism, or even to commit oneself to it, by talking action-language at however subtle and intuitive a level. Even in the case of the subtlest novelist's analysis of motive and character the analysis will never imply an obscure realm of entities to which it applies.

1.7.4 It seems, too, that the weakest account which might base non-deterministic properties on deterministic ones relates them by supervenience. (See Kim 1978 and 1982.) A property P_i is *supervenient* on a property P_j if things (events etc.) may not differ in respect of P_i unless they also differ in respect of P_j. Trivially, any property supervenes on itself. A common example from physics is that the temperature of a gas is supervenient on the mechanical state of its constituent molecules. The temperature of a gas is its mean kinetic energy. Many different micro-dynamical states of the gas yield the same mean kinetic energy and so the same temperature. But the temperature of the gas (its mean kinetic energy) cannot change unless the micro-dynamical state of its molecules changes too.

1.7.5 However, this example suggests a rather stronger form of supervenience than is likely often to be the case. Since we count the mean kinetic energy of a gas as a dynamical state of it, we can identify temperature with a dynamical state, thus gaining a reduction of temperature. But mean kinetic energy is not a micro-dynamical state save by courtesy, rather as if we supposed women whose heights, weights, and so on were average to possess a property of being average. We cannot reduce temperature descriptions to manageable descriptions of micro-dynamical states which tell us the detail of molecular numbers, masses, and velocities. They are far too complex for us to traffic in them. In the general case, where we have no such conceptual device as averaging over states, we ought not to suppose that supervenience holds much hope of reduction in the sense of useful conceptual replacement. Let us look at another example in more (though incomplete) detail.

1.7.6 Consider a printer's block for newspaper photographs. It is, say, a collection of 10^6 dots, that is 10^3 rows of 10^3 dots. Each dot is either black or white. Each assignment of one of these colours to each of the 10^6 dots defines a *representation* (as I shall call it), only some of which constitute *pictures*; that is, only some of which can be interpreted as pictures of people, animals, cars, natural scenery, and the like. A basic dot description of a representation simply lists the ordered pairs of natural numbers (the first for the row, the second for the column) of dots that are black. Let us not make it a necessary condition of a dot array's being a picture of something that it be intended by anyone to represent anything, or that it be somehow causally related to the represented thing.

1.7.7 Now consider the property of being a picture of Igor Stravinsky at the age of 60. It need not be a photo of him nor drawn from life; it need not be meant to depict him. Some things will be enough like Stravinsky to count as recognizable, some will count as pictures of someone or something else, and a number of pictures will be either too vague or ambiguous in how like him they are to count. I ignore the last lot, and assume that pictures of Stravinsky's double are also pictures of Stravinsky (which allows me to evade some knotty details). Now, within the practices, conventions, and institutions of picturing, being a picture of Stravinsky is almost a supervenient property of the block and its markings. There can't be two pictures, one of Stravinsky and the other of someone or something else, unless they differ in the array of dots that are black. But many different arrangements of black dots can be alike in being pictures of Stravinsky. These similarities are constituted by various relations among the patterns of dots. No doubt there are similarities in arithmetical relation between reduced and blown-up versions of the same picture, expressed as sets of ordered pairs of numbers. For example, we would get a smaller picture if we divided each member of an ordered pair by 2, retaining only integral pairs; an enlargement if we multiplied each by 2, and a less 'grey' enlargement if we 'filled in' dots in a way easy enough to capture arithmetically. This is a bit like the way in which a wide range of micro-dynamical states of the molecules of various bodies of gas yield the same mean kinetic energy, that is, the same temperature. There is a rigid relation between a certain characterization of the basic, determining properties (dynamical state; enumeration of dots) and a more global one which, in turn, gives the supervenient description (a temperature; that it is a certain picture of Stravinsky). But there is no law-like connection between the description of the representation given by the set of ordered pairs and a pictorial description of it, once we allow representations of Stravinsky to vary as to angle of profile, inclusion of other parts of the body with the face, expression and attitude—frowning, smiling, standing, sitting, walking, or conducting. Yet these could be clearly pictures of Stravinsky and share an objective property of being so. Thus, members of the set of representations of Stravinsky share no learnable property at the level of dot distribution, even though the pictorial properties do indeed supervene. (Bigger-brained creatures might learn it, but we must despair.) Hence we may conclude that properties of pictures are not reducible to properties of dot distribution in representations.

1.7.8 To say that one property—more strictly, a predicate expressing a property—is not learnable from another is to draw attention to such facts as that an exact description of the block's basic properties (the structure of its dot array) would be useless in general in telling us what the block depicts. Given the wide range of newspaper photographs which readers can recognize as pictures of persons or ships or the sea, to say nothing of recognizing pictures of Bishop Desmond Tutu, the *Titanic*, or the sea from Port Campbell (in southern Australia), there clearly is only a disjunction of dot-array properties, both arbitrary and indeterminately long, that corresponds, by means of some true generalization, to any of these pictorial properties. No doubt there will be some true generalization, allowing only for vagueness, which describes what might count, under our criteria, as a picture of Stravinsky or of a man conducting an orchestra. But it is not one which we could hope to foresee, even if we felt we could foresee (as against readily recognize when we see it) what any picture of a man conducting would look like. Thus the generalization would not be learnable from the capacity to recognize the type of picture, the property would not be epistemically accessible or projectible, and the generalization would not provide a conceptual link between the two sorts of description.

1.7.9 This is because our picture properties are wide and conventional, not narrow and causal. They relate the block, by conventions of representation, to a world outside it, just as our action-descriptions relate agents to the language and culture which provide the framework of norms for rational explanation of what agents do in the world. It is because there is a world of people and things beyond the block that the dot arrays can have these objective representing properties. Nor are properties simple relations to things in the world outside. The block can picture a ship even without closely resembling any actual ship; it can picture a unicorn though there are no unicorns; it can picture Stravinsky even if he has an identical twin. The picture properties supervene not on basic properties intrinsic to the dotted block, but on various and complex basic relations between it and things beyond. These relations depend, too, on conventions of representation in cultures for which blocks count as pictures. That these conventions vary across cultures is no reason for regarding the blocks as not objectively picturing what they are used to represent.

1.7.10 It is obvious enough that even in a determined world, supervenient properties might play no role in laws. Especially, narrow basic properties place few constraints on wide supervenient properties. Yet nothing is subjective or fake about whether a dot representation is a picture of a person. Supervenient wide descriptions may be anomalous, irreducible, and unlearnable relative to narrow basic descriptions, not because of problems concerning the infinity of disjuncts in non-nomic bridging generalizations, but because of their relative arbitrariness.

1.7.11 I shall argue, in Chapters 2 and 3, that the language in which we talk about people is governed by ideals and institutions. These, too, prevent the adequacy of any relation of mere supervenience, complex as that is, between belief- and desire-descriptions, and descriptions of inner states. Yet there seems no reason to suppose that we need do other than ascribe these personal descriptions to human beings (not their inner states), taking persons to be natural animals whose nerve networks respond so wonderfully to the stimuli of their complex environments.

1.7.12 Thus we can freely talk about people's moral and emotional lives in the rich and imaginative way that novelists do, with an untroubled conscience about saying something which will betray us into bad metaphysics—into dualism, in short. Philosophers are not novelists or anything like them, yet they must, on the face of it, construct a philosophy of mind which makes sense of those cultivated disciplines, subtleties, refinements, and insights which make up the novelist's and dramatist's arts. That is surely as proper a discipline as that of playing fair by our scientific world-view, and surely it is no less rigorous. Neurophysiology must (and can) eventually rise to meet the richness and subtlety of full-blown language of agents and persons, perhaps in ways not yet easily envisaged. It is a mistake to ask that novelists or even philosophers gear down to what looks feasible in brain science as it is now. To speak of disciplines, refinements, and insights here is to speak of a stratum of concepts which depends upon institutions directing the criticism of rational performances, which has great power to generate understanding, which allows for a degree of prediction (though not permitting the formulation of powerful, non-trivial laws), and which is based on a cultivated practice refined over centuries. I oppose the view that these aspects of our culture make up a folk psychology.

1.7.13 It would prove a ruinous discipline on the work I hope to do here to eschew all opinion on natural human virtue and excellence till it were cleared by the standards of physicalism or another reductive philosophy. There are, of course, eminent attempts to do something of the kind—to construct a moral philosophy which transgresses no canon of, say, behaviourist psychology (Brandt 1979; Quine 1981). But any such attempt of my own to square what I have to say with the state of current cognitive studies would, however successful in ontic parsimony, fail in moral tact and sensitivity. Thus what I have to say is descriptive in that it is not reductive. But if there were some tension between an adequate account of virtue—adequately sensitive and sophisticated —and the demands of ontic parsimony, I would place the claims of the study in virtue first and leave the ontic questions open, at least in this work.

1.7.14 There is another motive for distinguishing a descriptive style from a predictive or explanatory one. Explanation and prediction bring what one says under laws; either strictly excep-tionless general truths, or those with a form of generality which, though weaker, nevertheless forbids interpretation as merely accidental. But there is a problem here for action-concepts in particular and, more broadly, for this personal style of account. We find that anything we say which is both sufficiently general and plausibly true is so vapid and truistic as to shed no light at all on what people are like. By contrast, we are quite familiar with the most trenchant, surprising, and apt observations on individual people, both in common life and in literature. Most of us are fertile and perceptive in singular description, but quite at a loss to provide any general principles which guide and invigorate these descriptions. I think that this remarkable fact is a significant one. (See Morton 1980.)

1.7.15 We might liken this to our attempts to capture, in pictures, our experience of faces. It is hardly a meaningful idea to picture a general anything, let alone a general face, though we might, for example, think of the outline figures displayed to distinguish male from female toilets. What is striking, absorbing, and graphic about faces is individual and even idiosyncratic. This is not necessarily a matter of detail. Drawings which are very economical in line can offer a striking uniqueness which captures our experience of looking at some particular face. We need from a picture enough to enable us to peer into a face, as it were; to dwell on its particularities, which may seem to us eloquent of much not readily put into words. We can say general things about faces—they have noses, two eyes, and the like—but these generalities do not provide an intelligible basis for the power of a pictured face to hold our attention and provide matter for inarticulate reverie. The contrast between the vividness of individual pictures and the vacancy of general descriptions of faces echoes suggestively a similar contrast noted in the last paragraph. I think this is a feature of the deepest importance.

1.7.16 We are apt to think that any true, general description of human nature must be rather vacuous. Yet that is not true of human anatomy: books in the subject are long and extremely detailed, yet quite general. On a non-theoretical level, we are familiar with the fact that in reasonable light, reasonably close at hand, people are seldom mistaken for anything else. Only people are much like people. Nevertheless this is consistent with our very seldom being confused as to whether someone before us is or is not a particular person whom we know. The visible uniqueness of people is quite consistent with their equally marked difference from anything but fellow people. Anatomy shows in detail how a vast richness of shared properties among people is consistent not just with a theoretical uniqueness of individuals, but with a visible uniqueness, discriminated at rather coarse-grained and casual levels of inspection. In particular, the nervous systems of people are similar in a copious range of structures and properties. There is no reason to be found in reflections on the idiosyncrasies of peoples and cultures to fear that there are no densely describable global similarities which would constitute a human nature.

1.7.17 In this connection, it is worth noting some aspects of the way in which anatomy is a general study, which is clear from the role in it of drawings and photographs. Every living human has a pancreas, but by no means just such a pancreas as that displayed in one's textbook. But it is necessary to draw something as detailed as some actual pancreas in order to illustrate how much, in every case, the concrete tangible organ presents to inspection. Another example: everyone has fingerprints. A properly detailed anatomical illustration of that part of the body's integument would be obliged to show some particular set of whorls and ridges in order to display what fingerprints are generally like. But, as we all know, any sufficiently detailed pattern will be distinctive enough to identify some individual person uniquely. Anatomy has its laws (though it is not much concerned to state them as such). No doubt, the structure of friction-ridges which constitutes the fingerprint can be described in a perfectly general way. Yet it would be a mistake, I think, to suppose that the use of illustrations, including schematic ones which show cross-sections, artificially divided parts, and so on, is not a crucial aspect of what it is to present anatomy in a way which best generates an understanding of it. An understanding is, roughly, a power to generate further relevant action, including discussion, not merely the rather specific and limited power to deduce theorems about the matter within some deductive system. In a similar way, a naturalized picture of valuing in persons calls for concrete, detailed discussions which are unfit for true generalizations. Yet they may generate real understanding.

1.7.18 The language of action-theory does not lend itself to the forming of interesting generalizations for reasons given in the next two chapters. It does lend itself to something like graphic portrayal of what we see as individual (even if it is not), as the art of portraiture does. In that way, it is like anatomical illustration. It works best when beliefs and desires are many and varied, interactive and complex. Its richness lies in density, not generality. Its lack of generality, its lack of ties to locality, propagation, continuity, and contiguity are largely responsible for its lack of fit with our best models of the sciences.

1.7.19 Is the idea of a person, together with the ideas that surround it, the product of a folk psychology? The view that it is pervades current literature. Its attraction lies in its patronizing our familiar vocabulary as the product of rude arts, ill considered and founded on vague observation. The label motivates the kind of revision of ideology which it is crucial for my enterprise to resist. The concepts that surround the idea of a person, which I shall call action-concepts, spring from no kind of science. Chapter 2 argues that they are tied to a human activity, at once older, more deeply entrenched, broader, and no less highly (though much more variously) refined and well-articulated than the sciences: I mean the activity of communication. Action-concepts are not grounded in particular theories, nor in other kinds of discourse that go on within language. They are tied to the general practice and institutions of speaking.

1.7.20 It has been suggested, perhaps partly as a rhetorical flourish (Churchland 1981: 75; Stich 1983: 211), that it is time to recognize that folk psychology is trapped in a degenerating research programme and is hardly more sophisticated now than it was at the time of Sophocles. This simply takes for granted that there is a folk psychology with an identifiable programme, an under-argued assumption rife in the literature at present. But what are its actual products, what problematic has it faced, which body of researchers is, or ever was, pursuing it and with what investigative means, and in what ways has degeneration dogged their footsteps? Churchland mentions a number of problems which, he claims, folk psychology has failed to solve; for instance, the problem of the nature of sleep. But it is unclear what contribution folk psychology is supposed to be making to this issue. It is not that the contribution is poor or bogged down; there simply is no contribution to the issues mentioned by Churchland. We do not find a degenerating research programme. We find no research programme at all.

1.7.21 Churchland (and Stich) at least half imply, perhaps unintentionally, that Sophocles was an early pioneer of this elusive science. It is hard to take this very seriously, for several reasons. First, and most obviously, *Oedipus*, for example, portrays an archetypal man caught in the toils of fate, of the unkindness of the world, and of mortal hubris. These are the themes of Greek tragedy broadly. But Sophocles does not generalize about the traits or characters of persons, the kind of beliefs and desires to which they are prone, or their vagaries of rationality. Sophocles is not the genius precursor, brilliant but crude, of the modern psychologist in the lab—a sort of Hippocrates of psychology. Simply, he was no psychologist at all. Second, suppose we stretched the title 'psychologist' to catch the art of vividly representing idiosyncratic characters, which is one aspect of the art of Sophocles. It is simply false that no significant gains in that capacity have been made in literature since the Greeks. In very different ways, characters in Shakespeare and Henry James are very much more vividly and densely realized, are more varied, surprising, compelling, and interesting. Third, if one took that account of what psychology is with any seriousness, one would have to conclude that modern psychologists are not able, in terms of their own art, to offer representations and interpretations of particular persons, real or imaginary, which rise to anything remotely approaching the degree of sophistication, delicacy, or flexibility which even classical tragedy regularly achieves. What they have to tell us is, in those dimensions, too general, too coarse, too superficial for vividness. However, it hardly seems reasonable to view psychologists as harbouring any such ambitions. The attempt to see them in the same category as imaginative writers makes no sense.

1.7.22 So much for general remarks of an unfriendly kind on the 'psychology' part of the idea of folk psychology. Equally many questions are begged by the description 'folk', whether this be aimed at an explicit or implicit body of principles governing action-concepts. It suggests that action-concepts find a use only in our more naïve, unlettered, or unreflective thinking, and play no part in the more distinguished and cultivated non-scientific disciplines that make up our culture. That is plainly false, as suggested already. In law, history, literature, political analysis, and elsewhere, the vocabulary of intention and action proves itself, in work after work of the utmost refinement and, indeed, of greatness, to be flexible, accurate, sentitive, and richly generative (of understanding rather than of generalization). Perhaps it will seem no recommendation to modern philosophers to point to the closely reasoned and imaginative philosophical literature which has been written in the vocabulary of these ideas (and, indeed, in that timidity about our subject there is food for a good deal of thought, but I will not pursue it now). Their role is central in a wide variety of arts and disciplines whose place in our culture is, very rightly, immeasurably more secure than psychology's is, ever was, and probably ever will be. I am talking here of what may fairly be regarded as the most finely wrought and enduring landmarks in the history of our culture, ancient and modern. Since it can never displace the ideas of an agent or a person, psychology may be doomed to remain of little broad cultural interest. I say nothing of powers to manipulate which it might bestow; these seem more likely to be sinister than the opposite.

1.7.23 Philosophy needs to guard itself against both an arrogance and a timidity in its relation to scientific thought. It is like a science in some ways: it aims to explain, to seek the truth, to sustain objective enquiry. But it ought not to confine itself to the aims of science, which are to explain everything there is by means of laws, and to view the world from the standpoint of manipulating it (2.2). One aim of philosophy must always be to keep questions alive, to trouble dogma, to articulate and challenge the assumptions without which other disciplines cannot proceed, and to maintain a vigorous scepticism in the life of enquiry. We must be wary of accepting the picture of our subject as ancillary to the sciences; it is our duty to challenge that very picture continually. Another aim of philosophy must be to give an account of all the aspects of our culture which fits them into a synoptic picture of what humans are. It will seem to some a mark of intellectual softness to look at a great novel or play, or at music, and ask what it says about us that these things help us to make sense of ourselves. But it is surely timid and soft to feel that ground which has not already been clearly marked out by science is not for a philosopher to cultivate.

2

Of Science and Reason

2.1 Attitudes and the ideology of freedom

2.1.1 Scientific explanation is different from the rational explanation of actions but not opposed to it. Rational explanation is tied to the ideas of action, agency, and personhood, and to concepts of value. In this chapter, I compare these differing styles of explanation by finding their sources in two global attitudes, images, or ideologies (each of these descriptions has some merit). Each explanatory style yields a mode of understanding distinct from the other. Science and agency (and personhood) are equally primitive and equally indispensable ideas, each obliged to take note, in its own way, of the domain proper to the other. Every event in personal life (and every event beyond it, too) must be explained in a way which conforms to the ideals of scientific explanation; whatever activity lays claim to being scientific must conform to the ideals of rationality which are deeply embedded in the structure of our action-concepts. Science cannot have its own rationale as one of its outputs; the ideas of action-theory cannot tell us about how we are related causally to the physical world in which the concrete tasks of personhood must be solved.

2.1.2 Many writers (Strawson 1974, MacKay 1962, Van de Vate 1971, Dennett 1978) place the concept of a person within a distinctive *attitude*, of a quite fundamental kind, which we adopt towards our fellow humans and towards ourselves. The next three paragraphs follow Strawson (1974).

2.1.3 Some familiar compatibilist theories of freedom fail in a particular way. A deference to determinism prompts us to look at persons simply as one class of causal objects among others; that is, to place them within the objective world of science, and to try to find the basis and explanation of their autonomy within that objective stance. We confine the ideology of our discussion of this ethical idea to causal language or to what we are confident will reduce to it. Thus, Schlick (1966) defines responsibility and freedom by means of the effect on agents of practices of praising and blaming them. This procedure makes us look at the agent (ourselves or another) as an object to be manipulated or prodded, shouted at or soothed, not reasoned with. It is within this attitude that we may shape others, perhaps at their own request, by means of surgery, drugs, or hypnotherapy. Here, we do not properly talk *with* another, praise, resent, or portray his behaviour to him in a moral or other reactive light— or if we do it is because, for the time, we have stepped beyond the objective attitude and into an *engaged* one.

2.1.4 Now, while we might, and sometimes quite properly do (in medical contexts, for instance) adopt an objective stance towards another, it is simply not there that the concepts grouped round the idea of freedom have their foundation. In particular, we can find in it no basis for the idea that praise or blame may be *deserved*. A sense of desert springs, in turn, from some reaction we may have to what another agent does (or what we ourselves do). It depends on a judgement we make which is not an objective judgement. We are then engaged with another. We can understand praise and blame only in the context of having appropriately, taken engaged attitudes to another person. We can appraise our stance as just or unjust, but we can find no reason for taking it *from within the objective attitude* to the world and its contents, typified in the sciences. Yet we could not decide utterly to forgo the engaged attitude, most particularly towards ourselves. We may say, roughly, that to take up the engaged attitude is to treat another as a person; as someone who deserves that attitude. Only within that attitude can we make sense of responsibility, freedom, desert, and resentment. Schlick's account, then, is not just awry in some of its details. It is the wrong *kind* of explanation.

2.1.5 Taking an engaged attitude is not a matter of being forced to a conclusion, or even of being justified in drawing it on the basis of evidence, observation, or theoretical reasoning. From the viewpoint of the objective stance, we find nothing which obliges or even entitles us to adopt another attitude, however careful and ingenious our scrutiny and reflection. To say this is not to condemn the engaged stance as unreasonable, as if it required the support of reasons from the objective stance. It makes little sense as some sort of appendage to that stance: it must be explained as something independent. I try to defend this and expand it by taking both attitudes as primitive in a way described in the next section.

2.1.6 I begin by working towards seeing the objective attitude as an attitude: as something adopted without justification, intelligible only within its own posture of thought and plan of activity. This may help us to see each of the attitudes as different, yet not competing, modes of practical life for agents who are thinkers and observers, creatures with a range of needs and capacities. To stress just the engaged stance as unjustifiable and the choice to adopt it as primitive and radical is to give the objective attitude too much, or perhaps too little. We must see it as no less in need of reflection on its sources and no less one attitude among others; it needs locating among the rest even if none of them forms its basis or justifies it.

2.2 Cultural practices and images of man-in-the-world

2.2.1 Sellars (1963) places the origin of the objective attitude within the engaged attitude, though he uses the metaphor of images rather than attitudes. The scientific image of man-in-the-world evolves from the manifest image of man-in-the-world by means of a growing sophistication in each of them. Sellars regards the scientific image as maturing out of the manifest image by means of a progressive depersonalizing of nature. In the beginning, everything was seen as personal (runs my slanted version of Sellars's Just So story), as amenable to propitiation by processes falling within the engaged attitude—praising, bribing, sacrificing, casting spells, exorcizing, worshipping—aimed at inducing gratitude, at placating resentment and other reactive attitudes on the part of natural forces. '*Originally* to be a tree was a *way of being a person*' he writes (1963:10). The march of science begins with steps away from this personalized view and the capture of territory in which the objective attitude, in some version, can hold sway.

2.2.2 This may help to motivate my own Just So story: that two modes of practical life are each deeply primitive and separate in their geneses. (I take the phrase 'man-in-the-world' as referring to man as agent, leading some form of practical life. I will seldom use the phrase again.) The basic practices of the first mode begin, primitively, with literal manipulation: grasping, lifting, pulling, squeezing. The second mode begins, primitively, with the practice of changing certain things on the scene by laying information before them in various ways and by responding to information which things lay, intentionally, before oneself. Obviously, the most fruitful and flexible way of doing this comes to be by *talking* to some of these things—to other people, that is—and listening to them. But that does not exhaust all the techniques available. Gesture, facial expression, or the presentation of objects may change people and animals in ways practical people want.

2.2.3 In these different modes of practical life, language plays equally complex but intricately different roles. One difference works like this: language is a primary tool for the engaged mode of practical life, being our most precise and handy tool; it is marvellously apt for presenting information and goals and permits a range of linguistic performances (Austin 1966; Wittgenstein 1958). Language also plays a role in the first, objective mode but at one remove; clearly, it is not a direct and primary tool of manipulative practice. But it enters manipulative practice wherever engaged attitudes play a part there. Language has ancillary roles in sustaining systematic observation, in articulating and objectifying techniques, plans, and so on, both for work groups and individual toilers each engaged only with himself. One cannot use language at all without engaging with someone, even if just with oneself. Its main role in the manipulative practice, at one remove, is to present one's workmates with information simply to direct their work; one may be engaged with oneself in a similar way.

2.2.4 Another difference of role for language lies in the place and evolution of theory and explanation under practical pressures. Action is behaviour which is guided by information-processing to which the agent has access. Persons act, but not only they are agents. The theory and explanation of action is moulded by a quite particular form of interaction among quite particular sorts of being. One agent lays before another perceiving agent information which will be processed in ways at least some of which agents can access. Within the engaged attitude, one understands target-beings largely as one understands oneself; action-explanations are agent's explanations *of agents*, and are moulded by the norms which govern how information is received and processed by them. In particular, they are shaped by institutions and ideals that govern language, in ways described later. Manipulation is plainly something that agents do, but it has no such restriction to a form of interaction with objects; rather, it is all-in causal, that is, it is what bestows on the growing body of science (the theory which guides manipulation) its conceptual freedom and, in the long run, its conceptual power.

2.2.5 We get a fresh view of these contrasts if we refer back to Strawson's critique of Schlick, but from a slightly different orientation. Magic can be seen as the improper intrusion of the engaged mode of practical life into preserves proper to the objective one; incantation and propitiatory rites try, impossibly, to play the role of manipulation. By contrast, the attempt to explain human freedom and responsibility from within the objective attitude or the scientific image is the later, and somewhat more sophisticated, intrusion of manipulation into preserves proper to changing people by informing them—something rather subtler than the practice of magic, perhaps, but like it. Refined versions of the objective practical attitude are found in the practices of pure science; refined versions of the engaged one are found in logic, law, literature, and history.

2.2.6 The distinction between attitudes, like that between images, depends on differences in these distinct and fundamental forms of practical life. To speak of attitudes here, or of either form of life as unjustified from the viewpoint of the other, is to use a metaphor. It is meant to capture the fact that, as a primitive practice, each is a form of intervention in the world, an intrusion into it (to choose an expression which is aimed at stressing its activity and its unwarranted wish to meddle) which relates the objects dealt with to oneself in quite different ways and seeks to change them through quite different processes. To speak of each as a commitment is again a metaphor which casts as radical decisions on our part what are, in fact, scarcely avoidable ways of practising and pursuing a cultured human life. There are useful analogies with scepticism here. Arguably, we lack any conclusive *a priori* theory which would oblige or entitle us to leave general sceptical doubt behind. But no general sceptic can be an agent, for lack of real options among which to choose. Man-in-the-world cannot be a sceptic. Just as general sceptics cannot be manipulative agents, so sceptics about other minds cannot be engaged agents. It is inconsistent with that style of practical life. To see agenthood as a primitive, unwarranted intervention in the world is simply to acknowledge a spirit in which one might put scepticism away.

2.2.7 Sellars's contrast between manifest and scientific images is not intended as a contrast between the naïve and superficial, on the one hand, and the sophisticated and discerning on the other. The manifest image is refined and penetrating, though I will argue that Sellars fails to characterize these strengths correctly. The phrase 'manifest image of man-in-the-world' is unfortunate, I think. 'Man-in-the-world' can properly refer only to man engaged in some practice. But then, what Sellars tries to characterize is not an image one has *of* man thus occupied, but rather an image which man, thus occupied, *has*. He has it of himself and others, so long as his practice is that information-transactional one. What defines the image is the practice of agents in a certain style of engagement. It inevitably belongs to interpersonal practice however deeply and theoretically that is pursued. It is the principal style of a cultural and moral (in a broad, deep, loose sense) interpersonal form of life. That is why it is at once sophisticated and causally superficial, and why it will never be eliminated by progress in sciences that refine our practice as manipulative agents. We cannot abandon that style of life without becoming unrecognizably and immorally different from what we are.

2.2.8   For Sellars, the conceptual difference between the scientific and manifest images lies in contrasting the micro-structural aims of scientific explanation with a probabilistic style of 'correlational induction' in manifest explanation (1963: 7). I think this wrong in two ways: first, it suggests that the scientific image arises out of our limited perceptual acuity; second, it underestimates what happens when one insists, within the objective attitude, that explanation ends only when we can appeal to strictly universal laws.

2.2.9   There is, I take it, a sharp difference between the scientific image and an (imaginable) 'manifest but magnified' image, by which I mean a more powerful perceptual grasp of the world and of us within it. We might imagine this as like what the microscope, the telescope, and other perceptual amplifiers have given us, but without the conceptual apparatus which accompanies *law-like* explanations of phenomena, and which, symbiotically, is both the product of that style of explanation and what makes it possible. It is surely false that there would simply not *be* a clash between the scientific and manifest pictures we have of ourselves if we all began life with sharper eyesight, transparent skulls, luminous cortical activity, and whatever else would make cerebral processes manifest to unaided vision. The simple discovery that there are things within

things at the minute scale, and stars beyond stars at the astronomical one, does not pose any conceptual troubles by itself, nor
does it give rise to a distinctive conceptual style.

2.2.10 It is worth reminding ourselves of what is, I suppose,
obvious: that the first main advances in modern Western science
made no appeal to unobservables and were unaided by the increased
perceptual acuity given by the microscope. True, the telescope
played no small part in the final overthrow of the teleological style
of explanation which, in however debilitated a form, dominated
what passed for science till the end of the sixteenth century. That
overthrow was the great contribution of seventeenth-century
astronomy, and it preceded the development of what is more
characteristic of modern science in its full-blown form. Galileo's
Dialogue, written in plain man's Italian, constitutes a kind of grand
detective story which places the sun in the dock as guilty of
occupying the central place in the local planetary system. It formu-
lates no law, reveals no hidden objects or processes. It provides a
new orientation in the manifest world. Kepler used Tycho's careful,
accurate, but entirely phenomenal astronomical plots and charts to
discover laws which he viewed as mere preliminaries to an essentially teleological explanation of the world-system, an explanation
which would reveal the harmony of the whole. Galileo, too,
thought within some such framework.

2.2.11 It was on such an observational basis that Galileo and
Newton built their astronomy. (Perhaps I overstate the phenomenological character of seventeenth-astronomy, but I hope that
the reader will forgive my use of an expository convenience.) Their
celestial and terrestrial mechanics are a different story, though not a
micro-structural one. Galileo's pioneering work on mechanics is an
attempt to find strictly universal laws. Newton's advance is to grasp
that they are not to be found without some form of conceptual
revision. Thus, weight is reconceived by Newton to be a local
property, mass being the truly universal one. New concepts such as
energy, momentum, force, and work are forged because they permit
us to write in strictly universal form laws which are foreseen as
universally confirmable. Galileo speculated ingeniously on micro-
structures (following the ancient lead of Demokritos) in the first of
his *Two New Sciences*, where he introduces the study of the
strength of materials, but his actual findings make no appeal to
micro-structural concepts. The real shift in conceptual style comes

with the vision of explanations which replace design and purpose with law and deduction.

2.2.12 What makes such a subject as mechanics fall within the scientific and not the manifest image of the world is a feature more fundamental than the fact that it aims to construct and define concepts which exhaust the properties of micro-entities. It invents and employs concepts which have no part to play in the manifest image and are maladapted to its forms of refinement. It constructs them because, in turn, the concepts of the manifest image—which in this context include the coarse ideas of everyday rule-of-thumb manipulation as well as refined concepts of agency—are not hospitable to *its* forms of refinement, that is, to the expression of true generalizations. The uniformities of nature are not expressible in familiar vocabulary. We need concepts such as mass, momentum, energy, and force to allow us to formulate generalizations which meet all of the following conditions: they are strictly universal, physically necessary laws; they are quantitatively precise, and confirmable by observations; they are about properties instantiated by every object and take the form of laws of continuous development and propagation. It is this explanatory ideal which drove apart the ideologies of scientific and manifest images. The abandoning of the last condition in quantum mechanics has done nothing to draw them together.

2.2.13 The role of the micro-structural in scientific explanation was accurately seen by Demokritos and by Galileo before there was any workable micro-structural explanation or anyone knew what micro-structures there might actually be. The nature of micro-entities was to be exhausted in primary qualities and in their interactions with the primary qualities of the micro-constituents of other things and, importantly, with those of our sense receptors: this was to explain the basis of the secondary qualities which we naïvely ascribe to things. This role for micro-structures also demands that the basic entities of such an explanation be not secondary-quality-perceptible. A way of describing the difference between primary and secondary qualities, on this view of them, is that primary qualities figure in the strictly universal laws about the world described at the end of the last paragraph. Thus, micro-structure is simply a way of implementing an ideal of scientific explanation, foreseen long before the advent of aided micro-perception.

2.2.14 Now we may fairly claim about the change to this style of description that it amounts to an attitude, a commitment to pursue a policy which has no justification apart from the successes it may have in carrying out its programme. Nothing can guarantee *a priori* that teleological styles of explanation will *not* work; nor, on the other hand, plainly, is there anything of the kind to guarantee that the search for nomological explanation *will* work. Indeed, in a very strict sense, it has never worked. There is a large number of locally true, rather rough generalizations, verified within normal limits of observation, which we can feel sure will not be overturned. But what pass for now as the most basic principles of explanation in physics, the truly fundamental, strictly universal, physically necessary laws, are almost certainly false if only because they are imperfectly exact. The history of science is littered with failed hypotheses which had their day as candidate laws. Indeed, that observation is now a commonplace. The Principle of Induction (whatever that might be) does not find even a circular backing in the realm of empirical tests of it. It has never yielded a true law. All the 'laws' which we use it to confirm probably are, as they have always turned out to be, strictly false. (It is easy to make too much of this likelihood, as Devitt (1984: 9.4) argues.)

2.2.15 This picture of the scientific enterprise is not intended to portray it as irrational. Still less is it intended to suggest the idea that laws are something which we can impose upon the world, thus rendering it law-like. The Kantian picture of *a priori* concepts and categories remains tied either to an insolubly sceptical distinction between noumenal and phenomenal worlds, or to a subjectivism which renders pointless the scrupulous pursuit of objective precision which has served the sciences so well. Rejecting teleological styles of explanation for nomological ones was a commitment, and it remains one. But, in it, we commit ourselves to a deep *truth* about the world that the search for strict, law-like explanations is fruitful—that they are *there to be found*. A brief example might clarify what I mean. Kant's metaphysical expositions of the concepts of space and time do indeed show that these concepts are not learned from, or constructed out of, other concepts. Nor can perceptual experience sustain our constructing concepts which unite phenomena so that every body is spatially related to every other, and every event temporally related to every other. None of this obstructs the evolution of these ideas under pressure from objective observation and experimentation. Our *a priori* concepts of space and time have proved eminently corrigible, though corrected late. The modern idea of space-time is very different from the ideas Kant wrote about, but its lineage back to his unanalysable, *a priori* primitives is unmistakable. That we commit ourselves in advance of our knowledge to ambitious ideas and styles of explanation neither renders us ineducable in respect of those commitments, nor protects them from eventual banishment from science, nor does it prevent those of our remarks which use the concept from making genuine objective comment on the world. The attitude of scientific explanation neither has nor needs a justification in terms of some commitment or attitude outside itself. But then, neither does the commitment to regard ourselves and other parts of the natural furniture of the world as persons call for external props.

2.2.16 These arguments aim to show that the scientific image of the world contrasts with the manifest image of agents in that each springs from its own fundamental, practical means of coping with things. The scientific image of the world is the product of cultivated reflection on primitive manipulative practices in the world. The manifest image of agents is the product of cultivated communicative practices in it. The two most salient and contrasting practical styles in the life of cultivated man are manipulating according to a theory, and talking with fellow culture-members. They are different, equally fundamental modes of understanding our doings in the world. Neither mode is expressible, nor does it need expression, in the conceptual style of the other. That view of the contrast stands outside both conceptual styles to see what practices they rest on, rather than attempting to contrast them from inside by means of the concepts that make them up. Though it springs from a kind of objective observation, this is a philosophical view, not a scientific one.

2.3 Cultural practices and the image of persons

2.3.1 At least a primary part of the manifest image of persons is rooted not in a theory but rather in a disciplined practice. It is my aim in this section to try to describe this practice more fully. It issues in a highly refined rational structure, or complex of them, which is not strictly a theory. Perhaps it is well to emphasize from the outset that the remarks of this section define just one aspect of the image. There are others. The main interest of the one in focus now is that, if I am right about it, it clearly forbids our eliminating the manifest image or reducing it to a scientific one. I look at just the action-concepts in the manifest image, for it is these which have a logic resistant to assimilation by a science. The problems of pain and sensation in the philosophy of mind (the issues of *qualia*, that is) are not my worry here. Nor is the state or the task of being a person.

2.3.2 From the ontic point of view, we are agents before we are speakers, for speaking is a form of acting; but, conceptually, the idea of an action is of a movement intelligible in the light of information which guides it. It permits explanation and justification in terms of ideas which are made definite in linguistic practice and are anchored in the deepest institutions of communication. From the ontic viewpoint, actions are always justified *by actions*, and it matters little whether this is by actions of verbal explanation or simply by the role of some act within a wider style or strategy of action. But the conceptual order is different: we need our implicit grasp of the institutions of speech before we can see any movement as an action, since an action just is a movement rationally justifiable in some weak sense by *contents* of guiding inner states to which the agent has access, and both the style of justification and the notion of contents are provided by language. It is content and access that distinguish action from movement, and content is intelligible to us only against the complex background of institutions of language. None of this requires that the agent be able to say anything with justifying content, or, indeed, be able to say anything at all.

2.3.3 Our understanding of action and agency does not consist in a body of doctrine. It is not approached in the generalizations of social sciences. Weber argued that social sciences could offer probabilistic generalizations about ideal types. But there is no plain reason for confidence that a systematic body of such generalizations is to be found; for any attempt to refine a vocabulary in which one could really expect a large body of even such weak laws to be written is likely to lead one quickly away from an ideology or vocabulary which bears a proper claim to be regarded as social. The social sciences differ from, say, the biological ones not in a difference in the stringency of laws, but rather in the role of culture in social studies. Sellars, too, envisages the refined manifest image as issuing in statistical laws (1963: 22–3), but I think this profoundly misreads the contrast (or the conflict, if there is one) between conceptual styles of the objective and the engaged, the manifest or the scientific, which it was Sellars's aim to capture and articulate. The basic schema of action-explanation is unlike the one for science described in 2.2.12. It is no matter of laws and causes.

2.3.4 The image of agents is refined in ideals of rational explanation, embodied in what I will call institutions of language. A very rough model of principles which shape the idea of a rational agent can be found in logic. Logic is a normative, not a descriptive study. It does not tell us how we do think, but how we ought to think—as Aristotle told us some time ago. Indeed, as it advances in refinement, it is less and less accurate as a law-like empirical account of the thought-processes of personal thinkers, yet is more and more powerful in respect of its capacities to justify and criticize what any person may think. The model is rough because classical sentence and predicate logic are guided much more by their use of the simplest possible semantics than by any fidelity they have to the norms of actual human reasoning. The departures of logic from these norms are perhaps more striking than any fidelity it may preserve. Nevertheless, it offers some useful illustrations. Logic looks nothing like a science; it does not even begin to conform to scientific styles of explanation. We could call it a science only on pain of debilitating what we think a science is. It does not enable us to understand ourselves better, but rather to think more powerfully about any subject matter at all. Our image of justified believers and agents is also governed by principles broader than those in logic proper, principles which are the norms of objective thought quite generally. Some of these principles would be articulated in a successful theory of scientific method. But they do not constitute a science. In 2.4 and in 3.3, I try to strengthen this view of language as imposing cultural norms on information-processing by sketching what some main norms might be.

2.3.5 There is an ambiguity in what we talk about when we speak of science. We often mean the scientific image of the world; the output, that is to say, of practical scientific work. The output is a variety of theories in which we can see some hope of unity through assimilation. We sometimes, but less often, mean the cast of mind and set of disciplines that govern the practice and shape the output. But disciplines can be explained only normatively. Obviously, scientific output cannot contain a truly normative theory of anything, though a close look at scientific practice, a look which counts as scientific in being itself subject to the disciplines, may be a useful way of shedding light on what they are. That would result, we might hope, in a metascience. We see science's output as unifiable by processes of reduction and assimilation so that, in its last refinement, it is seen as issuing in strict laws that meet the conditions laid down in 2.2.12. But either that metascience gives some justification of the disciplines in which case it is not, properly, a science; or it is a properly empirical study of actual practice and is not normative. The justification of scientific practice is a cultural one.

2.3.6 Even at this late stage in the history of science, we seem to have only a rudimentary grasp of what these disciplines are and what would justify them, even if we could identify them with confidence. But there is surely something strange in the idea that an articulate theory of these disciplines would be mainly a natural rather than a normative one (an idea which is at least suggested in Kuhn 1969, Feyerabend 1975, and Quine 1969). Such a picture of it has been made attractive, nevertheless, to some extent, by various historical or quasi-historical studies. These suggest that our present scientific knowledge has not come to us through the pursuit of rational investigations, but by processes better understood sociologically. But it is not clear that this can explain how we can see with *hindsight* that the procedures by which we arrived at our present scientific theories were rationally unjustified, unless we can contrast the procedures with others that might justify them. We must concede either that we can *now* justify our scientific world-picture, despite the errors of our forebears, or that our scientific world-picture has no more right to our credit than any other picture could claim. Further, the historical studies that purport to reveal this lay claim themselves to being natural and scientific, and must do so to jusify the conclusions they reach, or else, they give us no reason to believe them. To write about the methodological failures of an earlier age can make sense only against the background of at least implicit canons of reason by which they are judged to be faulty.

2.3.7 Part of scientific practice is a rational practice: it justifies the sayings and doings, the theories and the activities of an organized group of persons, and the progress of science lies in the refinement of this practice quite as much as in the advance in our theoretical world-view. To articulate the cultivated practice would be to propound a normative study, loosely modelled on logic; theoretical advances in it might add new power to exercises in the practice, guiding it normatively as logic guides workers in the foundations of mathematics. However, just as it is clear that logic is always open to revision or expansion from new formulations of patterns in thinking at large (think of the push towards intentional logics, relevant logics, quantum and modal logics), so any theory of the rational disciplines of science is open to criticism from unarticulated practices which serve us so well in objective enquiries, but which not all of us are bright enough, careful enough, or agile enough to follow all the time—but others are sometimes ingenious enough to invent them. (See 3.4.)

2.3.8 Ideas on rational practice—normative ideas, that is—are not the output of scientific study. No part of the scientific world-picture includes the justification of rational practices, nor could it do so. It aims to explain everything there is from the viewpoint of its nomological necessity. Its aim is universal: there must be a sense in which it explains persons, all their activities including scientific ones, and all that happens to them. In that respect, the mode of understanding which sees us as agents is the more fundamental of the two.

2.3.9 Action-concepts rest on two primitive ideas: that of an action and that of an utterance of a sentence or, for brevity, a *saying*. Roughly, an action is a movement of an animal which can be understood by reference to contents to which the animal has access, and which guide its action. The animal has beliefs, desires, intentions, and their kin; they are somehow in it. The content of a belief (a desire) is the content of some saying. It is an atom of information, in the sense that an atom of language—a sentence—can express it. Thus, the identity-conditions of beliefs, desires, and their kin spring from the public, social, practices of communication in language. We know little about how any literally inner, physiological states which occur in the 'processing' of these contents might function. These states are not beliefs and desires. We characterize beliefs and desires essentially as communicable information-atoms whose structure is determined by the social needs of speech about the world common to speakers and hearers. I conjecture that our style of explaining action by belief and desire springs from the ancient practice of social debate about the justification of human doings. Perhaps the rest of the action-concepts can be arrived at by analysis from these as primitives (see Loar 1981). I use them as a blanket reference to all ideas about action.

2.3.10 Very roughly indeed, saying is believing. That is the best first step in a conceptual account of belief. In a different grammatical mood, and no less roughly saying is desiring. The presumption of language is that the speaker of an indicative sentence voices her belief and that the speaker of an imperative or optative sentence voices her desire. That presumption does not rest upon laws of nature, for it is surely, somehow, cultural; nor does it rest upon convention, since it is not a presumption we might change within language; nor is it a feature just of some languages and not others. Various writers have offered to explain it as necessary for the survival (or at least the continued efficacy) of language (see Dennett 1978: 18–19, Griffiths 1967: chs. IX and XI). Last, most familiarly and most remarkably, the entrenchment of the presumption does not depend upon its truth in any case. Though it has the 'hardness of the logical must', little useful light is shed on its status by calling it a logical or conceptual fact. I shall call it an institution of language. That it is indeed an institution is well-recognized, for it underlies the familiar pragmatic or veridical paradox presented by the sentence '*p*, but I don't believe *p*'. There is a counterpart paradox for the imperative and optative moods, of the form 'Let it be that *p*; but I don't want it to be the case that *p*'. The institution is not something we can override, however clear it may be to all parties to the conversation—in cases of blatant deceit or defiance—that she does *not* believe what she says. We can even exploit the institution in irony and sarcasm, where speaker and hearer equally recognize the falsity of the presumption and are understood by all parties to recognize it. But irony depends on its being inescapable that, standardly, speaking presumes that one is to be understood as saying what one thinks. This is one main way in which belief is conceptually tied not to some causal theory of human behaviour, but to the practice of communicating.

2.3.11 Many sayings are not believings, and vice versa. A belief is defeasibly related to a saying in two main ways. First, the saying, like any other action, is liable to subtler interpretation in terms of beliefs and desires which give the reasons why (or that for the sake of which) the saying-action was done; thus a saying may be rationalized, that is, non-morally justified, by means of contents other than the content of that saying itself; second, the agent has many more contents that can be interpreted by sayings than there are utterances he actually says. But what is going on in him which allows us to interpret his action can only be given by contents which are assigned to utterance types. The content of a belief is thus determined more by our picture of the practical relation of the believer to the world in which and of which we speak than by any picture of the causal role played internally by the neural state whose content it is.

2.3.12 But we need a broader perspective on action than this. It is not only speakers who have beliefs and desires. Still more importantly, by no means all the action-guiding information digested by information-processing organisms can be ascribed to them as beliefs and desires, even when they are speakers. Consider a cat's high leap to a precarious vantage point. The precision, delicacy, and economy of such leaps are remarkable. The information-processes which monitor such actions are dense and subtle. Though the cat has nothing to say, she leaps because of what she wants and believes. Nevertheless, we would not expect to exhaust the content of the information which is accessible to the cat, and which guides this precise and delicate action, in any set of beliefs or desires which we might plausibly ascribe to it or to an equally deftly leaping person. What can be said about these matters?

2.3.13 Agents do not have access to all the information that guides their actions any more than they have access to all the stages of processing which go on when they perceive something. Beliefs are information-atoms of a sort to which we standardly have access, and use in the conscious information-processes of deliberation. It does not follow that we always have access, in fact, to all we believe and desire. Further, some of the information to which we have access, even some to which we attend in deliberation, is unverbalized and even unverbalizable, either because its riches outrun description, as photographs of people outrun even the best police descriptions of them, or because we have yet to learn, or yet to articulate, apt concepts for it. We may think of all information consciously processed as requiring concepts. This would make some concepts inarticulate, and only the remainder linguistic. Even so, information available to deliberation is communicable, socially available information. Though the idea of content is dependent on language, we comfortably stretch it to allow non-sentential but accessible items to count. We can gesture to this kind of content as evidence, represent it in mime and by pictures. We can find ways to draw the attention of cats, dogs, or chimps to it. Despite all this, the idea of belief (and desire) remains tied to linguistic enterprises because of the justificatory style of action-explanations, whether verbal or gestural. Each sentence identifies an information-atom in socially usable style, and models the way in which we conceive of content generally. To ascribe actions, desires, beliefs, and intentions to the inarticulate—human or animal—is to see them as more or less likely to make certain movements when presented, in whatever form is envisaged, with information the content of which is, in principle, given in sentences and seen as accessible to the agent in some form. That is the theme of the next section.

2.3.14 We have good reason, from facts about feral children discussed in 1.2.4, to think (against Churchland 1979, and Churchland and Churchland 1981, for example) that specifically linguistic processing of information adds quite dramatically to the conceptual prowess of persons in processing information. Churchland argues that, on the one hand, the behaviour of the very young infant does not invite characterization in terms of belief and desire and, on the other, that 'the basic parameters of rational intellectual activity are the same at whatever its stage of development, notwithstanding the increasing degree to which that activity becomes "comprehensible" in terms of propositional attitudes' (1979: 129). Churchland concludes that the approach of folk psychology to an understanding of the growth to maturation of intellectual powers 'is pursuing what must be superficial parameters. That is, sentential parameters cannot be among the primitive parameters comprehended by a truly adequate theory of rational intellectual development' (1979: 128). I find this implausible. In known cases of isolates, functional intellectual impairment is massive and largely irreparable. Of course, linguistic mastery is underpinned by neural information-processes which make that mastery possible, and these very probably are ill-characterized by sentences. But the functioning of a computer is by no means necessarily better described by detailing the function of its hardware design than by the software programme it is currently

running, to exploit a familiar style of analogy. That seems the more
so when the programme is user-friendly, as it generally is with our
own programmes. The conclusion drawn simply fails to follow, and
there is some empirical evidence for its falsehood.

2.3.15 A deep tie between belief and the cultural, convention-
bound activity of communicating at once disqualifies belief and
desire from any key role in a rigorous natural science, and assures
their place in any recognizably human culture. A properly rigorous
investigation, which aims at highly general truths (no less general
than those of anatomy, say) and which accepts the need to find a
vocabulary in which these truths may be written, could hardly
confine itself to the ideology of belief and desire; that is, of a
convention-bound, cultural practice. If one seriously wanted to
predict the behaviour of people in the way one predicts the
behaviour of planets, billiard-balls, charged particles, and the like,
why would one ever think that this might be accomplished in the
highly specialized, sophisticated, and encultured concepts which
spring from and gravitate round linguistic activity? How could one
expect to succeed if one adopted the self-denying ordinance of
observing things always from the perspective of having to interpret
the meanings (the content) of their movements? The hope that one
might find, within so confined a perspective, the means to mount an
aspiring causal theory of those movements is baseless.

2.4   On rational explanation

2.4.1 Let us look, then, at the explanatory role of belief- and
desire-concepts. We need to distinguish several roles. Let us begin
with the first-person case. By another institution of language, when
I explain one of my current beliefs my explanation standardly
purports to be a justification of myself as believing it, or of the
belief itself as proper for anyone to hold. This is a second
presumption of language. That is not at all to say that what I offer
by way of explanation *will* justify what I believe, any more than my
saying '*p*' guarantees either that it is true or that I really do believe
it. What I offer as an explanation can be any nonsense whatever,
and the degree to which, as a justification, it may be inept will not
at all affect its purporting to be one. Though not all first-person

explanations of belief justify, I argue that such explanations are a dominant form.

2.4.2 I can certainly explain my present belief by telling you what caused it—I believe she is here because I saw her; I believe there is a mouse behind the wainscot because I heard what sounds just like that. Perhaps these figure better as answers to questions of the form 'How do you know . . . ?' than 'Why do you believe . . .?', but I do not wish to pause over that. After all, it is obvious enough that not all first-person causal explanations justify. If I tell you that I think no politician is to be trusted because that is what my best friends say, that provides me with no title to believe it. Yet what I take to be the dominance of the first-person justificatory form emerges if we consider what happens if I offer a causal explanation of my current belief which would show the belief to be *un*justified if offered by another person about me. The curious fact is that the pragmatic function of such an explanation from my own mouth is not of a purely causal explanation, but of a bizarre, ineffectual attempt to *justify*. I take this to be an important fact, which the following example illustrates.

2.4.3 Suppose I try to explain to you why I think I am unusually good at distinguishing fake suicide notes from real ones. I bring myself under what appears to be the quite robust generalization from experiments on belief-perseverance (Ross *et al.* 1975). I describe how the experimenter made encouraging noises to me as I made my judgements on apparent cases of suicide notes and also how she told me, later, that this encouragement actually bore no correlation to the genuineness of the notes; I go on to cite Ross's paper in detail, set forth its findings about irrational belief-perseverance intelligently, and say how common such irrationally produced beliefs are among even well-educated and practised reasoners. Whatever I might *wish* to be doing in this explanation, what I *am* doing is presenting you with a purported justification of my belief. Never mind that it is not a successful one, nor even that it actually undermines the reasonableness of my belief. It may well be, of course, that I really do have that belief and that there is a causal explanation of it along just such Rossian lines. That is irrelevant. The example suggests that there is no way in which the findings of a psychology, folk or non-folk, will empower me to explain, in non-justificatory ways, beliefs I declare myself to hold as I explain them. No such finding can be relevant. It is my claim that the concept of belief has its roots in the institutions of language just described: that, very roughly, saying is believing, and that the primary form of explanation of belief lies in first-person justification. Neither of these is the result of choice on the part of speakers, nor do they rest upon a changeable convention in the language community. Each lies at the foundation of communicative practices themselves in a much more deeply seated way. Finally, neither of them has to do with a psychology, nor could a psychology shed light on the nature or status of either.

2.4.4 Not all belief-explanations are first-person ones, quite obviously. Nevertheless, in most contexts, or at least in standard ones, my explanations of her beliefs, or yours, or my own past beliefs, are explanations which presume the justificatory style, even in criticism. If I want to explain why Adams wrote to the Astronomer Royal urging him to turn his telescope towards a certain part of the night sky, my explanation will not bring his behaviour under some rule of thumb, or even some sophisticated and well-confirmed natural law: what natural law could it possibly be? Of course, his action was guided by a knowledge of natural laws, but without falling under any that I could use in explaining it. My explanation will justify his belief that a new planet would be seen as predicted. It will not be a bit of psychology, folk or other. It will rationalize his belief, present an argument for it, not a cause of it. Of course, the explanation can be amplified with truisms about people usually doing what they want to do. But the addition is incongruous as well as trivial if I am right in thinking that desire- and belief-explanations appeal crucially to norms, ideals, and institutions. The causal looseness in such (superfluous) additions about belief and desire is no ground of complaint and does not weaken their entrenchment in rational explanation. In other cases, even when I explain my past beliefs critically, I may present what I took to be a justification and explain why I thought I could take it so. I may say, for example, that I converted an *A* proposition. Alternatively, I may explain another's belief by showing his purported justification to be insincere, or his reason to be clouded by self-interest. That is to say, I place a purported justification in a context in which it can be seen either as a mask for another justification which, though more rational perhaps, is morally deplorable, or as a confusion between one justification and another. Conversely, even when I know that a certain phenomenon is common enough among agents, I may still feel that it is inexplicable, if it seems just too silly. Think, for instance, of those people who take TV actors to be the characters they act, to have their personalities, and to be involved in their doings; what about those people who ring up actors and remonstrate with them about their fictional deeds? Perhaps these actions fall under a robust generalization, but in a real sense they are inexplicable because so daft.

2.4.5 However, one cannot sustain the view that all explanations of personal behaviour are, in one way or another, justificatory in style. Perhaps we can recognize a genuinely folk psychology, after all, in observations ranging from the proverbial (e.g. 'Spare the rod and spoil the child'; 'Birds of a feather flock together') to the more or less responsibly statistical (e.g. 'Delinquent children are likely to come from disturbed home environments'); from real rules of thumb to sober judgements on the basis of some incipient form of systematic and insightful observation. I am rather inclined to think that a good deal of such psychology is unreliable and explanatorily meagre in the way that Stich and Churchland deplore. But such observations are not the judgements of our non-scientific culture on the role of action-concepts, nor do they give these concepts the vitality and sensitivity on which I have been insisting! That is not to say that there is no distinguished work done in that style which has quasi-scientific status. We find, I think, in the pages of Freud or Jung the productions of poet as scientist; something deep, serious, moving, and insightful, but hardly science proper.

2.4.6 It is no matter of human quirkiness, of universal or individual pride or guilt, which determines the form one's self-explanation takes. Nor is it a matter of breachable but unbreached convention that determines self-explanation to be dominantly justificatory. Some may try to forestall criticisms of their irrationality by suggesting either that they are too stuck in the mud, too partial, or too prejudiced to have the right to believe what they assert. They suggest that they are not lost to all remonstrance, despite their persisting belief in what they disparage. But the institutions of language are unyielding. The suggestion declares, willy-nilly, that they do not seriously believe what they are saying; either their 'explanation' is an incipient retraction of the belief, or the persisting belief brands the concessive noises as spurious and insincere. Sometimes one may be genuinely puzzled by what one has just said and be at a loss as to what demands or even permits

its acceptance. But this puzzlement gives notice of conditional intention to quit: it is a kind of undertaking, a recognized obligation to reconsider, and a disavowal of future responsibility to maintain, what one has claimed. There is no way simply to evade the onuses which underlie the basic structures of communication, save in silence. Any first-person explanation of presently maintained belief offers an obligation or a permission to say and to think the proposition believed. Anything less propounds a doubt, a hesitation, a withdrawal of commitment, or else it pragmatically impugns itself as no meaningful offer at all. Such a discursive structure is ethical through and through.

2.4.7 Thus each of us thinks as she takes it she ought or may. She may believe, with Pascal, that the heart has its reasons which the mind cannot know. She may rejoice in the discovery of contradictions in holy doctrine which establish the need to found her belief in faith and commitment, thus constituting her permission to believe. Let the proposed justification be as bizarre as one can imagine, it nevertheless functions, in first-person mode, as her reason. Further, first-person justifications offered to oneself must be, in some real sense, sincere. I may explain to you, insincerely, what requires or allows my sayings and believings. But to explain them to myself is to offer a justification and to be satisfied that it does justify. Of course, there is all sorts of room here for self-deception and bad faith; nevertheless, I cannot simply tell myself how my beliefs were caused or under what generalizations about human credulity, of however broad scope, they fall, unless this aetiology is also seen as either permissive or demanding of belief—unless, of course, I do this as I query or abandon my beliefs. I cannot, for example, tell myself that I think that p because doing so resolves cognitive dissonances, unless I can also see that resolution as possibly rational (whether or not it really is); if not I shall just be unable to retain belief.

2.4.8   What sort of inability is this? Is it that human credulity is too feeble to rise to such occasions? Not at all: we are quite credulous enough—some of us credulous enough, it sometimes seems, for anything. But credulity rests on our leaving belief unexamined and unexplained, or on our accepting purported justifications much too easily. The oft-repeated fact remains that self-explanation cannot erode justification and be sincere. The source of these 'musts' and 'mays' and inabilities lies not in empirical laws and human limitations but in the nature of the dependence of belief on the institutions of language.

2.5 Self-encounters of the conceptual kind

2.5.1 Sellars writes: 'Man couldn't be man till he encountered himself' in the framework of conceptual thought (1963: 6). But he also foresees the possibility that this encounter might lead to the end of man (of persons); the picture of himself which he finds in the sciences might show that the very idea of himself which defines him as a person is ill founded (1963: sect. v). Since we have noted two primitive forms of practical life, and a distinct conceptual cultivation for each, we can expect two forms of conceptual self-encounter. It is the ideal of science to account, in its own explanatory schemata, for all things, events, and processes; this will include the activities of agents seen as events and processes. It is the ideal of the engaged stance of rational explanation to give action-explanations of all agent pursuits, including the pursuits of science.

2.5.2 The life of persons is dialectical, caught up in evolving conflict. We see the first signs of that movement towards rejection and recapture in the context of encountering ourselves as objects for scientific scrutiny (see also 5.5). Persons, once they form the ideal picture of their explanatory and predictive abilities in the sciences, must look for a scientific picture of what they themselves are. To achieve that vision of ourselves must be a central aim of culture. We would betray our personhood no less deeply by 'going soft' in the pursuit of it than if we discovered thereby that our idea of a person was somehow untenable. The aims of this book require that persons have a scientific view of themselves which is complete and exhaustive within its proper disciplines. That there may be other and independent disciplines in culture cannot weaken the claims of science.

2.5.3 We need a scientific theory of what we are. But it is no less vital that man encounters himself in another framework of conceptual thought, constituted by action-concepts. Science is the product of agents, whose actions are explicable, justifiable, warranted, or unwarranted according to the canons, implicit and explicit, which help to define the idea of a person. Unless we justify science as a global activity of persons in substantially the same ways in which we justify particular actions and sayings, we will impeach the scientific image from outside it, as the earlier image of the world based on teleological principles was subverted. Man's self-encounter in the form of 'reasoner encountering scientific practitioner' poses the problem of scientific method. I shall not pursue it here, but take up a related cultural theme.

2.5.4 If the divergence between scientific and action-theoretic styles of explaining human behaviour really were an inconsistency, then this might be resolved at the expense of either style. However, the prestige of science may make it seem inevitable that its superior mass would crush our understanding of ourselves as persons. Such an outcome would wholly destroy ethical life, for we would lose the means of formulating the aspirations and ideals, the self-exhortations and the demands of virtue, which provide intelligible goals to aim at. We might hope to translate existing rights and duties, unmasked as mere licence and taboo, into the expurgated and expanded ideology of a new science. But it is not the least bit clear how that might be done without complete loss in their directive force. There is no suggestion how these might become autonomous goals for us. It hardly seems adequate to our sense of a meaningful life to let our ethical pursuits drop because they are tinged with some obscurity, or with the naïvety of imperfectly warranted information.

2.5.5 However, the ideas of personhood run too deep for a clash of that sort between them and the sciences. To encounter ourselves in the disciplines of conceptual thought requires not just that we should have a scientific view of ourselves. Science is not produced by faultless gods, but by ourselves—some of it well produced and some of it produced poorly, ineptly, dishonestly; it may be slipshod, dim, or barren. To separate the gold from the dross in this vast outpouring is to estimate putative contributors as persons, rational, scrupulous, or inventive, whose justifications of their claims are adequate or not. This is a task which we have the capacity to perform, and we cannot possibly be less confident of the rigour and precision with which we can apply these tests than about the power, elegance and reliability of the scientific theories themselves. It is no impossible task, however dimly grasped in principle. Teachers do it, journal editors do it, fellow aspirants to the profession do it, the committees of learned societies and academies do it. What they do is to employ, either well or badly, crassly or with delicacy and strength, criteria which implicitly refer to persons, to what they are, what disciplines and institutions define them, and what norms they pass or fail by. Were scientists not persons, following personal skills with high excellence, we would have no grounds for accepting science. It would seem, then, that the overthrow of personhood by science could not leave science standing. Like a blind but mighty Samson tearing down the fabric of the temple of Man, it would engulf itself in that destruction.

2.5.6 The manifest image of man-in-the-world includes the idea that there are persons. The manifest image may seem to be undermined by the scientific image, even though science arises only out of aims and enterprises peculiar to persons. Yet the scientific image can have no claim on the beliefs of persons unless it conforms explicitly to personal demands of care and responsibility in observation. Science may find no persons in its final look at the world, yet its methods of discovery must fit what persons require, else there is no reason to believe it. To destroy the older image must be self-destruction, for only in it can we find sense for the idea that thinking needs standards which link what one thinks to what anyone ought to think.

2.5.7 Nevertheless, I must not overstate what these presuppositions of science can establish. They offer no simple guarantee that science will never overturn reason and personhood, but only that, in the event of its doing so we will not have an intact science which there is some motive (if 'motive' is not too personal an expression) to pursue. The structure of any *reductio ad absurdum* argument envisages the refutation of the presuppositions on which that very argument is conducted. These may just as well be the general principles of rationality themselves as any premiss of argument. But if reason were reduced, by reasoning, to absurdity, then we would have no *reason* to accept any remnant as a replacement for reason. The New Humans—those who have ceased to employ the concepts which define persons—may, by some impersonal techniques, succeed in getting us to behave in some ways rather than in others, including ways of speaking; perhaps they will do so mainly by speaking to us. But if these sayings are not reasonings, then we have no other model for their efficacy than to see them as commands, threats, cajoleries, spells, and incantations—as generally coercive or seductive. Perhaps this reads like an accusation of bad faith or the sounding of an awful warning—all that is intended, however, is an expression of puzzlement as to what this vision of the future is really supposed to be, a puzzlement based on the view that the idea of a person is really as deep-seated both in our conceptual structures and in our lives as, *a priori*, one would expect it to be.

2.5.8 It is not easy to see what would lead us to abandon reason. Would we not need some *reason* to do so? Somehow we would surely follow a path which it seemed we *ought* to follow, and what would this 'ought' mean, if not that there was some possibly unprecedented reason to follow it? If there seemed to be nothing we ought to do, it would not seem that we ought to abandon reason.

On the State of Being a Person

3.1 Persons as communicators

3.1.1 I want to explain valuing by showing it to be part of what humans do when they attain their natural state. Living in a culture, using a language, makes a natural ambience for humans. In this chapter I want to argue, or, more candidly perhaps, to claim, that whoever uses a language in a culture is in touch with what can usefully be called a project of being reasonable, or even a life of reason. This, in turn, puts the person in touch with the projects of valuing. I suggest some broad analogies between the life of reason and the good life which explain the claim, I hope. The analogies need more justification than I give, but the argument would take us far afield into philosophy of language and I could not firmly establish them even then. Nor are the analogies between reasoning and valuing so detailed and systematic as to warrant a long discussion. But whoever is a speaker in a culture is in the state of being a person—in touch with valuing, he understands what valuing is, and can be himself appraised as a valuer. It does not follow from this that the person pursues what he understands, that he undertakes the tasks that make us more and more fully persons. So describing the state does not yet tell us all that a person is. It merely connects valuing with human nature.

3.1.2 Persons who are merely in this state may fail to embark on valuing and on the self-excelling tasks of being a person which are my main concern. Some will be disabled; others will not yet be able, and still others will be past being able to deploy more than the most elementary of rational and linguistic forces. Some of these are persons not so much because of what they are as because we have taken them into our moral family, made them ours, and taken up duties towards them. There is a very different class of persons who fail to take up the tasks of valuing and self-excelling because of depression, accidie, weakness of will, illness, despair, or misanthropy. These last might be seen as pursuing the life of reason in some measure, but the first as pursuing it only marginally. Yet all of them have some conception, however dim, of values and valuing. They have a grasp of self-excelling, but have either turned away from it or are incapable of rising to a practical pursuit of it. However, it is not these problems, but rather those of what mastery of language in a culture brings us to grasp that I want to shed light on in this chapter. I begin with some analogies between what speaking demands and what personhood needs.

3.1.3 Clearly speech needs, in some form, reciprocal recognition of speakers and hearers (1.1.10). Primarily, we speak to those who have mastered the capacity to reply to us, a capacity virtually identical with their ability to understand us. A speaker adopts higher-order intentional attitudes to hearers and vice versa. A speaker aims to get a hearer to realize that he is speaking with the aim that the hearer learns something; if he is to understand what is said, the hearer must understand this aim (following Grice 1957). Thus, in communication we take higher-order attitudes to others and to ourselves.

3.1.4 Grasping a concept calls for an understanding of what is universal in two ways: speaker must use the word, or hearer understand it, in the way anyone uses or understands it; the rule is applied, in asserting or understanding, without regard to anything but the general character of the objects which fall under the concept grasped. As Sellars, following Wittgenstein, puts it 'there is no thinking apart from common standards of correctness and relevance, which relate what I *do* think to what *anyone ought to* think. The contrast between "I" and "anyone" is essential to rational thought' (1963: 16–17; italics in original). Thus speaking begins a practical enterprise in which one treats oneself as just an instance of being a communicator. Therefore, to grasp a concept is to be schooled in things which are basic to any understanding of moral appraisal.

3.1.5 This self-evaluative process at the core of language-learning is weakly analogous to elements that lie in the pursuit of virtues and in being a self-evaluating person. An immediate result, though at rather a tangent to our main direction, is that Hume mischaracterized a problem (Hume ed. 1888: 469) in supposing that an 'ought' must somehow derive from an 'is'. The idea of what one ought to do (in the form of what one ought to *say*) is fundamental to the grasp of any sort of conceptual skill at all.

3.1.6 Yet the reflective self-evaluation we practise in language-learning does not resemble in close detail the reflective self-evaluation which underlies the transformation of desires into values. It is *contrastive* self-evaluation (4.6.5; Taylor 1977) that we practise in forging values. This requires that we have (higher-order) desires about some of our (first-order) desires not merely as the result of a contingent clash among first-order desires, but because of an estimate of what anyone *is* in acting from some first-order desire. In communicating, anyone has a first-order desire to talk which leads to a usually lifelong, though intermittent, project of saying things which are more or less significant. This desire leads us to reject, or otherwise monitor, aspects of our linguistic performance. However, this monitoring process is not, in any evident way, generally powered by second-order desires. But we do criticize our own and others' performances as correct or incorrect and see this success or failure as necessarily connected with prowess as a communicator. The intentions and beliefs involved in speaking form a small but well-structured hierarchy, so that in monitoring linguistic performance one is an object of one's own criticism in the *social* role of communicator, an object of one's own higher-order attitudes.

3.2 Culture again

3.2.1 Concrete, objective, cultural conditions and processes are necessary for certain sorts of consciousness, including self-consciousness. They are necessary for the use of any language. Forms of consciousness spring from social conditions and in turn mould them; this may happen dialectically in breeding conflicts internal to a culture, leading to resolutions which, to some degree at least, reconcile the contradictions. Though the laws that human life must conform to are fundamentally relations among quasi-Aristotelian universals (Armstrong 1983; Dretske 1977; Tooley 1977), it is only in concrete and particular cultural circumstances that they can have instances and the laws and universals take on reality. The conflict, resolution, and growth attach to their concrete embodiments rather than to universals viewed abstractly. This is the broad theme of Hegel's *Phenomenology* (Hegel ed. 1977) and I take something like it to be true. Hegel is as much concerned as

Marx with concrete embodiments and processes of conflict by means of which these universals are instantiated in the concrete world at the same time as they guide its evolution.

3.2.2 To illustrate—Marx thought that an idea of property would have been meaningless before the social institution of division of labour in the production of material wealth: that is a clear and plausible theory. So is the further view that wrongs such as trespass could have no meaning before a post-nomadic agriculture arose which farmed land set aside for that purpose. Hegel thought that this dependency of subjective consciousness on concrete social processes extends to a very wide range of thoughts involved in human action. Actions, we saw (2.3; see also 3.3), have meanings. Meanings cannot be just subjective, for there are no meanings outside the social structures on which language depends, nor can there be meanings unless there are objective properties of things to constitute the similarities on which concept-formation depends. Fundamentally, it is in social contexts and only against the background of social institutions that there are meanings. Various things might be meant by this. Let us glance at some of them.

3.2.3 As argued in 2.2, it is within co-operative tasks and information-exchange that movements began to be seen as actions, though we may guess that extension beyond the area of co-operative work was rapid and wide-ranging. So actions depend on social institutions for their meaning in that weak sense first. An interesting account of our more developed explanation and justification of action (Pettit 1986*a*) is that we understand someone's doings by bringing them under a *norm*, a socially recognized and accepted pattern of aims and ends which make up being a certain kind of person (a gardener, a mechanic, a carpenter, to mention conceptually simple examples). Pettit (1986*b*) calls this view social holism and I follow a form of it: I claim that many of our actions have their richer meanings in the light of evolving traditions—of courage, of greeting, buying, or making. It is not that actions can be explained only when they conform to these social institutions, understandings, and enablements, but that their reform, challenging, and development are all involved in our understanding conceptually what persons do and in our explaining it in the language of action-concepts. We may say, at least, that any effective hierarchy of explicitly self-evaluating states of consciousness depends on concepts that are products of some social processes which at least approach the cultural institutions of personal life.

3.2.4 Hegel was right in saying that we must wrest our consciousness of self—of what we objectively are—from the recognition of others. Certainly it is only within culture that an utterance of 'I am hungry' means what it does. Just so (but more speculatively) it is only in the light of cultural patterns and traditions that my actions can have enough intersubjectively recognizable (even if unrecognized) structure to count as having integrity or courage. That my will has triumphed, and that an opponent has submitted in a combat in which honour was placed above life, depends on cultural institutions. These enable us to see whose intentions have been fulfilled and what makes the fulfilment concrete, what counts as combat, honour, and submission. The meaning depends on institutions just as much as it does on individual intentions in acting. This is made particularly clear in the famous master-and-slave passages (Hegel, ed. 1977: 111–19). We need to formulate conceptual tools which allow us to identify observers, appraisers, and agents. These need to be precise enough to allow us to distinguish what does the observing, appraising, and acting from the objects of these activities, especially when the objects are persons. This need for precision is especially acute when a person is the object of his own observation, appraisal, and of his consequent activity to change himself as appraised and observed; he may, indeed, want to appraise his own performance as an appraiser. Only in a culture can disciplines and practices be formed which allow such precise conceptual tools and the self-criticism and self-excelling which are crucial to being a person. Mastery of language needs a background of observaion and appraisal thus providing a deep tie between reaching the state of being a person, and being in touch with valuing and the tasks that being a person sets for us.

3.2.5 Finally, on these themes, what must be rational if the idea of a person is to make sense is not individual reasoners, but something like a *cultural* verdict on reasoning. Lakatos (1976: 146) puts the matter as follows:

But mathematical activity produces mathematics. Mathematics, this product of human activity, 'alienates itself' from the human activity which has been producing it. It becomes a living growing organism, that *acquires a certain autonomy* from the activity which has produced it; it develops its own autonomous laws of growth, its own dialectic. The genuine creative mathematician is just a personification, an incarnation of these laws which can only realise themselves in human action. Their incarnation, however, is rarely perfect. The activity of human mathematicians, as it appears in history, is only a fumbling realisation of the wonderful dialectic of mathematical ideas. But any mathematician, if he has talent, spark, genius, communicates with, feels the sweep of, and obeys this dialectic of ideas.

3.2.6 This Hegelian passage makes clear sense of the way in which individual practitioners of cultural enterprises, especially those who succeed in them, can see an enterprise as a discipline. Individual reasoners may be as incompetent as can be without disturbing the cultural sense in which we are rational animals (Stich 1985). This view implies just the theory that laws of nature rest on relations among universals and that this gives them their necessity; it lends cultural enterprises the possibility of a correctness or aptness ultimately constituted by the relations among these universals. It gives mathematics, logic, or scientific method, among others, their objective standards of success and correctness.

3.3   Propositions and other ideals

3.3.1 Some of the ways in which ideals, institutions, or norms are part of our language-skills give rise to a project of being reasonable, even to a life of reason, for some speakers. This is because the ideals are part of an ineliminable practice. No scientific concepts could play the idealizing roles in this practice which they, together with our agency-concepts, fill.

3.3.2 The objects of belief are *propositions*, true or false. My task is to sketch the idea of a proposition less as the concept of an abstract, normatively neutral entity with elusive identity-conditions and more as a demand of communication, a *value* which one must always aim at. It is the idea of a *need*, not of a thing. It might be likened rather to a goal in the language-game, to something scored; or, better still, to a mark in Australian football and a fair catch in American. For speaker must pass and hearer intercept in a certain way without fumbles. There is nothing mysterious about the *ball* when a goal is kicked or a mark taken.

3.3.3 Suppose we construe *modus ponens* as a rule of proof. It tells us that if $P{\rightarrow}Q$ is a line in a proof and P another line in it, then we may write down Q. Of course, it is useless to us as a rule unless it corresponds to semantic relations of logical consequence, though this distinction need not take up our time now. But how can we apply this rule in the real practice of argument, if we can apply it at all? Only if two distinct sayings can count as the same substituend for the sentence letter P (or Q). That gets cloudy, quite obviously, when the sentences used begin to contain indexicals, ambiguities, or change in sense of subtler kinds as we move the context to different times and places. It may well turn out that the sayings (utterances) substituted for P, $P \rightarrow Q$ are true, yet the substituend for Q false. The proof may be invalid.

3.3.4 Problems of vagueness, indexicality, ambiguity, and the like induce mismatches between your remarks and my responses so that we miss each other's contents and my objections pass your claims by. (See Kaplan 1968; Dennett 1982.) The central observation which I wish to make on all such loopholes is that they are intelligible only in as far as they are remediable. The very articulating of the gap teaches us the linguistic performance that will close it. It is the ideal of a matching of contents among speakers which the very concept of rational debate is founded upon. That is no cure for scepticism, however. I claim, later, that the practice of being reasonable is inexhaustible in any body of doctrine; that implies that the possibility of objections is, in principle, never exhausted by any list of ways of framing them. But the idea of a proposition is just the thought that communication may (not necessarily does) succeed, and succeed ideally. (Quine's 1960 view that translation, hence meaning, is indeterminate is a radical form of scepticism about these matters. It is underargued in the light of the immense strength of the conclusion. My view of the issue may be found in Nerlich 1972 and 1976.) To reject an ideal identity of content in favour of a regularly attainable similarity as the best possible approach to matching contents is to settle for something too thin to establish the possibility of searching, rigorous, valid argument. Where we envisage failure of content identity, there we foresee a gap in validity. Logic tells us nothing about how this ideal may be attained, though it plainly presupposes that it may be. Logic is like an ethics, therefore, in postulating ideals without specifying real examples that embody them, or recipes for attaining them.

3.3.5 I am suggesting, then, that contents are constructed or abstracted from sentence utterances by the use of dimensions of criticism to which purported logical arguments have been or may be subjected. Differences among contents, either of type-sentences or of token-uttered ones, are fixed by the styles of effective critique in reasoning to which they are subject. It is only in rare and contrived examples that criticism is about disparities between the speaker's notional world and the real one, rather than about careless or imprecise matchings of content. We articulate as best we can the concrete needs which rigorous argument ought to meet— which concern what we *ought* to say and think, or what we *may*. We can never be certain that an unforeseen challenge may not succeed and a mismatch be found.

3.3.6 The main point here is not to explicate how propositions and beliefs are determined just by properties that belong intrinsically to individual believers and sayers in concrete environments. It is to illustrate how communication gets to be rigorously precise on any occasion in virtue of a complex range of cultural relationships which await full elucidation but which involve, in complex ways, all of the following: speakers, hearers, the general language community, its practices, and the range of things that lie beyond this and make up what it is that they may talk about.

3.3.7 It is another ideal that language should permit the statement of every theory, so that any theory and its negation may each be framed. Our ideal is of a medium of representation which, in its conventions and structures—the usages by means of which we exploit it—contains no theory which might conflict with something we might want to represent. Given the complexity of the formal, structural resources of language, that sounds like a very tall order to fill. Nor would we easily know whether the ideal was met. What makes the ideal vivid is the prospect of its failure, as is the case with the ideal that there are propositions. One way in which the ideal might be thought to have failed seems to be universal across languages. It is a task of philosophy to probe such failures, whether real or apparent.

3.3.8 There is the problem of time and tense. It is often argued (I have argued it in Nerlich 1979) that languages do, in general, contain at least one ontological theory in the very ways they are constructed: they are ontic in concerning both the ontic structure of time and the nature of the basic members of our ontology. Despite what is sometimes said, all languages at least hint that, at any time, times other than that time are not real. This is tied to a particular sort of basis for ontology—continuants. (Tenses are less central to this implied ontology than is the posit of continuants.) At the very least, language resists the clear, direct expression of the ontic view that the structure of time is analogous to that of space, in which places other than the present place are just as real as it is. So language fails to admit the idea one struggles to articulate, and which would allow one to speak of things with both spatial and temporal parts to which continuants would be somewhat obscurely related. The case is specially noteworthy not merely because it is there, but because our best theories of the relevant aspect of the world (the theories of space-time) lead us to think that what has been built into language is actually false.

3.3.9 Thus mastery of language requires at least a grasp of how such ideals of communication may be pursued. It puts one in touch with a form of valuing.

3.4   An ethics of belief?

3.4.1 We saw that when anyone undertakes to explain why she holds some current belief, the dominant form of her explanation is a justification for believing it. Characteristically, she gives the reasons why she believes it, rather than the *aetiology* of her belief. She shows how the belief is reasonable, or more narrowly, how she is reasonable in holding it. She is reasonable in holding some belief either if it is something she ought to hold or, more feebly but perhaps more frequently, something that it is permissible for her to hold. The 'oughts' and 'mays' gestured at will be ethical in some clear sense if they relate clearly to the pursuit of a value. That is precisely what is the case.

3.4.2 The capture and exploitation of truth is a major aim of communication. Truth is a value of linguistic life—*the* value, since imperatives, optatives, and the like loom less large in our talk than indicatives do. The pursuit and capture of this value through a variety of forms of linguistic life is common to every culture in which humans become persons. If the use of language in the forms I have been discussing—which is something more than grunts, cries, or the display of plumage—is the pursuit of value in a culture (of truth, that is), then the norms of practice in its pursuit (norms we still cannot articulate fully), and the strengths and skills which maximize our achieving the value, make up an ethical practice. To speak of truth as a value, one needs to speak of the field within which one nourishes, grows, and harvests it: the field of linguistic discourse.

3.4.3 These reflections again link with Sellars's claim, already quoted in 3.1.4, that 'there is no thinking apart from common standards of correctness and relevance, which relate what I *do* think to what *anyone ought to* think'. Thus to explain, even to oneself, why one thinks what one does, why these and not other concepts apply, is to show why anyone ought to (may) think it by offering what purport to be *reasons for anyone*, as well as mere causes of belief. That this is inescapable does not lie in the inaccessible natural cognitive processes which underlie our language capacity. It is inescapable by the nature of the practice of communication which we learn. It is a cultural inevitability, or part of the 'logic' of belief and reasoning (if the last phrase seems illuminating). The inevitability is best thought of, I suggest, as an ethical 'must' ('may'), or connected with ethical 'musts'. More broadly, I am proposing that at least one way to pursue epistemological problems is not to naturalize them, but to replace the attempt to specify what belief, reason, and truth are with an account of what they ought to be and why. The push towards an abstraction or supernature (towards Platonic propositions and facts, for instance) is a mistaken direction for the push from what is the case towards what needs to be.

3.4.4 Let us consider reason. Reason is not a set of contents (truths). Reason is reasoning, an activity or an active commitment; rather a project or a form of life than a body of doctrine. It is *being reasonable* that is basic. We all need to know how to be reasonable, for to communicate at all is to acknowledge that onus, though by no means necessarily to fulfil it; we need to know that one ought to believe some things but not just anything. To be a speaker, to be in the state of being a person, is to be *in touch with* being reasonable, to understand, without necessarily taking up, a commitment to the pursuit of a value in the practice of a virtue which peculiarly belongs to the value. To be reasonable, however, is not just to acknowledge that onus, but to try to meet it as well, by committing oneself to being reasonable with some assiduity.

3.4.5 It is sometimes said that reason is, at bottom, just a faith, like any other, in some body of doctrine that defines what reason is:

the laws of logic perhaps. The grain of truth in that argument plainly is that the chain of reasons which anyone can give for a belief ends somewhere. If, in order to be reasonable, one could accept nothing unless one had a reason for it, no one could be reasonable. There need be nothing ultimate or privileged about one's stopping-place, on some occasion of reasoning. There is no place at which reason-asking loses point. There are no ultimate doctrines which reasonable people must accept as beyond question, as views which they can query or allow others to query only at the forfeit of their title to rationality. Every doctrine proposed to define what reasonableness is has been rationally challenged, and so things will go on. One need only glance at a text on alternative or deviant logics to see that reasonable people can properly probe and challenge any doctrine which offers to state the fundamental principles of reasoning.

3.4.6 Part of the reason why such challenges and probings are pertinent and interesting is that the principles of logic which are presently central to the subject fail to yield, or can plausibly be argued to fail to yield, a complete picture of our reasoning even when we confine it to strict deductive techniques. Our ordinary reasoning does not seem to be truth-functional, and the handling of intensional constructions in formal logic is still uncertain. It is an open question whether the relation of logical consequence, as classical logic defines it, captures what we mean by entailment. These few suggestions by no means exhaust the ways in which the adequacy of classic logic, merely in respect of scope, may be questioned.

3.4.7 But more fundamentally, being reasonable can never be exhausted in embracing some doctrine; no doctrine unchallengeably exhausts reason. For once we formulate it, we thereby present ourselves with the formal opportunity of asking whether it is true and what reason we have to accept it. Any doctrine, once explicit, immediately becomes a formal candidate for doubt, objection, for drawing support from other principles, or for confrontation by fruitful practice which departs from it. Of course, the formal sentential means of question and objection are one thing; making the question or objection good is quite another. Any question will be idle outside some dawning perception how the answer might be 'no'. That is, we must know how to go on *in practice*. It certainly had better not follow that just because we can frame, grammatically, a question about our principle or formulate its negation, its status is undermined. Yet any doctrine appears on the stage of reason as matter in the form of a rationally challengeable thesis.

3.4.8 These reflections show that reason as a practice lies deeper than reason as a doctrine. That does not quite capture the whole point, since there can be complete theories of at least some practices. But reason is a self-evolving practice, the formulating of rules that make up a theory of existing practice providing the occasion and the impulse for the practice to evolve a little more. That is, doctrine might change the practice by shaping, guiding, and extending it. It may then cease to describe it adequately. In any case, it is always reasonable to doubt that we have fully articulated rational practice because it is part of the practice to alienate and appraise (transcend, if you prefer) its own theory, though not always in an explicit metatheoretical way. Thus reasonableness is always open-ended in practice. This makes a dawning sense of the idea of a project or a *life of reason*, a life which continually probes and extends reason by adventurous practice and by formulating doctrine about the adventures.

3.4.9 It is not for us to decide, as a culture, what is reasonable. We can impose no rational structures on the world. Articulating theories of reason and expanding, perhaps inarticulately, its practice are subject to stringent disciplines by the unaccomodating, objective world, no less than other theories and practices are. There are things to *get right* in theory and practice. One of them is the idea (or ideal) of sentences as atoms of information, as complete thoughts, which may be true or false. The universality across languages of the tie of truth to message-structures makes it look too inevitable for it to be regarded as a convention, yet it is notoriously hard to make sense of the idea that the world imposes that structure on language and thought. Our holism needs the discipline of a considered atomism.

3.4.10 There is a sense in which whatever practice purports to yield justifications of belief will count as trying to be reasonable, even when the justifications are limp or worthless. 'Being reasonable' may refer both to this practice and to the virtues of the practice. Beliefs are justified (well or ill) as true; when permitted, justified as likely true or possibly so. Hence, truth is the value pursued in this practice; the practice aims to maximize the value. So epistemology is the ethical theory of how to arrive at truth, but also of how to appropriate and exploit it; how to understand it. Truth is the value of this ethics; knowledge is the grasp, appropriation, and possession of the value; and reasonableness the characteristic of successful practice in achieving truth and knowledge. It is the virtue of the practice. We can find counterpart features in other value-areas where we can speak of values, their appropriation, and the practices of winning them. Thus once a human has reached the state of being a person, an articulate thinker, conscious of self and self-evaluating of at least some of its characteristic performances, it is in touch with the concepts of value and with the task of making of itself a particular person.

3.5   Culture, meanings, and understanding

3.5.1 In the end, it is culture that sustains the ideal expressed in Sellars's phrase that there is no learning language without understanding that what I do think is related to what anyone ought to think. So language will determine the content of my sayings, where this includes the rules which interpret a speaker's utterance in context. Ideals of language take the determination of content out of the hands—more literally, out of the intentions—of the individual utterer. Humpty Dumpty was quite wrong: ideally, words are masters. Here again we find a requirement of reason: what allows you to dispute the very claim I make is that language mediates impartially between us.

3.5.2 This relates, in turn, to something else noted in a Sellars epigram: that in the case of persons, the impact of the environment on the individual is mediated by the group. This does not mean, merely, that the survival of species members to breeding-age standardly depends on membership of group, pack, herd, or flock as it does in many species. No doubt there is such dependence in our species too. But for individual members of non-linguistic species, the environment does not impact on them in the light of an *understanding* of it, through concepts culturally forged.

3.5.3 The cultural relation between the group and its individual members is complex, as Hegel was the first to spell out in any detail. In some sense the relation is dialectical, though it seems here to be more a dialectic of mutual presupposition than of opposition. The individual member of a full-blown culture can think, invent, challenge his cultural milieu, and, quite broadly, enter into his unique, idiosyncratic conception of his style of life within the culture only by the route of universalizing his grasp of the world and himself. The peculiar flavour of his life, in so far as he is the comprehending author and voluntary director of it, is grasped and foreseen in concepts forged by a rigid orthodoxy which ruthlessly expunges all attempts at individualism in the determination of content: what he means when he acts, speaks, and thinks is what anyone must (ought to) think and mean who exploits these resources of conceptual thought in just these ways. He perceives his originality and idiosyncrasy in *universal* terms, the contents of which are fixed by general usage of them.

3.5.4 But just as there can be no deliberately pursued unique patterns of life without the existence of a sustaining culture, there can be neither culture nor language without individual, inventive exploitation of it to give it sense and life. The range, diversity, and novelty of personality among those who appropriate cultural resources together with the unique and peculiar items in their individual experiences make room for the novel and the odd within the range of general description and understanding. The quirks, however idiosyncratic, make a place for themselves as rare, new, strange *properties* of the items, a place in what is general.

3.5.5 To no small extent, these reflections suggest that the ideal of sentence-content as inflexible to individual intention is something of a myth which practice leaves unrealized. Language, after all, grows not by atomistic accretion of concepts but evolves under a continuous variety of pressures for change. Nevertheless, the ideal of language, an ideal set by the needs of rigour in reasoning, is an ideal of settled usages and institutions. A creative thinker and speaker may reach among these for a verbal tool with a standard function which she can rely on its accurately performing and which she *ought* to employ to that end. If she finds she can use this tool in the course of some quite new job, then that facility depends on an agreed recognition (at least potentially universal) that anyone always ought to have been able (permitted) to use it for that kind of job, had that job been anticipated.

3.5.6 If we look at science, or indeed at any other institution within culture, we can see a case for saying that the unit of understanding is not the individual student but the cultural community. There is, very probably, no one person who understands the whole of physics or chemistry, let alone one who understands the whole of science. Science is the result of invention and discovery by individual people (or by smallish teams of them), yet each of these discoveries depends on the work of others, either as to the results of a range of investigations into which the new one fits, or by the use of the concepts and conceptual techniques already formed. This happens, to no small extent, even in periods of revolutionary scientific change. But the understanding of science, even more than its invention, is achieved and appropriated finally by the culture. The standards which settle how discoveries are to be presented and to be accepted or rejected are culturally set. One can appeal over the head, so to speak, of some local stronghold (local temporally or spatially) to the broader, more deeply entrenched culture, as Galileo did with the intransigent Aristotelians and the Church. Though the local battle may be lost the war may yet be won, as, once again, was the case with Galileo.

3.5.7 This does not make for a cultural relativity in any debilitating sense. Just as, whatever explanations I may offer of my own beliefs, they appear as justifications, so every publication of scientific results is offered as a justification of them. Whatever laws of cognitive science may be instantiated by the explanation of conclusions in a learned journal, a place will be made for them in science only if there is a properly rigorous justification for them. What is properly rigorous is fixed by the corporate understanding of the culture at the time. This understanding will not be something which it happens to have gained some consensus about. It will have been scrutinized and criticized by every interested intelligence, many of whom will have wanted to find every possible flaw, and we may assume that little will escape the net of practical reasoners. Nevertheless, that an explanation of one's beliefs comes to be seen as a justification does not mean that it is a justification, not even when we see it as the final limit of ideal scientific practice. Whether it ought to have been argued as it was argued is a question which remains askable and might, at any time, have been made intelligible and practical by an ingenious critic. However brilliant, quirky, novel, and unprecedented the processes of scientific invention may be, the presentation and explanation of it must exploit (or invent and introduce) cultural norms of rational practice. In the end, the total world-view lies beyond the reach of any one individual and is arbitrated by the world itself.

3.5.8 Thus anything that is a person, in command of a language and a cultured agent, is not merely in some socio-linguistic state, but is in touch with valuing, with ideals, with cultural and linguistic norms which point out, without dictating, the tasks of personhood.

4

Persons and their Desires

4.1 Desires are not beliefs

4.1.1 The concepts grouped round those of an agent and of a person may be represented, a little roughly perhaps, by two simpler core notions: belief and desire. The concept of belief has been very intently scrutinized for a long time. Desires are much less well understood; higher-order desires scarcely understood at all. They are belief-like in some of their properties, though irreducibly different from beliefs. But putting them under the microscope for a brighter, sharper focus obliges me to begin by considering ways in which belief and desire work together in voluntary action.

4.1.2 Hume (ed. 1888: 415) told us, in his outrageous way, that reason is and ought to be only the slave of the passions. His deeper meaning is that if reason, belief, and information play a role in voluntary action then they do so in subservience to, or at least in co-operation with, some desire, inclination, or passion. Reason cannot oppose desire and passion but only deals with factual matters. Rewriting Hume a little, we may say that there are three main ways of expressing desires: indicative formulas like 'I want . . .', and counterpart sentences in imperative or in optative moods. To the latter, one cries 'False!' in vain. They are not the sort of things that can be false—or true. When an 'I want . . .' sentence is false, that is just because the speaker does not want what she says she wants, not because there is some error made in the wanting. To say what one wants is not to endorse a judgement about what is good or worthy of desiring. (See Stocker 1979; Smith 1988; Pettit 1987.) Hume's idea demands, I think, that beneath these linguistic facts lie deeper ones about the nature of the claim that wants, but not beliefs, make on us and on the world.

4.1.3 But Hume was wrong to place the difference of desire from belief in the subservience of belief. Or, at least, the converse of this point is a theorem too, and perhaps that is also widely agreed among philosophers. Nevertheless, I wish to argue for it briefly, since I find it somewhat more elusive and, arguably, it has the authority of Hume against it. Paradoxically, perhaps its elusiveness lies in the fact that very often the relevant information is so obvious, pervasive, instinctual, and non-verbal. The argument proceeds quite simply by assembling reminders of this fact.

4.1.4 Imagine an acute case of a simple, familiar desire: thirst. Someone has been lost for days in the hot sands of the Sahara, let us say. To what voluntary actions might acute, simple thirst prompt this person? Perhaps to staggering off in some direction. But which? If the person has some belief about where water might lie, then in that direction. But if not, then at least away from the present area which she perceives to be so dry. Why does she not sink to all fours, lower her head, and go through drinking motions, which are perhaps the actions most directly, simply, and naturally related to her desire—assuming that lapping at pools is natural—and to which she would be most immediately driven if desire could act without information? Because she believes no water is there and without the relevant information (it need not amount to knowledge) the desire is not a desire to *do* anything at all. Even when she sights water, no drinking can go on until she relates where it is to her own place, until she can continuously monitor her changing body-position so as to bring her lips and the water to a conjunction. All this rests on a kind of information which, in general, is too obtrusive for us ever to seek it, and which is so highly reliable and so pervasive in experience that the shock of losing it is not readily imaginable. Much of the epistemic climate in which desire may lead to actions—to simple actions such as scratching an ear—is so constant and inescapable that it takes some effort for us to attend to it explicitly. But once we make ourselves conscious of it, the converse of Hume's claim appears obviously correct. Desire can issue in voluntary action only if directed by some information. We might throw down an aphorism to challenge Hume's. Ignorance is and ought to be the jailer of the passions.

4.1.5 The deep difference that splits belief and desire apart is basic to the style of explanation which constitutes the engaged or intentional attitude. The primitive, unhelpful, obvious truth about desires is that it is they, not beliefs, that move us to act. It may help to explain, and perhaps justify, the idea of an irreducible difference to reflect on how desires can and do conflict.

4.1.6 Hume claimed that any passion is an 'original existence' which 'contains not any representative quality' (ed. 1888: 415). This may be true of appetites but, I think, true of no other desires. Desires standardly contain representations, so bare appetites are not typical desires. Even the appetites, as the examples just given show quite clearly, play no part in voluntary, deliberate action—in true agency—unless directed by information. In general, I avoid the appetitive and instinctual models of desire since they are more confining than explanatory. Appeal to instincts in humans sheds little light and gives a largely spurious sense that we are comfortably in line with sound causal, naturalistic principles. It inclines us to overlook the fact that for cultured beings in circumstances of even moderate plenty, perhaps the majority of their desires are interests. I do not mean prudential interests only but also projects of more or less enduring scope and seriousness, pursuits taken up out of curiosity, out of absorbing interest, which amuse us, which enlarge our capacities, or which are ends in themselves. It is not plausible to suppose that these contain no representations.

4.1.7 Standardly, then, a desire contains representations of states of affairs in the world. In the simplest common case, there is a temporally ordered pair of representations, a before and an after, or a first and a second member. The first representation portrays the occasion for a dispositional desire to become occurrent. The second will standardly differ from the first. Desire, that is, is usually desire for *change*. This need not be so. I can want a state of affairs to persist, and my desire may give rise to considerable anxiety if that state of affairs seems precarious. But desire for change remains the standard case.

4.1.8 In general, we can perhaps best talk about the logic of desires, and thus of conflict among them, by talking about the representations which they contain (Sartre 1956: 433–8) even though these are by no means the most significant features of desires. In general, two desires conflict when the (temporally) ordered pair of representations are such that the *before*-representations are identical, and the *after*- inconsistent, with each other. That is, the after-representations depict states of the world not jointly possible. To be sure, this is a highly schematic model of conflict, since desires are frequently far more complex than this in their representations; further, the inconsistency may well arise only

when we conjoin with the second (the after-) representations some
class of statements (physical laws, technical means) relative to
which they can be assessed as jointly possible or not.

4.1.9 It is irrational to harbour two *beliefs* which one sees to be
inconsistent, or to be jointly impossible relative to some other body
of information which is seen to be not negotiable (for whatever
reason). So how does it come to be rational to harbour *desires*
which conflict? (For doubts that it is rational at all, see Jackson
1985.) Well, obviously enough, perhaps, because the second
representation does not have to project more than a *possible* state
of affairs. It is its mere possibility that is the cue for action. The
object of even the simplest desire is what is possible. Just as the
conjunction of two possible statements need not be a possible
conjunction, so it fails to follow from the fact that I desire both a
state of affairs and its contrary that I desire their inconsistent
conjunction, though if I do I am, no doubt, irrational. Even when I
act so as to realize one of the states of affairs and choose between
desires, the conflicting desire on which I do not act, which I choose
not to satisfy, need not simply cease (though it may quite simply do
so). I can go on urgently wanting to do X all the time I am
deliberately doing something with which X is not jointly possible. I
can, plainly, go on feeling very much like eating all through my
chosen bout of fasting; I can desperately want to do something
amusing all the while I listen to a harangue which I recognize an
obligation to attend to. Certainly, we ordinarily speak as if we
thought it common enough to have conflicting desires. If I excuse
myself from my wife's outing by saying that I have work I must do,
it is a perfectly intelligible reproach if she accuses me of not *really*
wanting to accompany her. But it can be a reproach only if I can
both really want to go out with her and also really want to work
(contra Jackson, as I understand him). That I want to do something
else more than I want to do X does not mean at all that I do not
want to do X. Since desires conflict like this, desires differ radically
from beliefs. For instance, a desire to do X is not the same as a
belief that it is good to do X.

4.1.10 Of course, possible states of affairs can also be objects of
belief, but some beliefs are free of modal structure, whereas desires
never are. Conversely, I can have desires which are more than
minimally structured, modally. I may want to be *able* to overcome
any would-be assailant with a karate chop, without ever wanting

actually to overcome anyone that way. But the desires of a rational person may conflict, may be known by her to conflict, and may persist with unabated intensity without reproach to her reasonableness, because the objects of desire are always possible states of affairs. Reasonable persons may characteristically be strongly moved to act in conflicting ways; they do not strongly believe conflicting propositions. It may be, incidentally, that our having a concept of the possible derives from our concept of desire rather than the reverse. In any case, we could not identify a desire with the ordered pair of its component representations (beliefs), the second member being a modal belief. Desires conflict. These ordered pairs of representations do not.

4.1.11 I mention in passing that conflicts of desires naturally give rise to cases of occurrent desires which issue in no action. We might call these defeated, frustrated, or disappointed desires. They may influence some aspects of behaviour because they give rise to emotions such as regret and others appropriate to disappointment and frustration. But this need not be so. I may simply set aside or neglect a desire from which I do not act. It may simply cease, by choice, and without more psychic cost than its having had no effect. We might call these lapsed desires.

4.2 Homoeostatic desires and open projects

4.2.1 What are we to understand by an appetite, generally? Appetites resemble each other through a cluster of features. Most appetites have most features. First, an appetite is a recurrent disposition. It is a disposition to eat or drink or whatever else; the disposition recurs, comes and goes, not just the eating and drinking. Each of us is subject to hunger and thirst and, in the ordinary course of affluent civilized life, is more or less strongly disposed, at regular intervals, to eat and drink, and, at similarly regular intervals, is little disposed to do so. Second, appetites, once the disposition occurs, typically grow more urgent and physically discomforting if long unsatisfied. Curiosity is not an appetite: it may be at fever pitch immediately one catches a whiff of scandal or notices something surprising, but may abate as other things distract us; the wish to play chess may persist neither diminished nor augmented over months without a partner. Third, the satisfaction of appetites is typically accompanied by physical pleasure, delightful tastes or thrills, or a simple glow of satisfaction. One's desire for chess is satisfied when one gets a game, and it may, indeed, prove enjoyable, but one cannot distinguish the pleasures of chess from the problem-solving, strategies, winnings, and losings that constitute the game. However, we can easily detach, in thought, the pleasure in food one chews and tastes but does not swallow from the satisfactions of fullness of abdomen and raised level of blood-sugar which satisfy hunger. These might be achieved by medical interventions which bypass the eating of food. Lastly, appetites may be surfeited though, alas for the portly, sometimes not so easily as their teleological role in bodily functions might suggest.

4.2.2 We already saw that not even the appetites can play a part in voluntary, deliberate action unless directed by information. Even so, we tend to look at desires on the model of appetites, as if information had little part in our understanding desire. This may make explanation by desires look suitably blind, hence causal and natural. It makes dominant over our thinking about desires a homoeostatic image of human beings. The image is false, and known to be false; but that seems little to weaken its power over our thinking. The image works as follows.

4.2.3 In any organism, motives are always directed towards restoring or maintaining an ideal balance in its physiological state. While it is in this state, the feeling tone of the organism is one of serene pleasure or bland neutrality. The feeling tone has psychological value which motives the organism to do whatever will produce or sustain it. Any departure from the balanced state may produce mental feelings of discomfort or pain; alternatively, a departure prompts activity (e.g. food-seeking) which, when it produces its physiological goal, rewards the organism mentally with feelings of pleasure. Thus all motives are directed at producing pleasure or extinguishing discomfort, where the feelings are correlated with definite physiological states. So every motive or drive is directed at an inner mental state which has some physiological homoeostatic mechanism as its correlate. The whole box and dice of motives subserves the evolutionary end of keeping the organism in the same balanced state.

4.2.4 Though plainly an empirical thesis, the homoeostatic image draws strength from philosophical muddles such as egoism. It is easy to see the influence of the image on our thought both at present and in history. In moral philosophy every hedonistic theory of morals has probably been based on the image, and even theories like Utilitarianism, which are immediately concerned with the objective consequences of actions, frequently come back to the idea that the moral good must be the maximizing of pleasure. Even Freud, though he often wrote as if he knew the image was wrong, based his psychoanalytic theory on Abraham's idea of erogenous bodily zones: oral, anal, or genital. Everything revolves round sexual instincts directed at inner gratifications connected with these zones. The immense prestige of Freud's theory makes it all the harder to rid ourselves of the idea that we are all really in pursuit of those inner pleasures or freedoms from tension which signal our return to the rest state.

4.2.5 The image has such power over us because we often find it obscure what our motives are, precisely. We know, or think we know, that we want something, without well understanding why. Together with this fact that our deeper motives are obscure to us goes an unwillingness to admit that we cannot fathom ourselves. To admit that your knowledge and power over your own mental being is incomplete and even fragmentary is very disconcerting. So we freely make up stories about how we tick and about how we can see, quite transparently, the way our inner wheels turn. The homoeostatic image of motives is only one of these stories. Another is the idea that each of us understands language by viewing an internal picture-show caused to arise in his imagination as a conditioned response to learned verbal stimulation. The falsity of this idea suggests a dim view of our powers of introspection which, in turn, makes plausible our dependence on the responses of others for much of our self-understanding. The homoeostatic image of humans is no less false, nor does it tend less to suggest that introspection is a poor guide to the structure of our motives.

4.2.6 This aspect of the spell of the image on us is connected with the theme of expressivism, and I will turn aside for a little to comment on it. In Sartre's philosophy, anguish springs from seeing that the project we are embarked on has no final claim on us, does not have a foundation in any *nature* that we possess and that, though much that we do is not arbitrary in the light of our project, the project is itself arbitrarily chosen. So we are subject to moments of anguished perception of the inescapable freedom to change our deepest project; that is, of the inescapable arbitrariness and absurdity of our lives. Typically, the anguished question which rushes in upon us is 'What shall I do?', and there is nothing about us to recommend one answer rather than another. Anguish, more widely, is the recognition that nothing determines what to do in circumstances that challenge the projects and styles of living which ordinarily content us and in the pursuit of which we try to conceal from ourselves that not even our deepest values *compel* us to any course of action.

4.2.7 I believe that this points to an area of real, practical moral difficulty. If life is largely a matter of sustaining a certain style of living, pursued more or less continuously, then at least some centrally important desires will be towards the continuous, not the discrete. 'Be generous, sensitive, tactful, compassionate, not envious, petulant, malicious, prejudiced, or cruel.' They will not be desires to return that book, avoid that lie, sign that petition, oppose that measure. We will want to be a certain kind of person throughout some occasion, or for longer. That may pose a particular sort of problem for us, since being a certain kind of person is just what we may find, in anguish, that we cannot guarantee to be and are quite uncertain of just when it is critically important to be sure.

4.2.8 It is not unusual to be ignorant of or confused about what one has done, is doing, or will do. I am not here referring to the labyrinths of the unconscious mind, but to more straightforward matters. Someone might equally well ask in anguish 'What *will* I do?' as 'What shall I do?', for it may not be indecision about what to do as much as uncertainty about whether and how he may, in some sense, escape from his own control and understanding in acting. Perhaps this happens because some project is wrong for him, or because he does not really understand it or himself. We may be caught in an inauthentic project. Contrary to Sartre, I take it that anguish, or something like it, need not spring from *knowledge* of the nothingness within us which constitutes our freedom. It is probably better understood as *ignorance* of what we are, of the nature of our motives and emotions.

4.2.9 This lack of self-understanding may be of at least three kinds. First, we may not know, as some quarrel threatens, a declaration of love is suddenly upon us, or a guilty confession begins, what cards we will play or just how we will play them. Will we be firm but reasonable rather than rigid and frightened, pompous rather than dignified, petulant or sentimental, do too much or too little? Second, as we are doing it, and even after we have done it, we may not know whether to see what we did as envious, forthright, awkward, calculating, destructive, or feeble. Third, we may not understand jealousy or lust or hatred or compassion even when we know we are jealous, lustful, or whatever is in question. We may not really grasp the nature of the threat posed by him of whom we are jealous or whom we hate which would explain the peculiar flavour and intensity of the emotion felt. We may fail to understand some emotion such as jealousy quite generally, not just in our own case. It may prove very puzzling what anyone is about, exactly, if he is acting with some nobility or integrity, even when we are in no doubt that he is so acting.

4.2.10 In fact, there is a motive or spectrum of motives, very widespread among higher animals, which seems to be both non-homoeostatic and of great importance to them. Animals seek a complex, stimulating environment and they manipulate it in a wide variety of ways in play or play-like activities. They are led to develop a more or less arbitrary array of manipulative skills and habits which allow control over the environment and free the animal to act in more diverse ways within it. The function in evolution of such behaviour is not to return the organism to an ideally balanced state. Instead it changes the neurophysiological state of the animal in a permanent way, without this change leading to the extinction of the drive. I will call motives with this sort of structure *open projects*, even when they take specific forms such as bird-watching. But they lack terminating ends, unlike the desire to pursue karate to the level of the black belt, then stop. A broad open project has no very specific form—the project to keep fit is an example. There is no typical physiological state, correlated with feelings of pleasure or the relief of discomfort, which is a homoeostatic reward for acting as such motives prompt. The acting simply increases the efficiency and diversity, the uniqueness and personality of the animal which exploits it.

4.2.11 A focus on open projects provides a useful counter to an appetitive or instinctual model for desire. Briefly, an open project is a general drive which neither ceases nor abates when satisfied by achieving sub-goals. It has no terminating end, though the activities to which various open projects prompt us do have ends and goals.

Curiosity is a broad open project. It prompts me to find out just what Fothergill said to Penworthy to make her blush so. But though copious gossip may satisfy curiosity on that score—I can't intelligibly go on being curious about that—to discover it slakes not a jot my thirst for more tattle or closes my open project. Open projects are quite various. Among these are *self-sustaining* open projects, which have their own continuance among their goals; living is an example. One self-sustaining project is of central importance in understanding personhood, as I will go on to describe.

4.2.12 This fits with what we said before, that for cultured beings in circumstances of even moderate plenty, most of their desires are best understood as interests. They are, in a sense, ways of filling in time. That is, humans are active, they are agents, they will be doing things, they will work or play, no matter what. We need no theory of instincts to explain why waking people do not sit inertly about. If anyone feels more comfortable with the thought that we have an instinct to be up and doing something or other (even if that is simply basking or lounging), let him cheerfully add it to what I say, for there is nothing here inconsistent with that thought. This question of what sorts of desires are at work in the lives of persons needs more careful attention and calls for more ingenious and insightful development than I can give it. I offer some observations but not a comprehensive account.

4.2.13 The basic motive (4.2.6) plausibly underlies, or is at least akin in some way to, a self-sustaining broad open project which is at the centre of attention in this book. The project is no less than the development in each of us of personhood itself. Hilgard and Atkinson (1967: 129–32) describe the basic motive as one without physiological correlate. It is play, in a broad sense; or like it, at least. I find it plausible that play, or something play-like, acquires in us, who are cultured and linguistic animals, the character of a deliberate striving to realize a personal identity. How it might be thought to do so will be clear from the arguments of this and following chapters. But let me sketch it roughly now.

4.2.14 We are self-reflecting animals. We formulate pictures of ourselves and of our personalities. Our personality, or personal identity, is a diversified and differentiated complex of styles of action in which notions like integrity—the idea of consistency and persistence of character under stress—and self-knowledge play a fairly obvious part. A personality is diversified if it has many facets and does not fall into a few stereotyped responses; it is differentiated if its style of action is different from those of its fellows. Diversification is variety within a single person; differentiation is variety from person to person.

4.2.15 Only within a society, which may provide the fellowship of others who are diversified and differentiated, is there any likelihood that these sorts of variety can be achieved and consolidated. You need to see yourself as other people reflect you in their interpersonal responses to your freely inventive, experimental interventions in the world. No adequate or objective idea of self and character is attainable unless your actions and their values are objectified in another's responses. Without such an external interpretation of what you are, you can form no realistic picture of what you can aim to become as a personality or an agent. That interpretation is the matrix of the higher-order desires which give rise to the dialectical self-transformation described in 1.4. We need a mirror to discover what we are like physically and how we compare with others. Only then can we make the most of our visual appearance. Metaphorically, one needs the mirror of social response to discover the same about what personality one is. Either we find our identity in this social mirror, or not at all. We owe our identities to others. (The theme of personality or style of life as aims of the life of valuing and self-excelling is developed further in 4.6.) Each of us depends on the diversified and differentiated group within which he lives and among which he may realize himself. That is part of the role of culture in the life of persons. This then gives us the outlines of what the self-sustaining broad open project to personhood motivates us towards.

4.3 Notes towards a classification of desire

4.3.1 I distinguish between desired ends and desired acts, actions, or activities. Some comments on wishes will serve to introduce the distinction. A wish is an inactive desire, though not quite because it is a disposition which lacks an occasion. Wishes are things that one would like and, perhaps, like a very great deal. Would I like a million dollars? Most certainly I would! But I am not now in the process of acquiring that sum. This is not because the present occasion is inappropriate for gratifying the wish. Any time is a good time to get a million dollars. Rather, although one has here a strongly marked preference, which one would be hugely delighted to have gratified at any time, one wants *not* to do any of the things likely to gratify it, nor even to do the sorts of things which would bring in the maximum wealth one could possibly get. Nor is there any *conflict* among desires here. The alacrity and pleasure with which one might accept the sum need be clouded by no disappointment of other desires. So I call more wishes those end-states which are desired, perhaps quite highly, though we desire no course of action likely to achieve them.

4.3.2 A main reason for talking about wishes is, as I said, to give point to a distinction between acts and ends. An end, like a wish, is a final state considered apart from any action or activity which might achieve it. In the case of ends generally, the motives for abstracting the final state from any procedure of arriving at it may be as various as you please, but the end is the *state*, not the occurrence or the process by means of which it is achieved. My desire may be defined by its end, or alternatively it may be a desire to achieve the end by some quite specific process or other. I can attain the state of owning a Mercedes-Benz in various ways: by selling my home to buy it in cash, by saving for it, by buying it on HP, by stealing it, and so on. My desire may be fully specified not by its end alone, but by specifying, perhaps in considerable detail, the course of action by which I reach the end. Of course, it may be that I want to become a Mercedes-owner by hook or by crook: my desire *is* my end and does not merely contain it. But that is not the case in general. Desires are standardly desires to *act in definite manners*, not simply to act any way to achieve a definite end. Desires, then, may include adverbs of manner in their individuating descriptions: one's desire is to apologize, but not abjectly; to refuse, but gracefully; to accept, but with a coolness.

4.3.3 Within the class of ends, mere wishes are distinguished from goals. Goals are ends that one pursues, as I use the word 'goal'. To specify a goal is thus to provide a motive for an action which I am performing or trying to perform, or which I have performed, or which I will perform. Goals are not idle, though wishes and preferences may be. Specifying my goal need not specify my desire; it need not say which *action* I want to do.

4.3.4 Acts, unlike ends, include actions, courses of action, activities, and the like. I note that the distinction between states and processes is not so sharp as to forbid one's regarding processes as states, and perhaps vice versa, if one is willing to indulge perversely in formal gymnastics. This does not matter, so long as we can appeal to the distinction in cases where it proves useful and intuitive. I shall argue later that confusion readily springs from ignoring or confounding it. I also note that acts and actions are composed of activities in the sense of continuous, hence continuously monitored, movements. Some activities have no state as an upshot but are ends in themselves; some which are ends in themselves have, as their ends, simply their own continuance in some form. Among these are the self-sustaining open projects already discussed. The pursuit of an interest or a hobby or a deep study such as music or philosophy has no end-state as its aim, but rather the end that one continues to make music or to go bushwalking or sailing, even though each of these contains within it subprojects with definite goals.

4.3.5 It will be useful to group desires in a way which emphasizes what is important for the purposes of this book, but what may not be so important in general. I group them, roughly and maybe not exhaustively, so that those satisfiable in a more purely human way come first, though this does not imply that these earlier desires are not satisfiable in highly personal ways as well.

4.3.6 Let us put the appetites first. They are recurrent, grow urgent if unsatisfied, their satisfaction tends to be physically pleasant, and they may be surfeited. Often their main features as desires remain largely unchanged when we embed them in cultural life, so we think of them as human. The case of sexual appetite, however, suggests that it may not always be simple to make them part of personal desire.

4.3.7 Second, there follow desires for various physical pleasures —shelter, sunbathing, cool plunges and drinks, warmth, the scratching of itches, pleasant tastes and comforts, and relief from pain and discomfort. These merge into more active pastimes and pleasures—exercise, or gentler pursuits, easier-paced and agreeably free of stress, but like exercise in being active pleasures of a not very structured kind. They are activities, though, which fall short of making and changing things. These shade into a third category of the less active but perhaps more mind-engaging desires of the spectator—of watching, listening, or, more actively, observing and seeking out or bathing in, scenes natural or cultural.

4.3.8 Then, fourth and last, comes the great central mass of desires which differ, some more, some less, from the last lot in being desires to engage with the world so as to change it and oneself. A first subdivision of these is desires to manipulate the world, to change it within the objective stance. Curiosity leads one past mere watching and listening and towards experimenting, manipulating, probing, changing, and discovering how the world responds to one's doings and thus to the discovery of what one can do in it. This tells anyone much about what she is. There is the wish to develop and exercise skills and strengths—to make, build, plan, grow things, save and spend resources, model, and represent. There is the desire to *work*; that is, to produce, by labour, preconceived artefacts. These might include the moulding, or preserving in their virginal state, of natural amenities. To preserve a thing by refusing to change it at all is a limiting case of making something what it is.

4.3.9 A second subdivision within this category of desires yields those which aim at changing the world not by manipulation, but by engaging with parts of it from within the intentional stance. It is the engagement of agents with agents and, especially, persons with persons. In particular, there is the group of desires which engage any person with itself and seek to change it by reflections on what it is and what it might be. These will be the desires of self-excellence.

4.3.10 It was Aristotle's view that the satisfaction of desires in this fourth main group, and especially the last subsection of it, most reward us; Marx's view also that, properly conducted, they are most rewarding, and I shall go on to defend that picture of things.

4.3.11 The main upshot of this look at desires is the theme that so many of them fall into the last main category. This means that though we can call them natural under very general descriptions, and as driven by the basic motive discussed in the last section, many of them can be specifically characterized only as desires within a culture—as desires of persons. This is clearest once we recall the central place among them of work. Any useful reflection on practical problems they give rise to would have to be specific enough to bring almost all of them under some broadly cultural description which will relate them to the lives of persons. We then find that they do not sound like natural desires, yet it remains entirely natural to humans to find the deepest satisfaction in consciously planned intracultural doings and makings. Most of these are not just socially defined through their role in culture, but are themselves social, not solitary, activities in more or less subtle ways. Marx's example of the apparently solitary scientist using the conceptual tools of his absent colleagues and predecessors is a graphic case in point.

4.3.12 Next, the idea of satisfaction is best confined, for philosophical purposes, to a close cognate of desire. An occurrent desire is *satisfied* if (i) its goal is achieved and is reached by the actions one wanted to reach it by and (ii) it is reached in that one acted from that desire and no other and (iii) the desire has ceased because the goal is seen to be gained. (An open project will be modified by hitting an immediate target, but will not cease; my interest in astronomy yields me satisfaction when I learn of the Oort cloud and I no longer desire to go on hearing that there is thought to be such a cloud of comets, but my desire for astronomical knowledge is quite unabated, and may be enhanced by this satisfaction.) Thus, typically, satisfaction looks back at action just as desire looks forward to it. So, at least, runs a proto-account of satisfaction. I want to argue that there are reasons for focusing on satisfaction, which proves useful in an understanding of action both philosophically and practically. There is of course the important matter of psychic feelings, which ought to form part of a wider account of desire, and therefore of satisfaction, than I shall give in this chapter (but see 6.2).

4.3.13 Let me begin at a tangent, by distinguishing desire *de dicto* from desire *de re* in the context of choosing objects. As Quine neatly puts it, if I want a sloop then perhaps there is some sloop I want, or perhaps I merely want relief from slooplessness. The latter is desire *de dicto* for something or other that answers a description. To make a choice, I move from desire *de dicto* to desire *de re* by some not altogether simple nor perfectly rational process of decision (Dennett 1978: ch. 16). However, when the object of desire is not a thing but an act, choice cannot be the motion from *de dicto* to *de re* desire. The thing to be gained may already exist, to be known and chosen; the act cannot be known in that same direct, rich way till after it is performed. This has nothing to do with any supposed debility in the ontic status of future acts. It is a brute matter of ignorance prior to performance. One cannot know acts *de re* except after the event.

4.3.14 These facts about action induce an asymmetry between the ideas of desire and of satisfaction. Desires to act, and choices to act as well, remain typically desires and choices *de dicto* (though goals, perhaps, need not). Some aspects of the concrete course of action will satisfy (or dissatisfy) and others will be neutral. Satisfaction is more informed than desire because it follows action, so it can crystallize and give structure to an ineliminable vagueness in desire. Satisfaction yields a more satisfactory picture of what is desired than desire itself does.

4.3.15 The *de re de dicto* distinction helps to focus on this problem, but does nothing to solve it. The concrete granting of a wish may delight or horrify us with unlooked-for surprises. But that is not my concern either. W. W. Jacobs's story *The Monkey's Paw* (ed. 1975) is about the supernatural granting of wishes by events which, in the sum of their properties, are disastrous to the wishers. They get money, as they wished, but only at the cost of the death of someone beloved. As the example shows, it would only be in an ironical sense that one could speak, simply for these reasons, of satisfaction as informationally richer than desire. The added content would never have been desired and is no source of satisfaction.

4.3.16 The asymmetry I mean is an aspect of expressivism and it too is intentional because it is epistemic. Even without what is irrelevant to expectation, satisfaction is related more specifically to concrete action or activity (to a process, not a mere end or goal) than desire can hope to be, though related in essentially the same way. What we take satisfaction in may enlighten us as to how we desired to act. Of course, this may well be because some aspect of our desire was unconscious. My spite is clear to me only after the deed is done. However, that is by no means usually so. Much more simply, I often cannot foresee how the action I desire will progress even when I am sure of no ugly surprises. If my desire is not exhausted in my *goal*, but concerned with my actions and activities in the process of arriving at it, with my continuous monitoring choices in the twists and turns of the course of action, my retrospective judgement on my satisfaction or dissatisfaction will standardly change my understanding of what it was that I wanted, if only by enriching the understanding. Satisfaction, like desire, is found in an action *qua action with certain properties*. A range of properties in the finished action, if they are enough like those that made the desire definite, count as satisfying that desire, even though richer than those defining the desire. If you like, satisfaction is desire's backward look at what it did or would have done, but the backward look affords a characteristically better view of the end or action sought; it can characteristically be a new vision of what one really wanted.

4.3.17 Another aspect of this asymmetry, one which interests and puzzles me, is the way in which time and, less obviously, space demand a richness in concrete performance which desire can very seldom envisage, though satisfaction easily may. Once again, this happens when our desires are for actions and activities rather than mere ends. In almost any social situation, for instance, there is time to be filled in, not just in the ordinary sense that one must frequently wait for things but, equally simply, that time imposes a continuing style on us. As I talk to you, I say this and that, I listen, respond, laugh, shake my head in rueful sympathy, or whatever it may be. All this time I *am* something socially—tactful, amusing, entertaining, attentive, responsive, and some of these to excess, perhaps; or I may be inert, silent, distracted, vacant, wooden, awkward, distant, self-absorbed, abstracted. There is no voluntary escape from this; so long as the encounter goes on I am, inescapably, something or other socially well-defined in it, however few discrete acts I do, unless involuntarily unconscious. (Falling asleep as you speak, however, is something socially definite!) Whatever my intention and desire may be in any discrete act, I will be something or other stylistically appraisable throughout this time. Desire and intention cannot anticipate much of this in advance. Similarly, one's body will be in one attitude or another, expressive always of something, never of nothing (of insipidity and withdrawal if of nothing else), simply because it is an object in space, disposed therefore in one quite particular way and not another. This problem is part of what shifts the focus from discrete actions to a continuing style, to being a kind of person expressing a personality in an ongoing life.

4.3.18 For all these reasons, then, when I speak of satisfaction I do not introduce another topic than that of desire, even though to speak in terms of satisfaction permits one to say more than one might if one spoke in terms of desire alone, even on the rather abstract level on which I am operating in this chapter.

4.4 Decisions and the strength of desires

4.4.1 The idea of acting on a desire, *making it one's aim or one's will*, needs to be better explained than it is in any account I know of. It always used to be said, and perhaps often it still is said, that one acts from the strongest desire. But this is well known to be unhelpfully trivial; the sense of 'strongest desire' here is simply 'desire from which one acts'. Worse, it is also confusing in suggesting that it is the desire which does the choosing and the acting, not the agent. Some quite explicit account of what it is to decide something, which makes desires part of the process of decision but does not make the desire somehow *decide the agent*, is necessary if we are to avoid the fallacies of division and composition which have long bedevilled attempts to make sense of the plain fact that motivated decisions can be free ones. (The point is raised, but I think not settled, in Hobart's splendid paper (1966).) Daniel Dennett offers an account which moves in the right directions (1978: ch. 16, elaborated in Dennett: 1984). In this picture of decision, the agent halts the processes of deliberation in a more or less arbitrary way and, as it were, plumps for an option, realizing that deliberation has no natural end and might go on—but enough is enough! Deciders satisfice, in short—they decide easily for what's good enough rather than persist in arduous pursuit of what's best. But though this takes a long step towards ridding us of a picture in which our desires do the deciding, it leaves us with an element of randomness in decision-making that is far from satisfactory. Dennett has the input of factors to the decision partially random with respect to the tester-structure which satisfices (1978: 293–9). But this at least seems to mean that, in so far as this randomness is important to the decision's being mine, I have no guarantee that, in choosing a job, I will take account of such factors as salary. That is cold comfort for satisficers! So the vital aspects of deciding are not random, and partake of none of the conceptual advantages which it seems to bring. Randomness touches only matters that don't matter. But that seems to give it, after all, no main role to play. The full story of decision is a problem for philosophy of mind, rather than for moral philosophy. Nor do I know how to solve it, so I leave it aside. But it is of some importance here to focus on the *kind* of problems which confusions about decisions may lead us into when we talk of making a desire our aim or of acting on it.

4.4.2 It is because of such confusions, I think, that we may have an inclination to speak of desires as if all of them had some strength and as if the processes of decision were simply the outcome of balanced or imbalanced forces. It is quite wrong to speak, in general, of desires as having strengths rather than to speak of the strengths *we give* to them. To put the matter differently, our priorities do not order themselves; we order them. To be sure, the process of putting them in order is a voluntary one, sustained therefore by beliefs and desires which are relevant to it; some, but not all, of these sustaining desires are among the desires to be ordered. We need to call on the idea of second and higher orders of desire. Here again we have a common mental process not well understood in all the detail we want. An imperfect understanding of it may well obstruct our grasp of the role of desire in free action. Once again I offer no solution to the problem I pose here. But surely it is clear that, very largely, *we order our preferences.* Crude, mechanical models of preferences as competitors, the winner dictating action to us, should not delude us into thinking that we do not order them.

4.4.3 Desires can be strong, however; in particular, long unsatisfied appetites may be. A measure of their strength may lie in the discomforting sensations, the downright pain, which they cause us. Another may be the extent to which they incapacitate us when we try to carry on without satisfying them. Apart from such simple cases, we can sometimes measure the strength of a desire by some measure of our own strength: by the quickness and resolution with which we move to encompass the goal, by the vacillations and feebleness with which we pursue goals other than or opposed to it, and by the degree of attention we give to satisfying or opposing it. This ties up with my later, unhappily crude, attempts to define a labour theory of values in the life of virtue (in 6.3). But, setting aside the more purely physical effects of unslaked appetites, the strength of a desire is often a muddled metaphor for the strength of the desiring agent. No doubt more needs to be said on this topic for a good understanding of it, but the present comments may serve as a useful corrective for excesses in other directions.

4.5   Persons and higher-order attitudes

4.5.1 Persons are distinguished by the criterion that they have
higher-order attitudes: that is, they have attitudes towards attitudes
and, especially, attitudes towards *their own* attitudes. When I speak
of higher-order desires, now and later, I will almost always be
speaking of attitudes to oneself. So I focus on the fact that a person
has beliefs about her beliefs and also about her desires and the
voluntary actions in which they issue and which they guide; she
has, also, desires about her beliefs, her desires, and her actions.
That view of the status of persons falls squarely within a tradition
which, it seems, is at least centuries old and which, I suppose, Kant
and Hegel, among the philosophers before this century, discussed
with most ingenuity and explicitness. But some idea that freedom
and goodness for human beings is tied to their self-knowledge and
self-direction is as old as Western philosophy itself.

4.5.2 It is higher-order desires which occupy a main place in the
discussions that follow in this book. That is not because higher-
order beliefs, observations, reflections, and scrutinies are less
important, but because they are less puzzling and better examined
in the literature.

4.5.3 Harry Frankfurt's widely admired paper 'Freedom of the
Will and the Concept of a Person' (1971) makes second-order
desires—more particularly, second-order *volitions*—central to the
idea of a person and its freedom. It is by appeal to higher-, and
especially to second-order, desires and volitions that he aims to give
a strong sense of the notion that some desire or other is particularly
the agent's own. Though I think that Frankfurt's focus on desires,
especially those of higher order, does bring problems into clearer
view, I shall argue that his approach is in some respects unhelpfully
abstract. This will serve as a foil for a more developed view. To
make higher-order attitudes do enough work, we need a more
concrete, richer, more varied set of ideas about desires, and we need
to bring self-knowledge and self-direction into a more detailed
perspective.

4.5.4 To begin with a minor point, I find Frankfurt's account
of second-order volition unsatisfactory. That is partly because
'volition' always was tainted by muddled metaphysics, but more
because second-order volition is a somewhat limp-wristed notion,

as he defines it. He distinguishes between desires that one merely entertains and those that actually motivate one in some action, rather as I distinguished, within ends, mere preferences and goals. One has a second-order volition when one wants to make a first-order end one's goal, rather than merely entertain it as a wish. But this allows the second-order desire (which is this volition) to be itself merely entertained and its end not made one's goal—to be merely a wish. It is enough for Frankfurt (1971: 87–8) that the person is *not neutral* at second order. It would seem to me preferable to reserve 'second-order volition' for a second-order *goal* that one should adopt a certain first-order goal. But if one does that, one need not speak of volitions at all.

4.5.5 My main reservation about Frankfurt's approach to the question of self-evaluation is that it is too abstract to permit a satisfactory individuation of desires. Desires, he says, are desires to *act*, which seems to imply that the criteria for identifying desires are tied to those for identifying acts. But, as will soon appear, his actual treatment of desires individuates them no more finely than by their ends, so that the discussion neglects those aspects of desire which are directed at the course of action or activity which brings about a final state. This coarseness of classification leads Frankfurt to make the following rather puzzling and mistaken claim.

4.5.6 A person cannot seriously want to want to *X*—that is, want her desire to *X* to be her goal—unless she already wants to *X*, however idly. So Frankfurt claims that it is only if I desire to *X* in the first place that I can desire to desire to *X*-as-my-goal. I cannot coherently want to be moved to act on a desire which I do not yet have (1971:85–7). This seems to be rather clearly false, and, I think, it is only if it is false that we can give to second-order desires more than a purely formal role in personal life. Some counter-examples: an invalid may want to be hungry—to eat out of robust hunger and with the keen satisfaction in food that hunger promotes—without being the least bit hungry. Equally, a depressive may quite desperately want not just to join in activities, but to join in them out of real curiosity and interest, while feeling no curiosity or interest whatever. Third, to borrow an example from Michael Stocker (1976), going through sociable routines because one admires them, or perhaps envies genuinely friendly people the satisfactions of truly friendly motives, is to have the second-order want to be moved by friendly impulses, but it by no means guarantees that one is moved by affectionate desires or that one could gain their satisfactions.

4.5.7 What *is* true, no doubt, is that if I have a second-order *goal* that some first-order desire move me to action, then the goal of the first-order desire is also a goal of the second-order desire. If our invalid wants to feel hungry, then the goal of his second-order desire includes the goal of hunger—to eat. That he eats is an end common to both desires. But that does not make him hungry, even though there is a projection from one's second-order goals into one's goals of first order. The goal of any second-order desire includes the goal of its target first-order desire. The upshot of these reflections is that we clearly need to distinguish desires more finely than reference to their ends will permit. But we already distinguished acts and courses of action as *processes* from the final *states* or ends at which they may be aimed. So the counter-examples to Frankfurt's claim oblige us to make use of that distinction and to understand desire and its satisfaction so that desires may be individuated no less precisely than types of actions or activities are. So we must envisage, as targets of desire and objects of satisfaction, possibly enduring and recurrent acts and activities, both finely and richly amplified by adverbial clauses and phrases. I want not simply to touch but to touch delicately. It is only if acts may be understood as embracing detailed styles of life and possibly global enterprises and projects that we can grasp what the role of higher-order attitudes may be in the life of persons (as argued in the next section).

4.5.8 There is another way in which Frankfurt's picture of desire is unhelpfully abstract. This picture shows us nothing satisfactory about the role of second-order desires in making their target first-order desires peculiarly someone's own (Watson 1982*b*: 107–9). In Frankfurt's phrase, anyone is a *wanton*, in respect of first-order desires, who has no second-order volitions about them; that is, if one has no second-order desires to make some first-order desire one's *goal*. But suppose that you are a wanton in respect of *second*-order desires. Suppose, that is, that you have no third-order desire to make any second-order desire your goal. Why should second-order wantonness be no reproach to the freedom of your will, if that fault undermines freedom at first order? Frankfurt claims that higher-order desires may tower and totter neurotically, and are as destructive of personhood as wantonness is. In the main, he says, a person identifies *decisively* with a first-order desire by means of a second-order volition, and this decision ' "resounds" through the potentially infinite array of higher orders'. Thus 'no further question, about his second order volition, remains to be asked' (1971: 91–2). However, this fails to explain why first-order decision should not 'resound' just as satisfactorily as second-order volitions do. If all one needs is a resounding decision, why will first-order decisions not do? Whatever the rights and wrongs of this brief account may be, it can hardly be said to explain the allegedly crucial role of second-order volitions. This too, is a problem which I believe will yield to a more detailed, more concrete look at the structure of desires.

4.5.9 We might make second-order desires look more tangible by reminding ourselves how we are apt to comment in retrospect on whether or not we had the desires we want (or which others wanted us to have) when we acted. We say 'I take no pleasure in the fact that I exposed Jepson as a pompous ass' or 'I am proud that I was able to concede Houghton's point without rancour or envy' or 'I am ashamed that I can't accept her other friendship without jealousy'. What pleases me about what I do, what I take satisfaction in, what emotions are aroused in me by what I do, shows a great deal about my desires in action, once we agree that desires are individuated by the prospect of these satisfactions and emotions. Of course, this makes desire seem more self-intimating than it is. For instance, only when I feel an angry pleasure at what I did is it clear to me how much I was moved by spite. Perhaps I should add that emotions, as I conceive of them, are essentially judgements about the flourishing of our values, judgements which cause in us, and are at the same time the reason for, a range of psychic feelings (see 6.1).

4.6 Higher-order actions

4.6.1 If second-order desires are to be of use to us conceptually, the idea of second-order *actions* ought to make sense too. What are these? In Frankfurt's story a second-order action is simply the action of making a first-order desire my will, that is, my goal. This is nebulous. Something more tangible might be made of it, however, if we recall that second-order actions must be motivated by appropriate beliefs as well as by second-order desires. We said that beliefs direct action, so that no proper action springs from desire alone. Appropriate beliefs show desire where and how to press, mould, and move. If we are to regard the having of second-order desires as something richer than having second-order goals, then second-order *acts* must have a good deal of the structural richness already described for first-order acts, which was necessary for an escape from an empty formalism for second-order desires. Second-order satisfaction must be a clear-cut idea too. I shall argue that in second-order action of a certain crucial sort, we choose or strengthen our understanding of our own personalities or identities —our characters. Thus second-order action is mainly an *activity*, connected with being a kind of person or leading a style of life, rather than with choosing this or that discrete action. Higher-order satisfaction depends on our recognition of our own identities and characters.

4.6.2 To begin, I suggest—with some diffidence—that there are no second-order *appetites*, no second-order desires which arise recurrently out of natural processes, which grow increasingly urgent if long unsatisfied, which give physical pleasure in their satisfaction, and which may be surfeited. I infer from this, diffidently again, that second-order desires are occasioned by *judgements* upon our desires and that these judgements will, in general, begin (be learned) by retrospective assessments of our actions, satisfactions, and emotions. So the *occasions* for second-order desires are noticings about the desires, satisfactions, and emotions which are generally at work in one in doing first-order actions; or these occasions of desire are notings of the kind of satisfactions and feelings foreseen in action.

4.6.3 I set aside the problem of second-order actions specifically concerned with first-order appetites. There are tastier fish to fry. How can I make myself have wants of various sorts? Let us begin with wishes and goals, that is with end-states rather than processes, to get some formal structures clearer; though, as before, it is only when we move beyond desires, thought of just as ends, to consider more concretely activities and courses of action that we can find a useful role for second-order action.

4.6.4 In ordering first-level goals and wishes, one appraises a set of end-states in respect of their consistency or conflict and assigns to them some strength or priority. In ordering second-order goals and preferences one appraises a set of end-states, each of the form that a certain first-level end-state is one's goal (or, less pertinently, one's wish). Formally, this is entirely analogous to appraising states of affairs in which *another* agent has some end-state as her goal, or in which the other agent appraises the state of affairs in which the first agent has some end-state as her goal. These states of affairs may be end-states and even goals for the appraisers. In short I may appraise my having certain desires much as I appraise your having them. This structure of appraisal looks even-handed as to whether the appraisal is of the agent, as committed to such a goal, or of the goal, as harboured by such an agent. A vague admiration of, or an infatuation with someone might recommend a goal because it is part of a character *Gestalt* which one perceives but cannot fully analyse. In regard to one's appraisal of others, which, it seems, ought to be the model of self-appraisal, I shall be suggesting that both styles of appraisal have important roles to play, though some form of appraisal of agents as having goals is more fundamental. But in self-appraisal it can seldom, if ever, be right for me to think better of a goal (or worse of it) just because it is mine. However, the idea that one might model one's goals and preferences in imitation of, for example, Christ is neither new nor outrageous. Each of these looks like a schema for making oneself a certain kind of person, for forging an identity for oneself. Which of them, if either, is primary? I shall say that it is appraisal of oneself as desiring certain goals and actions, rather than appraising goals in terms of who has them. This sub-question will occupy us till 4.6.15.

4.6.5 To argue this, let us look into Charles Taylor's (1977) deep and subtle account of second-order desires in human agency. I give my own version of it in this and the next paragraph. Some second-order desires are *functions* of conflict among first-order desires (if I can use 'function' so loosely). Thus I may have a second-order desire not to feel hungry *as the result* of a strong first-order desire to keep slim. Second-order desires may play a mediating role in conflict among first-order desires. Where that is the case, the conflict, at whatever order, is resolved, one hopes, so that satisfaction or pleasure or happiness is maximized (though, of course, mistakes about this easily happen). The conflict of desire is then mediated by what the world happens to allow. Not wolfing the delectable contents of my plate is contingently connected with slimness. My consequent second-order struggle to repudiate hunger occurs only because I live in what turns out to be a fattening world. There is no suggestion that the object of any desire concerned in this is other than some kind of good. This sort of desire for (against) desires Taylor calls weak evaluation. It does not concern my evaluating my volatile hunger as a desire which characterizes me.

4.6.6 Things are different in more interesting cases. My second-order desire to resist hunger may be motivated by puritanism, or a bent towards being a person of more rigid will, or by a desire to avoid a demeaning sensuality. I see that the desire stamps me as weak, ignoble, or naïve. In such cases, I characterize my desire *contrastively*, as Taylor puts it. That constitutes strong evaluation of desires. First, I see my having the desire as revealing something about what I am or what I may be. Second, no merely contingent fact makes my wolfing food an instance of spineless surrender to appetite, or gross self-indulgence. One can understand what it is to preserve an intact and vigorous will only in terms of such resistance to appetitive desires (among other things, no doubt). Purity cannot be understood other than as a certain style of limiting the obtrusiveness of a quite well-defined range of appetites, passions, or lusts. I cannot know what purity is and fail to know what counts as corruption, nor understand bravery without understanding cowardice. So the desire for the (diminished) structure of desires which makes up purity or temperance is more complex than any higher-order desire involved in weak evaluations. Desires of any order may be strongly evaluated.

4.6.7 It is this strong evaluation of our desires and motives that sets us the task of making ourselves properly persons. The other conditions of personhood are simply necessary conditions which put us in touch with it. To be merely a weak evaluator of one's motives is to lack the emotional and conceptual depth which we require of one who has some attitudes about how he wants to excel himself. The possibility of such attitudes, their conceptual structure, is already there in the mastery of language and its concepts, in the ethics of belief, and in those institutions of language that define what it is to explain belief and action rationally. It is to extend that self-appraisal to one's conduct at large and to adopt deeper appraisals of what one is in the world than the consideration, merely, of the maximizing of satisfactions. (Taylor develops the concept of strong evaluation in criticism of Utilitarianism, but I make a different use of it.)

4.6.8 More interestingly perhaps, the characteristically Aristotelian virtues such as courage and temperance require that the agent has a right understanding and balanced ordering of a range of values in life. Courage, for instance, is not mere steadfastness, but a course of action taken under threat to a range of one's values; it lies in a properly considered ordering of them and of the best means of preserving them from threat. It may be rash, rather than brave, to risk one's life for certain values—it merely cuts a dash, say. But not for others. Aristotelian courage is a virtue only of persons already quite far-advanced in complex self-appraisal, involving a range of subtle beliefs and desires. To desire this virtue, to want to be moved by the motives that make up courage, is to have desires much more convoluted than are at stake in any kind of conflict among first-order desires, the satisfying of any of which is good in itself. It requires one to evaluate oneself as the subject of a range of desires and values each of which is itself appraised. One may want to be courageous on some particular occasion, of course, and this suggests a focus on one's act rather than on oneself. But courage is hardly intelligible save in the context of an overall style of virtuous living. The same is still more obviously so of temperance. So, strongly evaluative second-order actions depend on desires about oneself as harbouring certain goals, at least in standard and characteristic ones; we may regard such actions as paradigms of personal self-excelling.

4.6.9 This allows me to offer, at this stage, two preliminary reasons for thinking that at least a central group of these actions will be activities, taking the form of pursuing a kind of personality or a style of life. I will give another later (4.6.16–23).

4.6.10 Typically, when our first-order desires are problems for us, we have to deal with them, in practice, as dispositions. Standardly, we do not want to resist gluttony and rise to some higher aspiration just once. Our contrastive second-order desires may be unhappily short-lived, but even a fleeting wish to respond more nobly can hardly be a desire to do so just on this occasion, with no regard to any other. 'I yearn to be free . . ., to be the kind of person whose mere bodily appetites respond to his higher aspirations, and don't carry on remorselessly dragging him into incapacity and degradation' (Taylor 1977: 110). Thus the standard practical problems of the life of virtue for persons lie not in decisions about discrete actions and their consequences, but in activities, projects, styles, and patterns of life. They are not about what to do just here and now, but about a continuing character to be moulded, monitored, guided, and made free in its nature. They involve us in being a certain kind of person, building a free strong personality. That is a conclusion drawn more from a view of the *practice* of valuing, of the exigencies of the life of agents who must translate abstract intentions into concrete actions and processes of life, than from any theory of the good.

4.6.11 A second, deeper reason for considering higher-order attitudes in the light of higher-order actions is that valuing, like reasoning, is more deeply understood as practice than as doctrine. Logic tries to articulate the practice of successful reasoners. Ethics tries to do the same with the practice of persons who succeed in being virtuous. In each case, the articulation of principles modifies the practice even when it is true to it, by guiding, illuminating, extending, or formalizing it, or by making it more consistent and intelligible. Even so, the principles remain subservient to the practice, for it is in practice that one deals with the richer conceptual structures presented by concrete cases and circum- stances, which no abstract articulation in general terms can hope to present in full over a long period of ethical experience. Further, the formulation of any principle of reason or valuing always puts us in a position which we were not in before. It enables us to ask whether the principle is true, or whether we value following it. Lastly, practice faces us with dilemmas in which a choice must be made between incommensurable value-alternatives in a way which articulated principles do not easily parallel. Sartre's famous case of the young man faced with the choice between joining the Resistance and caring for his ailing mother is a graphic example of this kind of dilemma. Here, too, one can begin to make sense of the idea of a life of valuing (as in 3.4.8). But this is not the good life unless the values are correct.

4.6.12 Because the articulation of values in principles changes a practice to which it nevertheless remains true, and, even more perhaps, because it may be false to the practice it purports to illuminate, we regard ourselves as responsible for our deeper and more radical choices among incommensurable values. To make a radical value-choice, to articulate and thus to change and strengthen what we first did inarticulately in practice, is to choose what events and actions mean to us quite generally, and thus to choose the way in which we see ourselves as related to the world and as agents and valuers in it. It is like the situation of a writer deciding what to say to resolve some impasse or some unexpected obscurity in what seemed a plain tale. The resolution not merely changes what he will say next, but gives new sense and import to what he wrote, without puzzlement, before. Some of it seems quite wrong or strange or no part of his real intentions, another part of it seems to be suddenly deeper, more precise, richer in consequences than before. Our understanding of the world and its values shapes itself round a crucial choice to be a Resistance fighter, for example. We define our sense of personal worth in such choices and principles and our sense of which personalities we have and want. For all these reasons, then, a range of second-order actions will constitute choosing what kind of person to be and what style of life to follow. What makes these choices deep is not adequately represented by regarding them as choosing which desires to act from on some single occasion.

4.6.13 Second-order desires which are individuated in this contrastive way are not functions of first-order attitudes, then. However, they may well find their origins outside the range of one's second-order attitudes to oneself. Perhaps the crude beginning of this sort of education lies in powerful desires I have for others to like, respect, or at least not to despise or condemn me. This suggests social roots for contrastive desires and, perhaps at some primitive level anyhow, that they are social products, offspring of social, cultural attitudes.

4.6.14 Thus to have some sense of ourselves as persons who can determine what we are, we must—and it is of crucial importance that we may—contrastively appraise an agent as having a certain goal. But I think that we do not contrastively appraise goals *as harboured by agents*. To want to have have a certain goal because to do so is Christ-like or Stoical or ladylike is not to appraise the goal contrastively. To want not just to act like Clint Eastwood or like a fashion model but to have his or her desires and satisfactions (or lack of them) as well is neither an uncommon, nor a contrastive, nor, alas, a particularly exalted aim. To begin with, the complex of desires and emotions which makes up the character admired is seen as merely instantiated together, so long as it really is the case that we want the desire or satisfaction merely because another character fascinates us, without our having more than a holistic perception what this charm or force consists in. Such a choice does not define our sense of our individuality through the value-meaning of things and events in the world—through what we value or aspire to. It reflects too little perception of what we ourselves are, or what we might be; too little sense of what a higher-order desire, articulated as a principle of value, might say about us. It negates all we are, in favour of a style which merely happens to have come together for us as a chance *Gestalt,* and which happens to bewitch us. Such choices do not have the depth of contrastive valuing and are not properly to be seen as choices of self in higher-order actions. (This is not to deny that the style of another might show us a desire or pattern of motives in a new light, but if this is properly contrastive, we will have grasped the relation among them in a properly universal sense.) So to choose a personality in the paradigm cases of self-excellence is not to choose an individual model. Thus the central cases of self-design are those for which we are peculiarly responsible.

4.6.15 But let us come back to the question which began this section. How are second-order goals translated into second-order actions? Obviously, in a wide variety of ways. As soon as I realize that an impulse to cry in my beer while telling my story is not manly, I may find that I simply never have that want again. Simply the recognition achieves the second-order goal. Characteristically, however, second-order actions are ruminative, cogitative in style: I dwell on features of what I want to do; cultivate, by repetition in imagination, various emotional responses to the envisaged action; ponder and comment on—as well as bask in—the kinds of satisfaction or perhaps frustration which acting from such a desire may bring, direct the course of thinking and attention one or another way. But the range of actions one may resort to is unmanageably wide for neat classification. Notoriously, young people are exhorted to take cold showers and long runs when beset by appetitive desires which they find some difficulty in resisting. Though such actions are quite clearly powered by second-order desires they are, as actions, among the very simplest, most direct, and least reflective that we perform. We may also adopt a quite Pavlovian attitude towards ourselves and try to extinguish or excite desires by a range of positive or negative self-conditioning. Obviously, there is a wealth of procedures available for actions with second-order motives, but it is not my purpose to offer, in these pages, a manual on the power of positive or negative thinking about one's own desires and acts. I simply point out that the structurally simplest cases of desires as preferences or goals would seem to lead to structurally simple observations of the responses to oneself. (However, this need not carry over to simple assessment of the goals of those on whom one models oneself.) We saw that the range of actions to which these goals and observations lead may be widely varied. Yet we might still regard these as all second-order because of our reasons for the actions, even though they are not, in any other way, reducible to a category. Nevertheless, without some understanding of the actions in which second-order desires issue, and of the kinds of observation which give occasion for and direct them, our grasp of their role in the concept of a person remains formal and vacant.

4.6.16 Still, some more structured comments might be made on second-order action. One obvious sort of second-order action lies in doing something to frustrate some unwanted first-order desire in the hope, sometimes well founded, that the desire will atrophy. Or one may, equally obviously, adopt the policy, whenever an unwanted first-order desire is manifest, of doing something else very agreeable in the hope that this surrogate satisfaction will eventually erode the first desire. Ridding oneself of unwanted desires (as against appetites) need pose difficulties neither for one's will nor for making consistent plans for second-order action. Negative second-order action seems easily understood. But, of course, success in action may well elude us.

4.6.17 However, inducing desires one *does* want may be much more complex. There are several difficulties here which can be made plain if we consider spontaneity and unselfconsciousness. Neither of these is a desire in a straightforward sense, but rather a mental state, though to be spontaneous is to act from fresh and lively desires and, with luck, to get simple and direct satisfaction from one's actions in a way which forbids second-order monitoring. To want to be spontaneous is to want to act from a structure of desires which have a certain untrammelled simplicity—it envisages not just discrete action, but a *style* of desire and satisfaction in action. Two problems present themselves here: first, that the very *wanting* to be spontaneous itself provides the net which entangles desire, so that this higher-order want may defeat itself; second, if values really are dialectically transformed desires, how is it even intelligible to regard spontaneity and unselfconsciousness as values? Plainly, one cannot be self-consciously unselfconscious—the wish for artless action cannot be simultaneously steered by second-order motives. There are other desires and states which contingently pose the sort of problems for my theory which unselfconsciousness and spontaneity pose conceptually. Second-order action to acquire desires and valued mental states more broadly will often fail if it appears as a simultaneous higher-order monitoring *epicycle* on first-order action. (I call the theory that all higher-order action must be of this kind the *epicycle theory* of higher-order action. It is false.) So how can higher-order action gain its ends?

4.6.18 Various models suggest themselves. I mention two. Performing artists practise and rehearse both to present set pieces to audiences (rehearsal) and to improvise for them (practice). In neither case need this detract from the spontaneity or unselfconsciousness of the performance. Indeed, these preliminaries are closer to requirements of truly effervescent and original acting or playing than barriers to it. Of course, neither practice nor rehearsal is a second-order activity having an attitude as its goal. But the example does plainly show that spontaneous and unselfconscious performance is perfectly compatible with forethought and afterthought, though no truly spontaneous, direct expression of feeling or desire, or whatever else, is consistent with *simultaneous* second-order watching or steering.

4.6.19 It would be easy to overstate the case at this point. Perhaps an actor or musician is never quite unselfconscious as to how the performance is going technically. It is crucial, though, that she is secure enough in technique to bathe in the qualities of her character and feel that what is done springs from them, or to sink deep into the textures and musical ideas of the sonata. Spontaneity asks, as we often say, that meeting the technical needs of the performance has become 'second nature' to her. This is a useful and easy phrase, provided that it is not used to insinuate some kind of success in the programme of naturalizing ethics. It is a good metaphor for the way in which second-order action may be effective without being epicyclic.

4.6.20 Preparation for performance is very directly related to the performance itself when the preparation is a rehearsal, yet this is no conceptual bar to the vitality and freshness of the performance. It makes for needless problems to insist that one can never aim directly at spontaneity in second-order actions, just as it would to insist that one never directly aims at building a cupboard in the preliminary actions of buying wood, hinges, and so on from which to make it. Though the purchase is directly instrumental in building the cupboard, it is in no real sense a by-product of the purchase. Probably any kind of mental state can be a by-product in the very weak sense that one might set about preliminaries directly aimed to produce it (Elster 1983: ch. II to the contrary). This is not to deny that many desired mental states, such as spontaneity, might not prove elusive. All that is clear is that some of these states, just because of which states they are, forbid *simultaneous* second-order monitoring. The point is worth making because we tend either to think of second-order desire as issuing in epicycles on the same actions as are desired at first order, or as giving substitute motives for them—as going through the motions of amiability motivated by the feeling that one wants to be friendly, but without the affection and playfulness of friendship itself. But second-order desires can be satisfied *only* if the appropriate first-order desires are. Going through the motions misses the point.

4.6.21 Let us still keep in focus spontaneity and unselfconsciousness as models of states which are valuable yet seem to resist conceptually the possibility of higher-order supervision, and which therefore cannot be transformed into values in an obvious way. These pose a conceptual problem for the epicyclic theory, which helps us to focus on it; however, many other second-order goals make problems for an epicycle theory of a practical kind, one of which we shall look at closely in Chapter 5 in discussing sexual desire. We can find another model for second-order action by noting that much, and sometimes all, we need in order to be fresh and direct in response and action is to clear away the barriers to being so. We need only act negatively at second-order. We want to get rid of certain anxieties, preoccupations, doubts, or ambitions about ourselves, for they intrude and hamper us, tying our tongues, making our responses laborious, ponderous, hesitant, pompous, or repressed. Such clouds of self-absorption obscure from us what is really afoot, hide the opportunities and rewards in what we are doing, and sully the pure, direct engagement in things which is the reward we want. So far as that is the problem, we can achieve these valued states rather directly—in principle, at least—perhaps by a more just self-appraisal which gives us the confidence simply to drop these distorting attitudes, by a better sense of which rewards we really do most want, or the like. Life is, in fact, seldom so easy, but these styles of pursuing the prize are neither highly indirect nor conceptually absurd.

4.6.22 We can often achieve spontaneity by achieving a more specific *mood*. It is not absurd to intend to induce in oneself some mood or other. In fact, it may be easy to do so. Simply entertaining the prospect of being sociable this evening may put me in ebullient, expansive, and spontaneous mood—a mood to be as good and effervescent company as I can, without contrivance or even direct intention to tell funny stories, venture my wit, or be more lazily good-natured. There are many ways to put myself in a state which is a sociable one, in which I can, and probably will, be motivated simply and directly by amiability, affection, amusement, love, and fun, and so on. The mood is second-order intended; its satisfactions include my pleasure in being pleased by the first-order satisfactions of amiability, without there being any need or room for anxious second-order epicyclic steering as I joke, listen sympathetically, understand the emotions and share the responses of my friends. Mood-inducement is a perfectly possible, deliberate, conscious, non-epicyclic activity, which may fail of its aim for all sorts of reasons, but not because it is unintelligible to try.

4.6.23 Let us remind ourselves of the following: to be free in one's nature requires one to *be natural*, to act in *human* ways from *human* motives, though from human motives which persons want. A second- or higher-order desire is satisfied, not just by some first-order action but by a result—the result that one takes a certain kind of satisfaction in the action. This may well require, either in practice or for conceptual reasons, that second-order action *not* take the form of an epicycle on first-order action. In such cases, the result of the dialectic among first- and higher-order desires will take the form not of directly changing the first-order desire but of making room in one's character at large for certain forms of first-order desire. The alienation and transformation take the form of a reorientation of the desire, of achieving a perspective on it which resets it as a natural part of a generally cultivated personal life. The dialectical process still involves concrete processes of alienation and recapture, but the scope of the process is more global than a first view of the matter might suggest. It is still the case that such a desire has been given its place in personal life by a transformation which allows us to see it no longer as a desire (or structure of desires) which is contingent relative to personhood itself, but as a *value* of the person for whom it has taken a place in her whole self-perspective. It adds a further reason for our seeing second-order desires as aimed at a character or a life rather than at discrete, single actions. Second-order desires aim to make a self-excelling personality become a second nature for us. It is in regaining one's nature, becoming free in it, that the dialectic of valuing points to pursuit of a personality or a style of living.

4.6.24 A last, simple, but vital point: I have stressed how, in paradigm cases, a strong evaluator will see its higher-order desires as directed at being a kind of person or leading a kind of life rather than at particular actions and their outcomes. This does not mean that the life of virtue and excellence is inward-looking in some deep-seated way. This is clear enough from the examples already afloat. To have the higher-order desire to be friendly—that is, to be motivated by affection, the wish to share experiences and doings with others, to talk, joke, sympathize—is to want to be something for others as well as for oneself. It really does require that another's interests, pleasures, and satisfactions become one's own just because they are those of one's friend. To be a genuinely friendly person, and not just an anxious performer of friendly actions because one thinks one ought to be, calls for an absence, in those lower-order desires, of self-absorption and self-regard. Some styles of being a person may need the absence of epicyclic desires. It is the general point that matters, which is that higher-order pre-occupations with oneself as an object do not even begin to make one an inward-gazing personality at lower orders. However, we are not yet considering how valuing can yield correct values.

4.6.25 In the next chapter we will take a closer and somewhat more concrete look at what goes on in some dialectical processes by which persons mould desires into values. This will afford us a deeper, if more special and concrete, view of what higher-order action may be.

4.7 Higher-order attitudes in practical life

4.7.1 When we expand our horizons beyond goals and preferences to include desires to act—wants for various actions and activities—then the role of higher-order desires, observation, and actions (acts, activities) becomes very considerably richer and more intelligible. In fact, some comments on the sort of situations in which we act (with desires) may serve as useful reminders about what we can expect the practical life of higher-order desires to be like. First, our daily, weekly lives fall into a number of broadly repetitive patterns in which we pursue courses of action over longish periods motivated by long-lived, recurrent (that is, dispositional) desires. Next, our desires are predictive and vaguer than satisfaction (4.3.16–18); this is especially true of our second-order desires. For these sorts of reasons, second-order desires are apt to be focused very much on manners or styles of action or activity.

4.7.2 For example (let us suppose) I am obliged to attend regular meetings of a committee to disburse funds. I want certain decisions to be made and so I want to argue for them. I may like to irritate others in the course of this, or to revel in the rotundities of committee rhetoric, or to argue in a level tone throughout. At second order I may want to diminish the first two pleasures in my manner (satisfactions, that is) and intensify the third. The occasions on which the stinging quip will rise to my lips or on which the rounder, more dignifying phrases will occur to me are not foreseeable. Nor are the occasions on which my own feathers may be ruffled. I can prepare for these occasions only by adopting a general *manner of engagement* in the committee processes overall. My second-order desires, observations, and activities, in these altogether typical occasions in the problematic of leading the good life, are quite as likely to direct themselves at styles of activity and action as they are at end-state goals. It is these more concrete facts about the temporal scope of (especially dispositional) first-order desires and their second-order counterparts, together with the uncertainties in monitoring continuous courses of action, which help to make second-order desires naturally prominent. They also make more sense of why our appraisals of the actions of others are important in giving us models for the styles of our own actions and for the ways our actions satisfy us. It surely is important that we can see how various goals are won, desires satisfied, actions performed in the wider style of another's behaviour. It may be only by appraising Storer that I see the ugliness of strong conviction as fanaticism, only in Weller the surprising generosity and sweetness that can be part of resolute dissent.

4.7.3 We can now see, I hope, why higher-order desires, among all of a person's desires, are peculiarly her own. That is because some state of that person—in a highly general sense of 'state'—is the object of them. It is a person's manner of acting, her style of behaviour, her general plan of life which quite typically become the targets of higher-order desire, once we understand actions as more or less extensive processes and desires as vague.

4.7.4 Contrary to Frankfurt's claim, there is seldom a *practical* problem of the destruction of personhood if a person's desires increase and ramify in their orders. It seems to me, indeed, that it is by no means unusual for people to have desires about the kinds of self-assessment they undertake and about the kinds of second-order desires and emotions which empower and direct these appraisals. People are, in general, all the more free and comprehending of what they do when this occurs. But there is, I agree, a crucial discontinuity between first- and second-order desires which contrasts with a virtual continuity in orders above the second. Higher-order desires are all alike in that the desirer is the object of these desires, or that some state of the desirer is. More strictly, the object of higher-order desires is the agent *qua* agent; the springs of a person's own actions become the target of his desires and hence of his actions and activities. That does seem quite intelligible as a basis on which to regard such desires as intimately connected with the agent. It connects them with his freedom, in the sense of his self-possession and self-direction. This takes us significantly further than the formal freedom mentioned before. It is a necessary, though not a sufficient, condition of any moral self-appraisal that one have second-order desires, and of one's moral effectiveness that one can carry through some course of second-order action.

4.7.5 For essentially these reasons, it matters little where the ramifying higher-order attitudes cut out. At some point, they will simply do so, for we are finite creatures. Perhaps we need to remind ourselves that desires of order n have content only if there are active desires at order $n - 1$ and desires are active only if they are desires for change or motivated about anxieties for continuance. Where one is content at level n with one's desires at level $n - 1$, pursuit of reflections at order $n + 1$ will indeed be, for the most part in practice, exercises in a sort of formalistic rubber-stamping. I do not mean that contentment at level n might not be mistaken: it certainly may. Reflection at $n + 1$ might have revealed to the person a smugness, a dishonesty, a lack of care, a comparison with another occasion or another person which could have led her to try to change her satisfaction with her structure of desires. I see no cast-iron guarantees of success nor any reason to expect them. Some people are better at this than others or more conscientious; better, that is to say, at intuiting that a scrutiny of their higher-order desires would be merely formal. But we do not need an idea of *perfect* freedom, *perfect* self-knowledge and self-scrutiny, to make good sense of what we are pursuing. Even if we had it we could never justifiably apply it to ourselves. We do what we can. The crucial point is to begin self-scrutiny, not to complete it. Indeed the latter idea makes no sense.

4.7.6 I hope that it is now clear that second-order actions—that is, acts, actions, or activities aimed at lower-order desires—contain *judgements* on scrutinized desires and on ourselves as harbouring them. This allows us to avoid Hume's picture of reason as the slave of passion and to follow something rather more like Plato's, in which reason may oppose and overcome passion and desire, and in which one is free and a person in so far as reason wins in this conflict and makes itself the motivating force. (Plato, as I read the *Phaedrus*, personifies reason, which has its own aspirations and desires.) What is good, what is of value, is something which reason makes clear to us, and it is much more than what we simply want. These judgements are of a kind nearly appropriate to our having the good as a reason for action. I say 'nearly appropriate' because such actions and judgements are quite possibly tawdry, mean-spirited, vain, or trivial. One can want some movie star's heartless, cool detachment, for instance. In Plato's usage, reason is never allowed to get things wrong, so that one's values always radiate a reflected glory from the Form of the Good. I see neither need nor hope for the present arguments to encompass that. I note that we frequently reproach people for their sordid or their tinsel values. I have described a concept of value which makes *valuing* more central than actual worth. So I speak of subjective values. A person's values are her longish-term goals upon which her higher-order attitudes have passed a judgement which has made them her own. They articulate her sense of herself and of a meaning of things which seems to her deeper than meanings which arise from uncriticized desires. This articulation of self in principles changes what it tries merely to interpret, as already argued (4.6.11). Such a judgement will be as reasonable and as worthy as the person herself is reasonable, scrupulous, patient, careful, worthy. It is an account of what it is for someone to have values. It makes no attempt at defining the proper values for persons. Before we try to do that, it will be well to put under the microscope some special cases of the dialectical transformation of desire into value.

4.7.7 I have focused on desires and their ordinal structures virtually to the exclusion of beliefs. But any theory of valuing as intellectualist as mine must take notice of the evaluative scrutiny of beliefs as well. I do not pursue that theme in the present work, however, since the structure of beliefs and believing is so much more extensively examined in the literature than is the case with desire. Beliefs, especially about oneself and one's values, play a crucial role, but the main aspects of what this involves are already quite well understood.

$$5$$

The Dialectic of Desire and Value

5.1 Sexual desires

5.1.1 This chapter is about problems which fall into what I have been calling the *tasks* of being a person. Normal humans are defined as persons by their higher-order attitudes towards themselves; these attitudes make for inner conflict with a dialectical structure so that a person comes to evaluate itself in the strong sense already described. I want to look in some detail at two examples of this dialectical transformation. The first of them is about conflicts over sexual desire; I argue that here the dialectic takes the form of a global adjustment of personality rather than of an evolution of sexual desire itself. The second is about the transformation of our workaday concepts of observation into those of the sciences, so it pursues themes already treated in Chapters 2 and 3. I hope to show how the progress of the dialectical transformation of these problems leads us on to other puzzles and conflicts which take us into new dimensions of cultural and perhaps personal development.

5.1.2 Sexual desire is one of the appetites. As with other bodily appetites, it is a desire which a *human* person standardly admits to a central place among its motives. But further, it is a motive one urgently *wants* to weave deep into the fabric of personal life. More cautiously, it is the sort of desire which might be expected to occupy deeply any person who has it, though it does not always do so, nor have all cultures been equally concerned about integrating it into cultural life. In any case, not all our desires or bodily needs are caught up into what can properly be seen as personal life. The need to breathe, though it is certainly something which people do together, has no personal style to it. The prospects of alienating it, in any fashion, look dim. Our need to excrete, though we might indeed satisfy it in communal fashion, is seen in societies quite generally as offering few opportunities to catch it up into cultivated life. In many societies, excreting is alienated in that one retires to some sort of solitude to do it; in our society, there are socially provided and serviced means of solitude. Any suggestion that we might transfigure these human bodily functions, recapturing them in more exalted forms, has not been realized. We happily civilize them without entwining them into cultured activities. This is hardly surprising. However, the appetites of hunger and thirst lend themselves well to convivial, to ceremonious, to broadly stylized modes of activity; but they still allow us to snatch a bite on the run and not much is cultural about that.

5.1.3 Among appetites sex is peculiarly complex in ways which set it quite apart from the rest and make it particularly apt to generate both problems and opportunities for exploitation in one's life as a person. These produce a dialectical movement which makes our sexuality an interesting field for valuing and self-excelling and, for the same reasons, a common source of anxiety. Undoubtedly, sexual desire is a subtle thing in biologically normal people. Sexual responses of arousal and desire are intensional and have become highly cultivated states. Nevertheless, we also need to understand them as like sexual states in animals, including our allowing some modest intensionality to animal urges. The object of desire is someone desired as a particular, individual, embodied personality. Though one may perhaps quite readily come to desire another individual, an episode of sexual desire is characteristically for some individual for whom no other, however similar, may be substituted (Scruton 1986). My discussion does not aim to deal with all such aspects of sexual desire, but to show how a person's struggle to become free in its own nature may be resolved in processes of valuing. I am more concerned to make this clearer than to get the character of sexual desire into adequate focus. I said earlier (4.2) of appetites that they are recurrent, grow urgent if unsatisfied, their satisfaction tends to be physically pleasant, and they may be surfeited. For the most part, these features of appetites as desires stay largely unchanged when we embed them in the cultural life of persons, so we think of them as human or as animal desires. The case of sexual desire, as we shall see, is less simple, and it may become a quite crucial part of cultured life.

5.1.4 Sexual desire, then, conforms to these four features which pick out appetites from the ruck of our desires. But it is unique among them and, indeed, among desires at large. First, sexual desire is *ideational*. That is to say, its satisfaction standardly requires a flow of rather precisely delimited (though richly varied) thought about its object. We consciously dwell upon information in the course of sexual activity; we look or touch attentively; we have sexual dreams or fantasies. One can quench one's thirst in the course of intense concentration on matters alien to the ingestion of fluids. Talk about art, car-racing, movies, or philosophy need not be inimical to the pleasures of the table. Indeed, free-flowing conviviality looms large among them. Not so, in general, with sexual satisfaction. Sexual activity is thinking, noticing, exploring, sensing activity and has to do quite crucially with the rather concentrated savouring of what satisfies it, though it may be savoured only in imagination. Sexual satisfaction regularly requires our bathing ourselves, largely to the exclusion of other thoughts, in sexual ideas and perceptions. For example, in a sexual encounter observation, impassioned attention, and conscious thought standardly play a critical role in producing orgasm. Primarily what we desire to observe and respond to is not ourselves but another. This seems quite obvious. Yet it marks sex off from simple appetites and takes it into something much richer and more complex.

5.1.5 To make this quite clear (but I hope not offensively so) consider masturbation to orgasm. Simple manipulation is seldom enough. One standardly needs a flow of fantasy ideas simply to attain orgasm physiologically, quite apart from any question of enjoyment or satisfaction. A normal fantasy is of an encounter with another, or words, touches, emotions between two persons. It is not enough just to think about one's own sensations. Looking from the opposite direction. Masters and Johnson (1966) record that some women are capable of fantasizing to orgasm without physical manipulation. A distantly similar thing is true of men in nocturnal emission during sexual dreams. In short, sexual desire is much more than a homoeostatic drive towards a psychic reward of pleasurable, internalized climax.

5.1.6 Let me be more precise about the ideational content associated with sexual desire. Sartre says this 'I make myself flesh in order to impel the other to realise for herself and for me her own flesh, and my caresses cause my flesh to be born for me in so far as it is for the other flesh causing her to be born as flesh.' In less oracular (and less graphic) form this means that my sexual desire for another includes that she should desire me. So the flow of ideas which is characteristically sexual concerns not just more or less involved forms of bodily contact, pressure, and friction between two people. It is directed at the desire expressed in that coupling. The intertwining of bodies is the field of expression of the desire each wants in the other.

5.1.7 It makes evolutionary sense that sex should be like this, not just in humans but in higher animals generally. Suppose that the reproductive drive were not directed towards the arousal of another in its ideational content and that this content and its psychic reward were not correlated with mutual physiological states of arousal and readiness for impregnation. How would the sexual urge be likely to result in offspring which make possible the transfer and mixing of genes? Sex as simple appetite aimed at just one's own pleasurable inner states not only grossly falsifies our sexual experience; it is nonsense biologically.

5.1.8 So sexual desire has this reference not only to another's body and its sexual features. Sexual desire—considered straight-forwardly as lust—is desire not just for flesh, but for flesh animated by sexual desire, and sexual desire not just for anyone, but for the desirer; lust is not simply for bodies and bodily contacts but for mutually lusting bodies and for mutually lustful contact. Thus the activities of sexual arousal are aimed at inducing another to sink into this state of mutually desirous absorption in the body. Each is made flesh by and for the other, to return to Sartre's phrase. (See also Nagel 1979, ch. 4.)

5.1.9 For all this mutuality, sexual passion is animal passion. 'Goats and monkeys!' expresses Othello's horror at what his sexual entanglement has brought him to. Sex is a vivid reminder of our kinship with non-personal animals, for there are strong pressures in the ideational flow of sexual passion to exclude from attention in the encounter all else but the contact and envelopment of desiring bodies. One wants to be, in sexual episodes, a purely sexual being; to have one's whole being absorbed in and by that passion. This is just impossible, just as it is impossible to be, for an hour, a purely philosophical being with a colleague without also being either gentle, acerbic, confident, insulting, considerate, amusing, vapid, or boring (4.3.16–17). Just how to be a social person while being a sexual one may be a problem for persons.

5.2   The alienation of sexuality

5.2.1 Two features central to sexuality may lead us to alienate it, either by an attempt at celibacy, thus completely repudiating it, or by allowing some higher-order monitoring to reduce somewhat our absorption in our bodies, or by finding a place in personal life for episodes of bodily absorption. The first of these two features has already been mentioned briefly. It is that sexual desire is naturally absorbing. Complete sexual arousal is a kind of immersing or consuming oneself in the desiring body. It is accompanied by global (i.e. widespread) physiological changes which include a marked drop in perceptual acuity for sensations and perceptions other than sexual ones and a mental absorption in the perceptual input (or the flow of fantasy) which is peculiarly sexual. Sexually aroused persons are not readily distracted, not merely because they are strongly inclined to satisfy desire, but because of the peculiarly complete absorption in the body, the obsession with the sexual state of one's being, which is a necessary part of arousal—arousal being, in turn, a necessary part of vivid and complete satisfaction of desire. Conversely, distraction, intrusive thoughts, irrelevant ideas inhibit both desire and its satisfaction and may lead quite quickly to the relaxing of those states of physiological tension which play so prominent a role both in the passional and the physiologically functional (i.e. impregnation) sexual process. I assume, with Masters and Johnson (1966) and rather against Scruton (1986), that these global physiological changes play an evolutionary role, raising the likelihood of impregnation in sexual congress.

5.2.2 This desire for complete absorption in sexual thoughts and deeds is a desire to be human in the sense of wanting to be a human animal. Lust is, properly, sexual desire with that animal absorption. In sexual intercourse it may be fostered by a variety of doings, sayings, postures, and attitudes. It is a train of ideas in which our wish to be obsessed with sexual thoughts and deeds naturally and simply casts itself. This animality is true to the nature of the passion and true to the beings who take part in it. Yet it is also an *intended* state, conceived against a background of consciousness of oneself as also other than this, at other times at least.

5.2.3 But, secondly, however much one may succeed in sinking oneself in the desiring body and becoming absorbed in it, one can never become a purely sexual being (see 4.3.16–17). First, a central part of one's sexual interest lies in arousing another, and part of this process lies in presenting oneself as aroused and desirous. This will be done either candidly or not, considerately or brutally, with tact and grace or crassly, sentimentally, timidly, deviously in role-playing, or with integrity. Next, throughout the continuous activity of a sexual encounter, any caress or murmur shows what one is as an agent; it is matter on which to judge, conclude, appraise, however inconveniently, what one and one's partner *are* in this activity socially, as persons and as agents. The pretence that one can be nothing more than a sexual being, save for very short times, is just pretence. Finally, however absorbed one may be at the time, one will appraise the encounter later and one will have appraised it, as far as it can be foreseen, beforehand. The dream of lust, one might say, is for purely sexual, purely animal, and entirely non-personal behaviour. The dream, like dreams in general, is delusive. Persons are quite inescapably persons in sex as, indeed, in everything. That is a main source of sexual anxieties.

5.2.4 There is a practical contradiction here. One's primitive or animal lust leads one to invite, excite, and arouse an acute focus of another upon oneself as one who feels a similarly acute focus on this other. This focus, in lust proper, is not evaluative. But, for a person, it must always invite evaluation, judgement, and appraisal just because the relation is between persons. If one is somehow engaged with a person in any conscious role then one is, in that role, appraisable as a person too, whether one likes it or not. Thus, in company, however little one wants to be engaged, one must count at least as bored, distant, detached, or remote; if disengaged, as in an airport lounge, one is still considerate or boorish, noisy, intrusive, or inertly obstructive. Any such posture admits some appraisal of one's values, excellence, or failure, however unwilling a party to the evaluative enterprise one may hope to be. So, in a sexual encounter, one must risk personal appraisal, induce, excite, invite it, just when one is most intent on absorption in one's animality as a desiring and desired body. Further, this appraisal is to be made by one who, though one need not esteem him or her as a person or a judge, is the object of desire, is the partner of an episode in which one is passionately and intimately involved in such a way that one's satisfaction and pleasure pay a necessary tribute to the other's desirability, sexuality, vitality, satisfactoriness. Though this is not directly to value one's partner as a person and, thereby, as a judge, it can hardly escape some close relation to it. For if one does not value one's partner as a person, one thereby probably *dis*values her, through some insincerity, evasion, or brutality which makes lack of esteem concrete and may well make it plain—and plain, too, what manner of person one is in just that encounter. Sartre and Nagel, whose ideas deeply interest me, see in sexuality, as elsewhere, problems that are essentially insoluble for persons. I do not share their pessimism, arguing that success in personal life is difficult but possible even in practice, though dependent on luck. People can and do solve this sexual problem and solve it well. But it is there. The liberal slogan that anything is permissable among consenting adults may do for the morals of 'ought's and 'may's; it is inadequate for the morals of valuing and excellence.

5.2.5 A complementary source of anxiety lies in the fact that sexual activity and satisfaction are essentially uncontrolled. I offer some diffident reflections on anxiety about the role of orgasm, as a central event in standard sexual encounters. Orgasm need not be seen as the indispensable end of satisfactory sexuality in order to be perceived as playing a prominent role in sexual reward. What is true of orgasm' is, I think, true in some degree of much of the process of the sexual absorption in one's body that is necessary for acute sexual arousal and satisfaction.

5.2.6 Orgasm is a climatic moment in which you abandon conscious control of yourself so that something thrilling and pleasurable should happen to you. Orgasm is not an act nor the object of a direct volition. Of course, we voluntarily do things to precipitate it. Yet we are passive in it, we undergo it, we suffer it rather than do it. It is a helpless delight. It is a kind of surrender of yourself to your body so that your consciousness becomes, for the moment at least, purely sensual and carnal. In the context of a sexual encounter, it is also a surrender of yourself to the other, a kind of gift, because each partner has been made flesh by the other and for the other. If I thus surrender myself to another's beauty and vitality, this becomes, for her, a final reflection in the mirror of our encounter of what I have found her to be as flesh. It is, for me also, the moment at which, helplessly, my non-personal humanity is most fully revealed to her, most vulnerable to judgement and rejection, least able to resort to defence or subterfuge. Orgasm can pose a threat (and undoubtedly often does pose one) as well as offering a promise.

5.2.7 Thus sexual passion endangers to some degree—and the degree may be felt considerable—that very self-possession and self-direction which characterizes what one is as a person. There is no escape from reflective self-evaluation before and after those absorbing episodes of strong arousal, though one may well not reflect, during them, on what one is. Thus sexuality can seem to threaten one's being a person not so much in that one lapses from the state (as one does in sleep or, in a different way, in excreting) but in that one violates it, one tears aside cultural veils to allow quite primitive behaviour, one is no longer at all a gentleman (or a lady), or even a simple beast, but a person who deliberately gives itself up to highly energetic, non-personal forces in an encounter with another person. Thus sexual passion is a personal dilemma.

5.2.8 For these reasons, then, persons may be strongly impelled to alienate sexual desire—to be rid of it or to act upon it only in some transmuted form. The threat which sexuality seems to have posed for so long and in so many cultures is the threat of a revelation. This poses two main sorts of fear. First, one fears exposure as a beast. This is apt to have its comic side, since it has generally proved to be nameless practices that so dismay more prurient imaginations. A cool recital of the most ingenious and athletic sexual exploits fails to horrify, so long as the gyrations are not directed at the devaluation of another. Physical exploits are beside the point, since it is in the flow of ideas and attitudes that sexual corruption properly lies, and this may rightly disgust us even in the course of the most ordinary of physical sexual behaviour. Equally familiar sources of anxiety about sexual passion lie in the falsehoods and distortions to which its urgency may drive us— anxieties to which Shakespeares 129th sonnet gives eloquent voice:

> Th'expense of spirit in a waste of shame
> Is lust in action; and till action, lust
> Is perjured, murd'rous, bloody, full of blame,
> Savage, extreme, rude, cruel, not to trust,
> Enjoyed no sooner but despisèd straight,
> Past reason hunted, and no sooner had
> Past reason hated as a swallowed bait
> On purpose laid to make the taker mad . . .

Furthermore, sexual fascinations tend to blind us to where our other values and interests lie; their destructiveness in this respect is notorious. The film *The Blue Angel* shows us one of the faces of sex as decadence. However, the second, opposite fear is no less urgent. One fears to be insipid, tame, lifeless, or sexually feeble. For reasons canvassed in the next section, our sexual identity is, for most of us, deeply tied to a range of other values and choices. Our understanding of them defines for us the meaning of much else in our experience. So this anxiety may be vivid when we encounter the vapid self-portrait it seems to present. Our sexual lives are too close to our personal beings for us to let them unfold unscutinized, yet the absorbing preoccupation of sexual passion drives us towards just that.

5.2.9 Last, there is a human bent towards blindness and self-delusion which sexual passion notoriously fosters. It plays a part in answering some objections which might be raised to what I have been saying. Quite clearly, those whose sexual intercourse is for trade and gain may lead highly sexual lives, in one sense, but their desires can be expected to be far from what I have described. It may seem, too, that the passions of the rapist are too one-sided to allow plausibility to the idea of lust for *mutual* lust that I have put at the centre of sexual desire. I do not accept these objections. It is no small part of the prostitute's or gigolo's art to *feign* desire, if it is not felt, for the reason that it notoriously dampens desire to face boredom and distraction in one's partner. It would be an objection if a whore who read a book during intercourse lost no customers thereby, but I find that implausible. The case of rape is more complex, but, on the one hand, it is all too plausible that many rapists project sexual satisfaction—the counterpart of desire—on their victims; and on the other, that rape may be closely allied to the sexual perversion of sadism, which I discuss, consistently with my view of sexual desire, in 5.4. I shall be arguing that sexual actions that do not have the passional structure described are perversions.

5.2.10 What may need explanation is the notorious ease of self-delusion in sexual desire. I mean delusion as to response, rather than as to the general character of one who is the object of an infatuation. I do not know what the explanation is, but offer these guesses. It is sexually attractive to another, in general, to display desire towards him or her; it is an advantage to be persistent; it is easy to persist in desire in the belief that part of its object, a desiring response, is attainable—when one can persuade oneself that success is at hand. These factors obviously foster a tendency to project a desiring response on to another. Of course, if another is set rather against accepting one's desire, hopeful persistence can be irritating and offensive. Nevertheless, I guess that persistence in desire and expectation of its return is generally a rather successful biostrategy.

5.3 Paradise regained: sexuality of persons

5.3.1 There are powerful motives for making sexual action part of personal life and thus for projecting sexual desires into what turns out to be a range of values. The sexual drive is imperious; the affective costs of celibacy, in general, are high. Nature strongly impels persons to be sexual beings. Further, sexual intimacies may be the foundation of a range of other personal styles of involvement—of loves, loyalties, confidences, trusts, friendships, givings and takings. Our sex remains a main part of our sense of identity and of the direction of our aspirations. At least, that has been so in our culture and, lessening though it perhaps is, it is likely to remain central. A long, constant, much-celebrated tradition in Western culture testifies, often absurdly but sometimes with the deepest insight and subtlety, to sexual relationships as the key to a broad wealth of values in human life. All this is abundantly obvious: it neither needs nor can bear my enlarging on it. But it is quite essential to my picture of what induces a dialectic of sexual desire, transforming it into a value.

5.3.2 I will make some observations which, though they are not perhaps the main reasons why we want to regain our sexuality transformed, are worth mentioning because less platitudinous than the main reasons. Sexuality transformed is sexuality still; it is sex for persons. I mention, first, the problem of reaching *objective* self-knowledge, of finding yourself objectively in the interpersonal mirror of impassioned relations with another (3.2).

5.3.3 A very large part of our interpersonal relationships is carried on verbally. But words are limitlessly malleable. Speech can distort, mask, or set us at a conventional distance from others. It need not do this, but it very frequently does warp and cloud the interpersonal mirror. This is both an escape and a burden. Carrying our personality on words alone makes it easy, for example, to present for reflection a mere vulgar urbanity, polished but hollow, of cigarette or cosmetics commercials. This is an effortless refuge, on the face of it. But it is liable to a form of corruption in bad faith. It may also become a burden, since we begin to lose the real diversity and uniqueness of our characters, both for others and for ourselves. The verbal surface becomes an empty shell which is all that one's manner allows others to reflect. Identity and integrity blur and fade. Since words lend themselves to falsehood just as easily as they do to truth, what I display of myself verbally may be only my own subjective view of myself at this moment. Or, often, it is just the image I would like you to have of me. Of course, other people frequently see straight through this image to what it is an attempt to mask. But even if they do, their response to me will no longer be to what I simply, transparently am, but to what I am as stained by the verbal prism. Thus I lose self-knowledge. I am not fortified in being the thing I am, in authenticity. So verbal manner may become a cage I cannot easily break out of. Words can debilitate, for I might not find myself objectified in genuine responses from others. There is, therefore, a value in retreat from the purely verbal, cerebral plane of relationships.

5.3.4 We can put this point in terms of Sartre's image of finding oneself as flesh. Looking at the other and caressing her I find the reward of my being flesh, in that I can express my delight in her by awakening in her a counterpart discovery in the reward of her being flesh. I may discover myself as a unitary bodily agent, able to exploit all the resources of my intellect, emotions, and bodily abilities in bringing it about that she finds this for herself. But she also finds it for me in that the changes wrought by my caresses reflect what I am in that role.

5.3.5 The sexual desire of another for you is thus an inter-personal mirror in which you can find yourself reflected with an intensity, and from a variety of angles, possible in few, if any, other human relationships. Particularly in a series of sexual encounters with the same person, you are likely to have played a role overall in which you have been more completely integrated as a psycho-physical unity than in any other role common in human life. For you can be ingeniously sensual, inventively emotional, perceptively passionate. You may find yourself objectified with unrivalled clarity in the directness and urgency of your partner's response.

5.3.6 Thus sex, in particular sexual lust, contains in it a primary value. In sexual lust you act as a completely bodily agent. This is not something that people are very ready to do. The most superficial attention to the milieu of popular culture gives impressive evidence of how anxious people are at the thought of themselves as flesh—at the recognition in themselves of a little human reek and grubbiness. We do not like to think of ourselves as, among other things, animal bodies. But obviously this is just what we are. To be a properly and honestly integrated person sexually, you must come to an objective understanding of what you are and accept this in yourself. You must consciously be the body that you are, to realize yourself fully. That is the role of lust in the pursuit of virtue and excellence. What you act out, in lust, may not be the essential you, but it is certainly an essential part of what you really are. It requires, for a personal reward, that you are free in your sexual nature.

5.3.7 In short, sex offers unrivalled scope for objective self-discovery and for making yourself be, objectively in action, the integrated, many-faceted person you want to be. With luck, with honest and skilful playing of the sexual game, you are rewarded and reinforced in the role you draw for yourself deliberately and of which you are consciously aware. It is a quick, delightful, fruitful way to objective self-knowledge. That is part of freedom in one's nature. So sexual relationships have a particular ethical value.

5.3.8 My message is, then, that in sexual encounters, played through without evasion or subterfuge, we are reflected and objectified. Carnal knowledge is knowledge. Indeed, in orgasm, it is revelation: you are shown for what you are. If you think the truth about yourself or about your sexual role as you understand it is hideous or insupportable, you will be unable to leap the hurdle of that revelation when it appears or you will run for cover from the outset. That is why fear of sex is so widespread and why sex seems so horrible to many. Just because it reveals awful truths. Just because it is ethical.

5.4 Dialectical solutions and defeats: sexual perversion

5.4.1 I hope it is now clear which factors I am claiming make the adjustment by persons to their sexuality a dialectical conflict, which leads to a problem how to synthesize opposing desires, some of which are higher-order desires, of strong evaluators. But a solution which might synthesize this conflict is still not at all obvious. Indeed, the role of second-order action here is quite problematic. To see why, reflect again on the exclusiveness of sexual consciousness; intense sexual satisfaction requires that we think, in sex, about nothing much but sex. Being free in one's sexual nature means freely acting as one's nature invites and accepting this activity at higher levels, but without simultaneous intrusion of strongly evaluative attitudes. To see what all this means in practice, it turns out easier to focus on ways of botching the problem than on ways of solving it, and no less illuminating. This will take us to a new perspective on the pragmatics of personhood.

5.4.2 As we saw in 4.6, rejection of first-order desires can be straightforward enough; so can simultaneous monitoring of accepted desires. We learn the arts and crafts of forbearance, tact, politeness, and, more pertinently, we learn how to soften irritation and redirect selfishness without much conceptual stress. But the management of sexual desire is more subtle, since its exclusive, obsessive character either destroys or is destroyed by intrusive thoughts born of other attitudes. As with spontaneity, the descent into unselfconscious bodily obsession is incompatible with simultaneous self-conscious monitoring. We need to regain our alienated sexuality in a form very like that which we alienate. It presents us with a practical problem for an epicyclic view of the second-order actions which might make a value of sexual passion. It is not part of the very idea of lust, as it is of spontaneity, that in lust one is busy about sexual ideas to the exclusion of thoughts about the evaluation of one's desires. But it is entirely characteristic. So paradise regained, for sexual beings, lies not with higher-order steering of sexual voyages, but rather in finding the place, in personal life at large, for episodes in which values are made concrete, realized, and secured in very direct and unmonitored ways. I have argued that it is wrong to regard these first-order actions, desires, and satisfactions as eluding the attention of higher-order attitudes, though we need not attend at the time. So second-order action is apt to be subtle and even devious. For this reason, it is not merely hard for one to define, in philosophy, which second-order actions might regain sexual desire for personal life. The practical problems are subtle, idiosyncratic, and subject to complex circumstances; they forbid any general description.

5.4.3 We can speak of sex as being perverted just because it is essentially ideational. Sex is perverted when so great is one's fear in anticipation of making one's passion concrete in action, and of the revelation of objective self-discovery in the sexual role, that one must somehow change the ideational content of the situation. It is a perversion if one must escape the natural and straightforward content of the encounter by replacing it with another, either in fact or in fantasy. More accurately, it is sexual impotence or frigidity in the ideational content (including perception of the actual situation, correct judgements about the responses of yourself and the other) of a frank interpersonal encounter, where the impotence or frigidity is caused by fears that are strongly evaluative. It may help to stress the role of ideas to point out that, according to this account of perversion, homosexuality is not a perversion nor more liable to perverted forms than heterosexuality is. Every sort of sexual perversion, as I am defining it anyhow, arises out of some kind of self-rejection.

5.4.4 Put in this light, it is clear what we should say, morally, about sexual perversion. It is a moral failing. Whoever perverts his or her sexuality cannot face self-discovery in a fully objective fashion. His freedom and moral stature are stunted and diminished to the degree that he avoids confronting himself. But let us be clear, first, where the failing lies; it need not be in what his sexuality is perverted to, but in what it is perverted from, that he fails. A perversion need not involve the devaluation of *another* person. In so far as a person can sustain a relationship in which he discovers himself to some extent, is objectified and reinforced to some extent, we should count this as some kind of success. Nevertheless he fails, but in such a way, surely, as to call for our compassion rather than for our censure. Some perversions will not attract this forgiving attitude, however; extreme narcissism and necrophilia being two rather different, examples.

5.4.5 Sadism is an interesting case to start from since it is often a purely ideational perversion. Desire comes to be directed at another's fear of one, not a mutual desire. It is not hard to grasp what motivates this dislocation of lust.

5.4.6 The sadist cannot believe that he is acceptable, let alone desirable, to another, since he cannot accept himself. He cannot think himself into an imaginative grip on how he could be desirable. Desire in the other for him, not for his body but for his desiring body, points out the feared descent to a final revelation of the hatefulness and ugliness of his passions. In anticipation, that revelation presents itself to him as an overwhelming disaster. He will be judged and rejected in all the helplessness of surrender to orgasm. The escape is to give the other no real part in the encounter as a person at all. She must be diminished beneath the status of an evaluator, be utterly overwhelmed by aggression as the only safety in the encounter. For the power of this aggression is vividly reflected in the fear by which the other is diminished. This reflection of the sadist through desire is replaced, for him, by reflection in fear. The other becomes a harmless cipher whose acceptance is not invited and who is too defeated to judge, but who is still a witness to his power in the vividness with which her fear, pain, and defeat reflects it. But the agent's own defeat and incapacity are hidden in this process; he cannot reach the direct, spontaneous satisfaction of sexual passion, is defeated in his aim to be free in his own nature, and loses the prize of an objective confirmation in being what he authentically is (Storr 1964).

5.4.7 Masochism, notoriously, is the polar opposite of sadism. Let me quote from the fantasy-content dictated by an actual masochist (Storr 1975: 41).

> I like to imagine any group of men or women being led into slavery. Slave markets. Being stripped naked, examined as animals. Being sold, having a master to work for or submit to sexually . . .
> A slave has no past, he has no name. A master is beyond criticism, whatever he does or orders is immensely significant, he is incapable of evil or wrong, he cannot insult or degrade a slave. He can only honour him by noticing him. The only relationship the slave fears is that of friendship. This would be against nature and shatter his world.

5.4.8 Here again, we find that the retreat to a situation in which one plays no role as an individual with a variegated and differentiated personality is regarded as a refuge. To be treated as a child is to be a nonentity, beneath judgement and appraisal. Friendship would destroy the world just because it opens the door to personal involvement, to making desire concrete in action, to moral revelation and eventual judgement. The masochistic solution to this problem is to look for a relationship in which the acceptable role is like that of a child who is the object of the lust of a powerful, uncritical quasi-parent who permits the child no responsibility for what they jointly do.

5.4.9 Freud's essay 'The Most Prevalent Form of Degradation in Erotic Life' (ed. 1925) is about the widespread inability of men and women in Vienna at the turn of the century to act out sexual lust with partners whom they regard as equals. Such people married, commonly, with mutual respect and out of a kind of sexual love. But they could not look at their partners lustfully because they were convinced that this lust had something in it too bestial to be accepted by an admirable person. So men turned to whores, or to women whom they regarded as whores, for these women were seen as too degraded or too coarsely perceptive to pass judgement on what a man becomes who discovers himself as flesh. The fear of guilt of sexual revelation could be escaped. Yet these women were often the objects of strong affections (of a certain kind no doubt) of the men who thus exploited them, because they did permit the free expression of strong natural desires. Clearly this counts as a sexual perversion according to the account here offered of it as an escape from an unmanageable ideational situation.

5.4.10 I have dwelt on the ways in which the dialectical evolution of sexual desire may fail to solve problems for persons partly because this serves well to make clear the value aspects of the matter, and partly because a person's acceptance of this desire is so dependent on idiosyncrasies of culture, circumstance, personality, past vicissitudes of this and other relationships, and, doubtless, other factors. I see no way to make a coherent, properly philosophical commentary on the relevant positive higher-order actions. Perhaps novelists and playwrights can best inform us about them.

5.4.11 It is not only because sexual passion is an urgent appetite that people wish to slake it, despite the problems which this may pose for them. Nor is it because of the rather formal reason that without some first-order desires pursued in its practical living a person would be merely an abstraction (or rather, perhaps, a concrete being leading a life of almost unimaginable asceticism). It is because sexual encounters offer such rich opportunities for deeply personal life, not merely during the sexual episodes themselves, but in the broader communal life within which they occur. It seems plausible that the long-lived romantic myth of ideal love between two partners, each the supreme value object for the other, for which a sexual passion is the basis once the exercise of passion is firmly integrated in personal life, has at least some foundation. At the same time, there can be little doubt that the more extravagant versions of the myth are absurd, many of them destructive of realistic expectations of what some version of married life can be (*de jure* or *de facto*), many others portraying quite unacceptable roles of dependence, responsibility, exclusiveness, moral blindness, or sheer sentimental flabbiness for the partners involved. No doubt the best solution to the problem of sexual passions for persons, as I described it, does not lie in debilitating our absorption in and exclusive attention to the animal passions in the sexual episodes themselves; it lies rather in the way in which they are integrated into the rest of social life. We need not suppose that there will be no consequences, in the encounter itself, of the success or failure of such an integration.

5.4.12 Sexual passion is interesting to philosophy in its own right, in the ways I have been trying to articulate. Two more things might be said about it before I leave it. First, one ought not to forget the variety of contexts, projects, moods, and associations which may cause problems in sexuality which I do not wish to probe. Boredom is one of them. Sexual activity is necessarily tied to presuppositions of strong and obsessive sexual interest. The presupposition is by no means always met, either because custom stales, or because one is satiated when another is not, or, no doubt, for many other reasons. This presupposition obviously makes for a variety of subterfuges, role-playings, evasions of various sorts (some depending, doubtless, on ways in which the presupposition fails) which readily corrupt sexual life. More notoriously, urgent desire leads to the corruptions of lies, flattery, false promises, pretences about other than purely sexual desires, all aimed at getting another into bed. These have little to do with the dialectic of sexual desire or those features of it which touch on the idea of its perversion.

5.4.13 Second, sexual absorption simply is the most striking case of a much wider need for enrichment which can be met only by unreflective pursuit of first-order desires. Max Deutscher (1983) speaks of objective interest in things as an interest in which the properties of the object determine one's perceptual and more broadly epistemic responses to it. Although an objective understanding of something requires that one be on guard against all the ways in which subjective hopes, fears, and expectations may obtrude and obscure so clear a vision, the objective attitude must emphasize the role of pure, unscrutinized, unmanaged response to what is there. There is a similar moral need for the emotional, appetitive, unmediated absorption in pursuits at hand for which sexual desire has been offered as a model. There are, in a properly evolving culture, always two components in its dialectical evolution whether or not it concerns sexuality: pressures towards the reflective, artificial, mannered, cultivated styles of doing things, and pressures towards a direct, natural, unsophisticated absorption in life. Each is equally, though differently, also crucial to the life of persons individually.

5.5 Science and dialectic

5.5.1 One way to examine the dialectical structure of personal life is to look at the evolution of science. Its dialectic is not entirely typical of the evolving conflict one finds in more standardly moral dimensions of personhood. But it does illustrate the kind of cyclic structure I want to display and it does show how advance in one dimension of personhood may lead one to explore another dimension. Mainly, however, so much has been written about the structure and growth of scientific knowledge that I can treat it in a manageable length as an ethics of belief.

5.5.2 It ought to be a theorem—I showed its outline in 2.2— that the generality in my thinking what anyone ought to think has a particular outcome for persons in the case of manipulative knowledge. It extends to a corrigible, lately acquired, though *a priori* postulated requirement that our understanding of the world must aim at embodiment in law-like sentences. These state that the same hypothetical relations among properties hold at all times and places. That is not a new idea, of course; various suggestions have been made about it, but it remains unproved. At all events, I assume that knowledge that serves the basic manipulative practices of persons must have the sort of deductive power that general laws can give. So I take for granted that the form scientific knowledge takes is a function, in part, of prior demands which spring from a structure in the thought of persons.

5.5.3 That manipulative knowledge for persons is to be cast in the form of law-like statements requires also that it be written in cultivated vocabulary and focused on properties conformable to that ideal. That is to say, to find a class of sentences which are both strictly universal and confirmable by observation one has to construct concepts and discover properties which are remote from *human* perceptual contact with the world (see 2.2.12). The properties and concepts proper for personal forms of knowledge contrast sharply with those most significant and accessible to simple human touch or vision. Human perception is alienated in personal understanding of the world.

5.5.4 This is not the only way in which contingent facts of human perception obtrude upon systematic knowledge as pursued by persons, and therefore need to be transformed. We can know scarcely anything about how the world responds to manipulation unless perception guides us—which means, for humans, looking at things, touching them, and so on. But these perceptual techniques carry loads peculiar to the concrete causal processes they happen to be. This colours the properties that cause our seeing, and warps their appearances away from the law-like ideals which we pursue. So in an ethics of belief there is pressure to shed the tainted appearances and to alienate what is contingent to natural perception. In short, there is a pressure to prefer (something like) primary qualities to secondary ones. Personal perceivers attend to relations of observed objects to other observed objects; to their relation to instruments and measuring devices, rather than directly to perceptual organs. There is an advantage, too, if the relations of objects to objects somehow admit counting. What matters is not how long an object looks but which objects, when appropriately brought together, neither overlap nor are overlapped by this one. It matters how many overlap-equivalent objects, laid end to end, make a composite object overlap-equivalent to the target object. That is to say, we want to measure objects in terms of standard units, metres, grams, and so forth (see Campbell 1957).

5.5.5 I argued (2.2.9) that it is wrong to stress the role of micro-structures in the evolution of the scientific image of man-in-the-world as contrasted with the manifest one. Indeed, to call the latter a manifest image reflects the wrong contrast—that between the hidden and the apparent. But the properties which loom largest in micro-structural explanation all derive from macro-science. Time, length, mass, force, momentum, energy, and charge all sprang from the need, in phenomenal studies and notably in mechanics and electrodynamics, to select properties that figure in confirmable laws and which are measurable, primary ones. It is those epistemic needs, crucial for knowledge that persons want, which explain why immediate perceptual qualities are alien to science.

5.5.6 But though in the process of writing science as doctrine we must rule out human perceptual qualities as qualities of major significance for science, we plainly cannot get by in the practice of science without human perception. The property I wish to measure may be the wavelength of electromagnetic radiation, not colour. But unless I can distinguish colour boundaries I shall not easily read the dial of my apparatus nor readily tell whether the proper switches are on or off, whether the circuit is correctly wired up according to its colour code, and so on. There could be a blind experimental physicist or biologist, though her tasks would not be easy. But there is no way that a successful experimenter can fail also to be an acute, alert, sensitive human perceiver. What is alienated for some purposes must be retained and carefully exploited for others.

5.5.7 But perhaps more importantly, it is crucial to keep perception fresh, sceptical, and probing, however educated its glance or touch becomes One has to look with an informed eye but, no less surely, with one ready to see that what theory suggests is not there to be seen, and the reverse. One goes on needing a keen eye, a sensitive touch, a readiness to smell where smell may seem irrelevant. A peeled eye is needed to suggest where we might measure or bring in instruments. The eye and touch of the theoretician must not be hidebound by what theory tells her; she must be able to respond in an inventive, penetrating, quizzical, perceptive way to what she sees and touches. The scientist as observer must retain keen senses, and sharpen their capacity to tell her what she does not expect to observe.

5.5.8 That is a rather simple dialectical structure in the growth of knowledge for persons. A more complex structure is also at work in science. We have already looked at the tension between the scientific image and the manifest one. I shall argue briefly (since I am resetting what was said in 2.5) that this conflict is a dialectical movement.

5.5.9 The ethics of belief, which persons follow, requires that we construct a scientific picture of man, that human nature should be brought within the scope of scientific law. The resulting picture uses none of those concepts from which the idea of a person may be built. The manifest image in which, alone, humans may be seen as persons appears to be undermined and toppled by the scientific image, even though it is achieved by peculiarly personal enterprises. Yet the scientific image has a claim on the belief of persons only if science continues to be seen as a rational pursuit. In its doctrines, there is nothing which science describes as a person when it looks at the world, but its methods of discovery and argument must meet what persons require else there is no reason to believe it. If the scientific image did topple the manifest one, it would overthrow itself, for only in the manifest image do we find the concepts with which to relate what I think to what anyone ought to think.

5.5.10 Viewed as a dialectical process, the situation looks like this: science alienates the common properties immediate in and significant for human life prior to its use of law-like explanation. Eventually it presents its picture of (something like) mechanical man, an account of *human nature* in which describing things as persons has no place. It is through the alienation by persons of specifically human qualities in their observation of the world that we reach this impersonal view of human nature. But we must return to and regain the engaged attitude and the practices of rational explanation, in *philosophy*, to show how our being persons, though absent from this purged view of humans, is yet consistent with it. We must be able to identify, in the purged view, the very believers, reasoners, and self-reflective evaluators who discovered it, despite the absence of any entities, so described, from the view. Having strongly alienated our human nature as perceivers so as to pursue personhood as ideal observers—an alienation whose strength may be felt in the incongruity of scientific and manifest images—we are obliged to return, on a new level, to encounter our human nature all over again as science sees it. We must square personhood somehow with that. But this leads us to pursue the ethics of belief and understanding along a new dimension. It leads to philosophy, not to deeper science. Persons must now tackle, self-consciously and articulately, the problems of rationality, freedom, responsibility, and dualism.

5.5.11 The rather strongly dialectical structure of this process— this movement of consciousness towards its other which returns it, on a new level, to itself—is strongly reminiscent of Hegel. Something of this sort, though by no means always just this structure, may be found in a wide variety of human moral endeavours, and perhaps in all.

6

Emotions and Feelings

6.1 The structure of emotions

6.1.1 What makes someone fully a person is that he evaluates the kind of agent he is in a contrastive way, and is not merely in touch with the tasks that this evaluation reveals to him, but also undertakes them. But that does not mean that he spends much of his time preoccupied with the state of his own soul and pays heed to little else. It can, and should, leave him engaged very directly and immediately with the world, finding most of his rewards in a free, spontaneous, and other-directed life, taking satisfaction in the upshot of his activities in changes wrought beyond himself in the world and the well-being of his fellows. Before I can give a more complete story about what a successful person's life will mean, I need to take a close look at emotions and feelings. Some reflections on their structure and their role in valuing fill up this chapter. People are apt to find their lives meaningful and rewarding or not through their emotional experiences or lack of them. My view of the passions ties them tight to values as mainly outward and concrete, and indirectly, to the virtues as properly aimed strengths, skills, and perceptions in the enterprise of making values real and concrete. But my first aim here will be to offer a theory of emotions which captures much of what we believe about them intuitively; linking value to practical tasks; and analysing emotional pathologies or corruptions.

6.1.2 I examine some central cases of emotions and passions. A range of other cases cluster round them. These diversify and merge with things such as moods and manners. Thus, melancholy is not so much a passion as a mood, and exuberance neither a mood nor an emotion but rather a *style* of activity, a way of being moved or moody. The vocabulary of beliefs and desires frames my picture of emotions. People think that emotions are, in general, not chosen but rather suffered or undergone, partly because they often give rise not so much to action as to non-deliberate, even involuntary activity. Much of what we do in emotion looks purposeless; it seems either not adaptive, or maladaptive. I speak of these activities as *non-adaptive*, without meaning to rule out a function for them (6.7), though they are not *intended* when emotions are sincere. We also look askance at the emotions—especially impassioned ones— as potent dangers, likely to prove destructive to those who suffer them, as well as to those at whom they are directed. We tend to think of turbulent emotions as close to madness and vice versa; we think that the neuroses and psychoses are emotional pathologies rather than intellectual ones. We often speak as if we think that reason goes with emotional coolness and that the passions have no rational basis, but nevertheless that the heart should often rule the head when they (naturally and regularly, as we think) come into opposition. Much of this—it is a folk psychology, no doubt— survives, though changed, in what I have to say. I cannot give a full account of the emotions; it seems, still, that there is much we do not understand about them.

6.1.3 I begin with emotional episodes, occasions on which one feels an emotion; I set aside, for now, dispositions to emote, such as irritability. The 'agitation of the mind' which the dictionary speaks of refers to this episode sense of emotion. Emotions contain judgements. If some emotional episode happens to a person then she makes a judgement, either in acquiring a belief then or in having the belief then occur to her as something true. She judges not just in being disposed to agree to some proposition if asked about it, but in thinking it then and there (Solomon 1976; Lyons 1980: chs. 3 and 4).

6.1.4 The judgement is always about some object of desire or aversion which may or may not be a value. She thinks some state of desired (aversive) affairs holds in the world (has just begun to hold, persists in holding, fails to hold, or the like). Emotions are intensional events or states: they are about *objects*, which are states of affairs. An emotion may have a cause other than its object; something other than the object may be the cause of its occurring to her that the state of affairs holds (Kenny 1963). My tactless mention of apple pie may cause a companion a wave of grief, for it reminds her of the death of a beloved mother much given to the making of that delicacy. The object of the emotion is the state of desired affairs; the nature of this state of affairs tells us how to classify the emotion. Thus, grief implies a believed loss, fear a believed threat, envy a believed excellence in another which one

wants for oneself, and joy a believed gain or recovered loss of what
one values. Even in diffused anxiety or depression I judge the world
a diffusedly threatening or gloomy place. It is the desire- or value-
judgement that identifies which emotion someone has, rather than
the flavour of its mental agitation. Further, no emotion is mere
agitation of the mind. Nor is mere agitation of the mind emotion;
there might be a dispassionate, but active and global, dislocation
and upheaval of beliefs when we have to give up a central plank of
our thinking on some interesting subject. Emotions mean something: the meanings are the desire- or value-judgements about how
the world *is* (Lyons 1980: chs. 1 and 4). However, emotional
meaning is not primarily what we *mean by* our emotion, or what
our intention is in having it; Sartre thought it is, as we shall see, but
I shall disagree with him.

6.1.5 It is values and value-judgements that mainly concern us,
so I will speak mainly about them even though most of what I have
to say also covers emotions about states of desired affairs. But
emotions that arise from changes in states of affairs that we desire
may be crucially important because it may be some emotional
response which begins the work of dialectically transforming our
desires. These may be educative. Desires may surprise us in that it
may be their satisfaction or dissatisfaction that shows us more
clearly what both the content and the importance of the desired
state of affairs was to us. It may also be in our emotions that we
assign weight, strength, or preference to desires when we are
engaged in that part of our deliberations about what to do. There is
also a theme to which it is difficult to do justice in a work of this
kind; it connects with emotional responses to changes in desired
states of affairs. Many of our attitudes, including some of higher
order, are inarticulate in various ways. We certainly have access to
them as we do to the richness of perception which is not exhaustible
verbally. But perhaps we do not have access to all the processing of
them which goes on in the dialectical transformation of our desires.
Or, plausibly, psychic feelings are our only accessed response to this
processing. It is tears, laughter, tearing anguish, or delight which
give us some inarticulate grasp of what is happening. None the less,
what is happening seems best described in an intellectualist way. It
is the process of the dialectical evolution of first-order desires into
values, under pressure from the higher-order desires, which our
emotional responses either contain or occasion.

6.1.6 The occasion of a value-judgement on how the world is gives rise to feelings, which form an aspect of any emotional state. On the one hand, it causes various bodily changes which are involuntary, and only some of which are felt. Thus fear causes all or some of these: increased heart and breathing rates, pallor, dilation of the pupils, nausea, tensing of muscles. No one experiences the dilation of pupils, though they do experience the nausea, the pounding heart, and a sense of rigidity and strain in the body. Bodily feelings caused by emotional judgements are usually part of what we experience in emotion. On the other hand, the judgement is the reason for various *psychic* feelings, which are also involuntary but which are about the state of value affairs. These seem to be a different kettle of fish from the bodily feelings. We may, crudely, sort them into pleasant and painful psychic feelings; we can tie at least some of them to styles of activity in emotion which are not (obviously) adaptive or done for a purpose. We weep or laugh or act in more nearly deliberate styles, either more muted or more exuberant than is usual with us. The pain of such psychic feelings as grief or jealousy is not physical pain though somehow like it. Nor are psychic delights a kind of felt bodily pleasure. That is vague, but we will come back to psychic feelings in 6.2.

6.1.7 Emphasizing value and judgement makes emotions look more sophisticated states of mind than it is always plausible to think them. It seems plausible that animals have at least simple emotions; also plausible to attribute simple beliefs and desires to them. However, the judgement need be neither wise nor ruminative. One can lash out in anger at some real or fancied slight, never pausing to consider the merits of one's judgement. It is still instant rage *at* something one thinks was said or done. You cannot recognize a slight or insult without making a value- (desire-) judgement; no one spots a barbed retort unless he spots the hope or value stung by it. Unreasoning, instant rage is no objection to the theory (*pace* Lyons 1980: 87). The problem with flash responses among humans is like the problem of animal passions generally; value looks too sophisticated an idea to figure very plausibly in them. But the simplicity of a hot response does not argue simplicity in the value engaged. Of course, simple first-order desires will sometimes—not always—play the role I have given to value. I leave this complication aside. Human emotions do tend to concern values just because humans are so concerned with personal things.

6.1.8 This apart, desires are both like and unlike emotions. First, a difference: desires always contain judgements on how the world *might* be; emotions always contain judgements on how it *is* (was, or will be). Of course, either may also contain judgements of the other sort. Emotions are seldom intended: they are passive responses to how we see the world. We only sometimes think, in emotions, of changing what we see. Desires, too, depend on beliefs about how the world is, but yield intended, active responses to it so as to change it. Thus emotions are suffered, are judgemental, more like verdicts than noticed opportunities, whereas desires begin action: they suggest (are reasons for) initiatives, they lie behind intentions about what, deliberately, to do. Emotional responses can often be understood apart from plans of action, whereas a desire *is* the plan of some action.

6.1.9 We also think of the passions as suffered partly because they give rise to activity which looks purposeless, non-adaptive, or even maladaptive. Tears and laughter, we said, are obvious examples of this, but not the only ones. The phrase 'give rise to activity' is intended to steer a course between 'action' and 'behaviour'. Neither of these is quite right: the first because the lilt in one's voice, the mid-sentence sigh, or the tender smile are not aimed at anything and reach no *end* of the agent; the second because these lilts and sighs *express* our feeling while the involuntary tremblings and pallor of terror do not express, but merely accompany (though they may betray) it. Of course we can fake these expressions and do so to gain ends. But that is insincere; what we do deliberately has an effect only because genuine expressions of emotion have no deliberate point. These activities express our valuations through our psychic feelings; but trembling or gooseflesh do *not* express bodily feelings.

6.1.10 Second, desires may be related to emotions by being parts or aspects of them. A desire may be part of what identifies the emotion: fear entails a desire to escape the object of your fear, even though you might override that desire without ceasing to be fearful. Perhaps among the features that distinguish admiration from envy are the sorts of desires that characterize (and poison) envy (Deutscher 1983: 148–55). In other cases no desire is part of the concept of the emotion—in regret, for example. Yet again, some desire may be natural to an emotion without being part of what defines it; for example, its goal may include the goal of a desire which is part of the emotion. Thus jealousy does not entail that you desire to deride your rival rather than, say, to outshine him or her. But a desire like that is not just accidentally connected with jealousy, since jealous people want to displace their rival in the (perhaps only fancied) gaze of the beloved. Grief, in a somewhat more distant fashion, may breed the desire for revenge in some circumstances, though that is not usual. But here, grief would be (seen by the agent as) a *reason* for revenge, and not associated with it naturally, causally, or by habit.

6.2 Psychic feelings

6.2.1 Psychic feelings are puzzling. Much of moral philosophy which ought to explain them simply leaves them out. A full account of emotion must include them, but it is not clear just how they fit in (Stocker 1976 and 1983; Alston 1969). If we stress ideas of commitment, care, devotion, and faith (Stocker 1983), we talk about the will, not about suffered responses to a judgement. I offer an incomplete picture.

6.2.2 Psychic feelings are part of the agitation of the mind spoken of in dictionaries. Are psychic feelings actually bodily sensations—diffuse ones, perhaps? Well, psychic pains—the gnawing of envy, the grating agonies of remorse, the pangs of sorrow— are not literally bodily gnawings, gratings, and pangs. Yet they hurt in too real a sense to be merely metaphorical pains: they weary, debilitate, oppress us; we can say when they assault us, when they cease, how long they last, and how intense they are. Psychic feelings may halt us in mid-action, disconcert our fluency in mid-sentence, cause us placeable, datable tears or laughter or caperings or bouts of gloomy brow-hanging contemplation. Thus they are mental events and processes just as bodily pains are. Just as thoughts (thinkings) may be token identical with brain events or processes, so psychic feelings may be token identical with brain states, events, and processes. But it would be wrong to think that psychic feelings are bodily *feelings*.

6.2.3 Psychic feelings are intensional, in the way in which laughter and tears are intensional. They are about something; they have objects. One weeps for Adonais, for joy, for golden grove unleaving; one laughs at clowns, at pathos, at wit. The pangs of grief are similarly *at* loss, *for* one's beloved, *at* an excellence marred. So psychic feelings are intensional—at or for things. Weeping and laughing are *expressions* of psychic feelings, not actions done for some reason, nor are they yet psychic feelings themselves. They are not expressions of bodily feelings, certainly, for bodily feelings are not *at* anything (Bedford 1957). A pounding heart or gooseflesh are tied, causally, to fear, but are not at or about its object. However, laughter is not just tied causally to amusement. Amusement is the impulse to laugh *at* or *about* something. This likeness between tears and psychic pain should not lead us to think psychic pain *is* the impulse to tears, the felt tendency to weep. The pain is not an aspect of the intensional object of weeping, not what one weeps at, as a child weeps at physical pain. Yet painful thoughts are not the same as psychic pain, but rather the source of it. One weeps painfully in psychic pain. Psychic pain, in this, is not conceptually like physical pain but like pleasure, as in the pleasure of chess or of woodwork, and not to be separated from the activities, including the thinkings, of emotion itself. The agony of shame is not the thought that one did very wrong, for one may think that, quite sincerely, without the agony. Psychic feelings loom large in emotions, yet emotions are more complex than feelings are; our feelings lie just in the *response* to the value-judgement that identifies which emotion we feel. Finally, feelings of lethargy, drunkenness, nausea, drug-induced euphoria, or serenity differ again, since they have no typical intensional contexts or occasions; but they are not straightforward bodily feelings either, since they are not locatable, even diffusely, in one's body as gooseflesh is, or as sinking feelings or skin cooling are. These last are quite clearly sensations, not psychic feelings. P. D. Wall speculates (in a television programme) that psychic pain may somehow be physiologically akin to physical pain, which may well be right; yet my main point still is that psychic pain is always *about something*. Psychic feelings, I suggest, are not analysable into other sorts of mental states and are of their own kind, but this does not mean that we can say nothing useful about them.

6.2.4 We do not usually intend to have psychic feelings, though sometimes we do. I may want myself to feel the full weight of remorse in order that I shall not slacken my resolve to make amends. I may do all I can to savour joy or love. The tortures of jealousy may be feelings from which I urgently want to escape. However, there seem to be no second-order epicyclic actions which bring about our having these feelings, or losing them. Like gaining or keeping faith, we can only put ourselves in the way of them, not bring them directly about.

6.2.5 I want to go on, in the next section, to try to shed light on how we order and roughly quantify our values. It will be useful to offer first an account of the kinds of occasion we have for emotion, and see how a dynamical picture of psychic feelings fits in. For much the most part we pursue our personal lives in the spirit of monitoring a continually changing process. We make adjustments, change direction, trim our sails as our sense of occasion demands, and in one way or another, on this tack or that, move to encompass our values and make them real. Occasions for emotion are occasions for these moves and adjustments.

6.2.6 An emotional episode is an appraisal; either a local and sudden one, or a global and reflective one which reassesses the state of value-affairs in some large-scale project. A sudden rise or drop in the status of someone's value-objects leads him to marshall and deploy a set of skills, energies, and resources; alternatively, he finds that he can release these energies elsewhere. There looms a sudden access of or release from attention, care, concentrated scrutiny; we are unexpectedly faced with a large expenditure of energy in some act of defence or aggression; we are surprised by a need for sustained, delicate, meticulous activity. Both psychic and bodily feelings arise from these episodes of husbanding, gathering, organizing (perhaps unsuccessfully) resources; they also arise from episodes when we suddenly see how to avoid them. They arise because the *human* person has a natural dynamics of activity: our trains of thought or periods of rapt attention have a momentum; sudden changes in them, even in so comparatively value-free an emotion as surprise, disturb our progress or (to switch metaphors) create whirlpools, white water, cascades. We must adjust to these, take risks, digest and recompute things. These reverberations of reorientation and redirection are the agitations of mind and body, the feelings, both psychic and physical, for which sudden emotional judgements are both the reason and the cause. Feelings are the responses of *human machinery* to personal affairs; they are like the jars, shocks, frictions, and eddies of a particular embodiment of a certain range of Turing-machine states that may be a person.

6.2.7 Global, summary, evaluative reflections are also apt to create emotions. Lifting your gaze from the immediate task at hand to appraise the broader course of action—some wider project—and assess its costs and profits, what values have been or may be harvested, what lost, debilitated, corrupted, or threatened—this occasions emotions. You assess the demands your project will make on you. These are occasions for despair, hope, disgust, delight, and the rest. Emotions arise from perceptions of the demands our values make on us if we are to retain them and our personhood. This idea helps to explain some of the corruptions of emotion, as we shall see in 6.5 and 6.6.

6.3   A labour theory of value

6.3.1 Emotions attract a degree of respect for their place in our lives which makes sense only in terms of some such analysis as the one given in 6.1. Emotions can be *of* value only if they are somehow *about* values. Of course, that does not show that all emotional states are valuable, which would show too much. After all, what confers dignity, scale, and depth on our emotions is not the scale and depth of the agitation of the mind, the degree of excitation of the emotion. Agitation, just by itself, neither has nor lacks dignity or nobility. King Lear may cry 'Touch me with noble anger'; he has occasion for the nobility of anger in the object of it. It is the *value* of any passion that may make it noble. For contrast, it really is exceedingly annoying to have one's baggage sent on to Perth from Sydney when one saw it labelled 'Adelaide', and one may vent one's anger at the airline on a company clerk. But Lear's invocation, in the course of one's vigorous remonstrance, would be absurb. Anger is noble only in a noble cause. One's agitation, in such a matter, had best not be too extreme, lest its extremity show that one is foolish in one's anger. An intensely agitated emotional state, on some occasion, might rather make one ludicrous, trivial, shallow, and emotionally puny than majestic, deep, weighty, and emotionally rich. The *value* which is at stake largely, but not solely, determines the value of a passion, not the mere vigour and degree of its excitation, however spontaneous and sincere these may be.

6.3.2 If that is right, then it follows that emotions have enough that is cognitive in them to attract cognitive critiques. Emotions may be misplaced and mistaken in at least two ways; in each, it is the *judgement* that is faulty. First, obviously enough, someone can feel anger or gratitude towards another who is not the cause of the benefit or injury which is the object of the emotion. Notoriously, someone's jealousy may be misplaced; he leaps too hastily or too anxiously to conclusions about what he thinks he sees. Perhaps his beloved never glanced aside or perhaps she glanced at someone quite other than he thinks. You can be envious of another for a talent or trait which she does not possess or which you have yourself in greater degree. You can fail to see how your position disqualifies you from the general criticism of another; she could not have intended her remarks to apply to you, so that your resentment is based on an indefensible judgement. These are mistakes about the *foundation* of a passion and so described by Hume (ed. 1888: 416). But, second, the emotion may also be *disproportionate*, either in being excessive or in falling short of what is appropriate. Proportion must be a matter of the value of the emotion along lines followed in the last paragraph. So these are mistakes in the valuation of a passion. What do mistakes of proportion come to?

6.3.3 Anyone's values play a more or less prominent role in her active life. Let me set aside complications about the possible dearth of opportunities to pursue certain values; then the ranking of a value in someone's life is measured by her active commitment to it—a measure which, in turn, needs some explaining. But let me take up something else first. We can judge wrongly, in an emotion, in allowing the agitation, the psychic feelings of our emotional state, to get out of proportion to our real commitment to the relevant value. Thus we can see the childishness of a child's grief—the screams, the tears—in its readiness to accept another toy to replace the lost or broken one, in the ease with which it is distracted, in its not persisting in sorrow, in its scarcely remembering later in the day the violent, five-minute explosion of frustration or loss. Conversely, of course, we find it inappropriate that a person should have no agitated reaction, or a rather tranquil one, to some happening. The new security, erosion, or loss of some value surely must, we think, count in her judgement as a major change. Not to be delighted, anxious, or miserable is to deflate real values just as much as excessive responses falsely inflate others. The agitation is a measure of the values of desires concerned, a measure in a *human* metric. Thus one's emotional responses (or lack of them) to the vicissitudes which our value-objects enjoy or suffer are at least evidence about their role in our lives. The evidence may be conflicting. Surely the loss of someone's close friend must mean more than his present calm suggests, else we get puzzled whether we ever understood him.

6.3.4 I shall say that the value at stake in any occasion for emotion has a *field*. That is an agricultural metaphor. The field of a value is just the area of human life where it may be made real: cultivated, grown, nourished, sustained, and finally brought to fruition. It is also where values may be lost or destroyed despite our best efforts; become diseased, warped, and, perhaps, merely neglected. In general, values are not just there simply to be carried off, and kept. We have to make them real, bring forth embodiments of them, make them tangible, concrete, datable, placeable, accessible, so as to appropriate them. We have to make them or find them in events, things, or processes. We must preserve and cherish them. The values of such emotions as love, spite, or jealousy must be forged and nurtured in the concrete stuff of which human relationships consist. The field of such values lies in concrete actions, sayings, gestures, and glances. In these we find the material in which to embody and express the values of our passions either by benefits or injuries to others. This is a materialist or, much better I think, a concretist theory of value and of the requirement for it of *labour*.

6.3.5 Some materials in the field are natural, you might say. Physical injury is a natural material in which to make the value of hatred real. But some of the materials are created by us no less surely than the values themselves are. Obviously language is a powerful instrument for embodying values: think of the compliment and the insult as simple examples. On the micro-social scale, affectionate friends or lovers make use of, and make up, a diverse and flexible range of styles and rituals of action and response, both verbal and non-verbal. These embody and express the values of their emotions, but not in natural materials. The power and flexibility in language and gesture among friends and lovers are inexhaustible.

6.3.6 If values need to be created and cultivated by labours in the field, then our emotions do not only link us to our values. They make claims. Claims on our labour. Our labour in value-fields measures both the values we pursue and *our* value as pursuers of them. To be a careful, scrupulous, dedicated, and untiring cultivator in the field measures the value we really place on what we make real and objective. For labour is a cost, paid in time, energy, pain, boredom, or minute attention. But equally, once we declare our values, then that labour, or lack of it, measures us, says what we are as persons, whether light and limp, or resolute and resourceful. Our values themselves may be casual and shallow (though what this means awaits the story of Chapter 7). They may fail to show us as serious, and courageous, however assiduous we are in cultivating them. But the theme of this section is that we can order and measure *subjective* values in terms of commitment; and we can measure commitment by the expenditure of our human and personal resources in labouring to make values real and concrete. Perhaps our degree of agitation of psychological feelings can be seen as a human measure of our subjective values and our degree of commitment to labour as a personal one. These ought to be roughly equitable if, as I would like to think, the feelings are a response to the costs demanded of us in securing our values. It is in some such way that psychic feelings span a gap between the human and the personal in emotion. (Objective value comes to more than subjective values made concrete in particular events, processes, or objects; but we can expect objective value to be based somehow on subjective ones.)

6.3.7 Among things that most of us value are persons themselves. That is because they are at once inventors, perceivers, nurturers, and harvesters of value. Only persons are strong evaluators. We may not share their values, or find them valuable for reasons such as their being witty, affectionate, clever, obliging, beautiful. Simply in the fact that they are evaluators, labourers, and makers of whatever values, they will be of some significance to any person. They might, for these reasons, be of negative value, though I will argue that they are, objectively, a positive value. They are ends in themselves in at least this weak sense. They alone provide for there to be values other than oneself, and thereby provide the range of value-responses to one's own actions, without which second-order satisfactions must prove empty and personhood be lost. Still, individuals ought not to be regarded as instrumental to the general end that there be valuers.

6.3.8 A passion which does not meet the claims of its value by work in the field is a passion devalued. It is mere agitation of the

mind. The agent is devalued with it. Plainly, it is our values that
make us the persons we are, and not the mere casual, whimsical,
and wanton (though possibly urgent) desires that we (sometimes)
humanly have. Thus values make a kind of existential claim, for
they define anyone's personal life through her projects and lift her
above the merely impulsive, unprincipled, human thing she
otherwise is. What may be at stake, in an emotion, is one's
existence as a person, as something which cannot turn its back on
the demands of labour for its values without prejudice to its very
existence as a self-possessed, self-controlled, self-evaluating being
(6.5).

6.3.9 The labours of love (to use this as our example) go
forward, if they do, in the light of information and argument. That,
as I said before, is inescapable in voluntary action. The information
and the reasoning may be good or bad, but if bad then the
information will mislead passion as to how to make its value real.
In the making and sustaining of its value, love can be, ought to be—
and true love *is*—ingenious, perceptive, inventive, reflective, and
analytical, careful in its reasoning, willing to make hypotheses and
test them. All of that *thinking* lies at the core of all the claims on the
cares of love (or whatever else it may be). Without it the claims are
not met but botched, so the value is debased. Love becomes content
with mere feelings or with fantasies of value. Love which avoids the
labours of reasoning (the guide of all its other labours) reveals itself
as a passion too light to sustain the work necessary to create or
sustain its value. It is love without integrity, a shallow passion after
all; it is a fickle and trivial thing, no matter what its degree of
agitation. Thus, being reasonable is a crucial part of the responsibility and integrity of any emotion whatever.

6.3.10 However, there are at least two serious weaknesses in the
idea that labour defines, rather than roughly measures, the scale
and order of subjective value. For obvious reasons, the measure is
not the labour we do expend, but rather what we *would* expend—if
we had the opportunity and ability. If I cannot reach my toppling
child at the cliff's edge, or cannot staunch my beloved's severed
artery, my rigid ineffectual anguish in the disaster need not make
my grief trivial. But it is not satisfactory, I think, to rest the account
on subjunctive conditionals, either. Any counterfactual is true in
virtue of the truth of some categorical statement, and it will be this
that tells us what measures subjective value. I do not know what the

relevant categoricals are. Further, the formula suggests a kind of perspiration theory of value, as if sweat were the measure of all things. Some of us have the flair and the knack of the thing and are none the worse, as persons, for finding the good life easy. Others of us are doomed largely to earnest good intentions; we mean well but are maladroit; we till the field for our values but lack green thumbs. Such people are not the best examples to raise, if we hope to learn the art of life by seeing the thing well done. In the nature of the case, good luck, skills, and grace (for which there is no algorithm) loom much larger in the practice of the life of virtue than they can in its theory. Despite my dissatisfaction on these two scores, I persist with the labour theory; I hope to develop the idea that it is in pursuing values and making them real that we express what we are when we excel our natural selves in the dialectical tasks that make us fully persons.

6.3.11 Let us turn now to the darker side of the emotions. It will be clearer how emotions are tied to value if we look at ways in which a passion may be corrupt. I begin with a brief picture of Sartre's theory (Sartre 1962), in which all emotion is a degraded form of consciousness.

6.4 Sartre on the emotions

6.4.1 Sartre, in an arresting, paradoxical, yet highly suggestive theory, takes a dim view of emotions. I cast passions as constructive features of personal life and gave them a central role in valuing; that is how they are most often seen. But we often also think of emotions as dangerous and destructive, as distorting judgement, shattering peace and affection, subverting true values, tempting us to evil, subverting our dignity, and eroding the veneer of culture. This portrays at least some passions as fierce and animal.

6.4.2 Sartre accepts a bad image of the passions, yet also sees in them the strong cognitive features which I made central. For Sartre, all emotions are corrupted forms of consciousness; they must be corrupted forms, if they purport to overcome us in some way. For Sartre, radical libertarian that he is, nothing can predetermine consciousness by overtaking and colouring it in the way envisaged. We need not share this condemnation of all emotions as corrupt;

still, it will be instructive to look at them, with Sartre, in a less friendly light.

6.4.3 Sartre begins with the phenomenological point that we must understand the meaning of a passion rather than its cause. Thus the interpreter will plumb the waters of passion deeper than can the behavioural scientist, who only links emotions with their causes and behavioural effects. Sartre sees the meaning of emotion as what someone means by it. So he begins by giving emotion the character of an *intended action*, which has meaning in the sense of a *purpose*. Thus emotions are not suffered, as responses are suffered. They are doings of ours, to be understood as actions are.

6.4.4 What sort of doings? To adopt an emotion is to choose a (possibly brief) project for grappling with the world and under-standing it. Better, perhaps, it is a way of choosing to continue with some project, not in the light of a practical, realistic understanding of how to achieve its end but in the light of another, and inevitably debased, form of 'understanding'; a bogus theory about how the world bends to one's will. To follow Sartre's rather oracular style, one *chooses* the world as if it conformed to magical causes. The choice is not simply a mistake about causes; the chosen world is constructed as amenable to incantatory, sympathetic, imitative practices. What lies behind this resort to magic is that you repudiate your real capacities and, with them, the tasks and responsibilities they impose; instead, you pretend to do the tasks by magic and so only pretend to a serious commitment to the values of your passions.

6.4.5 Sartre's analysis of his examples is always imaginative and surprising (though some of them strike at least this reader as implausible). He suggests, for instance, that fainting in panic is the magical pretence that one can erase some great danger by blotting out all consciousness of it, or alternatively that one thereby escapes all responsibility for grappling effectively with the predicament and undertaking the labours it calls for. Similarly, resort to tears (in pleading, say, with an implacable antagonist) is an incantatory ritual which attempts to repudiate the idea that one will somehow have to cope, well or poorly, with the threatened situation. One pretends to a magical incapacity. The breakdown in tears is both a declaration of helplessness and a rite aimed at rejecting so intractable a world. A dance of joy at a long-parted lovers' reunion is an incantatory rite of immediate and complete possession of the other; the rite is performed to symbolize performance of the duties of continued living together in love. But despite the magical dance of joy, the rite cannot really make good in a moment all the responsibilities of tact, consideration, patience, tenderness, and generosity which love demands. These can be made real and concrete only in the longer, more arduous processes of actually maintaining love and making it real in a sometimes difficult world. One pretends that a momentary ritual may capture a lasting and complete harmony and unity with another. No such consummation can really be there; even the deepest love lasts for long only if its commitments are seriously pursued.

6.4.6 Thus, for Sartre, the emotional consciousness is a sorcerer's consciousness, spurious, debased, false, magical. Emotions are essentially self-delusional states, states of bad faith, in which one pretends to be what one knows one is not. The picture of emotions as overcoming us is not acceptable to Sartre's extreme indeterminism; it is this aspect of the matter which forces him to his deprecatory view of emotional life.

6.4.7 What these striking examples show us is that our passions may be, somehow, in bad faith without the obvious bad faith of deliberate insincerity. What Sartre really draws attention to is not that all emotional states are corrupted forms of consciousness, but that any may become so, even without lapse of simple candour. The non-adaptive activity in emotion may conceal a plan which the agent follows in bad faith, in self-deception rather than by conscious design. Bad faith is self-deceiving, though obscure to the agent in some way—we need not delve into just which way here—and so it is corrupt. In particular, Sartre's striking account for joy focuses on a corrupting style of emotion, in which non-adaptive activity does not express an impulse which overcomes us, but is intended and acted. Yet passionate joy may sometimes be a most constructive emotion. The non-adaptive behaviour, which forms one basis for the view of emotions as suffered, not acted, here gains sense and purpose in the magical plot to escape the claims which our passions make on us. Emotional *agitation*, its rituals and celebrations, its singing, dancing, exclaiming spirits on the one hand, its passionate storms of grief or anger, or its dead, flat calms of despair or inert resignation on the other, are at best only one measure of the high seriousness and moral worth of delight, bliss and exultation, or remorse and sadness. The agitation is highly serious if the engaged values are grand and grave and if the emotor's commitment to them is deep and faithful; but this same intensity of agitation may be false, light, and trivial, as we saw before, or devious, evasive, and irresponsible if it is inauthentic.

6.4.8 Let us now see how some such picture of corrupt and destructive passions fits into the frame for understanding emotion developed in the last section.

6.5   Emotional corruption

6.5.1 What can I take from Sartre's sketch and use for my own purposes? Mainly, I borrow the idea that we can offer a *cognitive* critique of the non-adaptive activities in impassioned behaviour; they are what led us, in part to regard passion as suffered. That is, we can find ways of probing what emotions mean, at least in some cases; we can hope sometimes to see an inarticulate strategy in them, but not one that will oblige us to deplore them. According to 6.2, these activities express psychic feelings, which are intensional states. Therefore, the critique will apply primarily to these feelings. There is a sense in which Sartre's theory denies that there are any emotions; whatever seems to be an emotion is really an action or an activity which pursues a plan. It is a rite, an incantation, a bit of magic to disguise the neglect of realistic, practical, but above all *painful* labour for value. I think that is wrong. An emotion is a complex involuntary state, usually occasioned by a sudden or global reflective appraisal of the state of some value-affairs and a consequent adjusting of one's labour economy (6.3); so it gives rise to an agitation of psychic and bodily feelings, perhaps to desires and plans, and thus, perhaps, to practical thoughts about one's position. A turbulence *is* suffered and comes over—perhaps even overcomes—one. We do not choose it; we feel it. Thus the account offered here leaves emotions as emotions in all these ways. Yet it will give room for us to appraise them as reasonable or not.

6.5.2 One model, somewhat different from Sartre's, for understanding certain emotions as corrupt and destructive sees them as obsessive. But what idea is that? As I use it, it is a distortion of scale or place in some (subjective) value; this is not simply a matter of pursuing the comparatively tinsel sort of gold at the expense of the true gold, nor pursuing the gold idly, laxly, fecklessly. Nor is it weakness of will. It is, rather, to magnify some value so that it becomes for us (at the moment, for the month, or forever) larger and more demanding than its capacity to enlarge, strengthen, and reward us could possibly account for. (That this capacity is one that matters is a theme of Chapter 7.) Often this is simply a distorted perspective on what is close or frequent. We allow our work, our garden or car to seem inescapable taskmasters. This may damage us—waste our opportunities, warp our sense of what is due to love, friendship, integrity, and self-possession. Perhaps it does so more than we are often willing to admit. But, for most of us, these are hardly obsessions in a serious sense.

6.5.3 One is truly obsessed when a distorted value displaces almost all others or when one pursues exclusively some inappropriate form or realization of it. I can think of two ways in which this might happen. First, this dominance of a warped value may be a kind of existential anxiety: a sense that one will be quite bereft of any intelligible project without it, that the whole of one's life as a person will be destroyed unless *this* value is gained and made concrete here, now, and in this object or episode.

6.5.4 Let me contrast this with the attitude of the character Parolles in Shakespeare's bitter comedy *All's Well That Ends Well*. When Parolles finds his treachery, boastfulness, and cowardliness ruthlessly unmasked and ridiculed, with all honour and credit irrecoverably gone he is still able to exclaim 'simply the thing I am shall make me live' (*All's Well* IV: iii). There is a kind of evaluative nudity about this attitude to oneself that few of us could accept. Parolles is interesting because he can give up the projects of personhood. He is someone without values; he is himself of no value in his own eyes. This does not mean that he has stopped being a person! He is still free, responsible, unprincipled, cowardly, dishonest, damned. Nevertheless, he is not so much vicious as robbed of all virtue. In the end he is accepted, evaluated as more than a nothing, by the very Lafeu who has always been his most scathing critic. The existential obsessive cannot face this loss of personal open projects, yet feels threatened by his fragile hold on those he has; he is fixated by a basic anxiety about what a person is and what his values are. He is convinced that without gaining some quite *local* end, so to speak, his values will be globally destroyed and he will become, as a person, a *nothing*. Like Othello, his occupation will be gone.

6.5.5 The true obsessive sees this threatened annihilation too early and in the wrong place. That is because the threat lies in the arbitrariness of his values. If the present project is lost, he can find nothing to give point to a further one, for the obsessive lacks a context of basic personal meanings within which to rethink his values. The mistake is cognitive, since the dialectical transformation of his desires into values is imperfectly resolved. The dialectic which transformed desire into value has somehow been, for him, arbitrary, either because it lay in mere conformity to uncriticized social mores, or because the theory on which he has proceeded is somehow false to his nature, or for some other reason (see 7.2). He has no basis on which to make a radical revaluation; worse, the values on which, in panic, he wants to rest all the others are fraudulent; he sees that they cannot really fill this basic role.

6.5.6 Other styles of obsession crop up in jealousy and resentment. There is a kind of resentment which one cherishes. It may seem to nurse and cosset itself, to grow and bloom and fill an obsessed consciousness with resentful thoughts, with the angry pleasures of self-righteousness and of a sense of undeserved injury. This obsessive growth feeds on a second-order satisfaction in the passion nurtured. It is, however, not the satisfaction of a strong evaluator's second-order desire, nor does it have the sort of structure which directs higher-order action at being a certain kind of person. It is the pleasure of an anger or a hatred that has found a rationale for which it has been searching. The satisfaction felt in obsessive resentment is hardly consistent with the emotion entertained. It springs from a sense of justification which is cherished because the anger or hatred is vivid and demanding whether or not it has the justification; or better perhaps, what one really resents cannot justify the malice one feels, though one finds that something a little like it can seem to justify it. The anger or hatred is a human response which rationally ought to be alienated, yet seizes delightedly on spurious reintegration in some fake value. An urgent human impulse wins a place in personal life which is undeserved. Alternatively, obsessive resentment might not feed upon satisfaction, but be an *agonized* resentment. It is the obsession of an impotent anger which sees no way to act, less because of sheer powerlessness than because it envisages no adequate, perhaps because no personal, response to an injury felt. It sees its response as petty or as betraying too much that is vulnerable, as too like a ruffled hen, or whatever else it may be that makes the scale of a response inappropriate to the scale and place in the range of values of what was infringed. It, too, is the obsession of an inadequate solution to a dialectical problem. It is confusion over the scale of what one values.

6.5.7 But how can one be confused about what one values or about how much one values it? Doesn't one know, simply? Of course, one can easily see that one might be wrong about one's best *interests*, understood in the light of common prudence, but to throw aside simple prudential values for others need not enmesh one in error. Quite the contrary: one ought sometimes to act from generosity and love, which are not prudential motives but may yield what one values more highly. One can also be in error about the consequences of one's actions and not see that what one values in pursuing some course is inimical to deeper values. But how can one be confused about what one values?

6.5.8 In two rather diametrically opposed ways, I shall argue. The archetype of the first way is infatuation with another. One has, to begin with at least, an inarticulate but absorbed interest in another's face (or figure, demeanour, and so on). One dwells, bathes, sinks in absorbed perception, watches for changes, absence of changes, expressions of this or that in a quite uncritical, unanalysing way. One is fascinated, besotted, blinded, lost, absorbed in a contemplation which is not an understanding. It is often said, and perhaps rightly, that one projects one's own ideals onto the face, onto the person, whose separate individuality offers no more than a pretext for the supposition that she is a value-object of an extraordinary kind. But infatuation is yet more blind, more inarticulate than this. For one can neither say nor understand intuitively what values, what expectations, opportunities, or hopes this person offers. So no well-understood, itemized, costed, determinate potentialities are thrown upon this person who offers, as it seems, such golden chances. Even so, infatuation is the excess of a necessary virtue; its lets the practical life of reasoning and valuing outrun what one's principles articulate.

6.5.9 Love is blind, we say. That need not be so. Your hope can be inarticulate, intuitive, but worth trusting, and so can your insight into how the hope is grounded in another's character. But, notoriously, they may well not be. So obsession by another, a delightfully inscrutable stranger kept at an uncriticized distance lest the hope be shattered—or, worse, kept inscrutable despite abundant evidence that the promise will not be fulfilled—may be destructive. If the hope is ill-understood yet urgent, grasping that one's Blue Angel is, visibly, a cheat, whore, and liar need not dampen one's ardour; its shapeless, cloudy toils may bemuse one all the more for remaining inchoate and unappraised. But this imbalance is the vice of a virtue, for many values need time and use before they will bear the wintry sun of a truly objective, explicit, and conceptual appraisal.

6.5.10 The second way in which we might mistake our values is ideological. But this too is the excess of a virtue, for it tries to guide practice by explicit principle. Principles expand our understanding of values and guide our pursuit of them. But explicit principles may nevertheless not exhaust what we grasp intuitively; precept may turn out cruder than sensitive practice feeling its way. Even more, the unforeseeable world, rich, concrete, and mutable, is apt to reveal the paucity of principle without insight. It is dangerous to tie our aspirations to explicit principles so firmly as to have no grasp of values but an articulated one. There is nothing to be said for keeping values inarticulate; the work in hand right now is to spell them out a little more. Yet we need a basic *practical* grasp, a know-how which does not depend on formulation, to direct our search for the articulate. A rigid sticking to principle may be the mark of one who lacks the know-how of her values, who can find the substance of them only in the letter. Without practical insight, one's values *are* one's principles; if the principles look arbitrary once questioned, one risks a total loss of them should the world grow awkward. Fanaticism is the ugly lot of those who trust an authoritarian source of principles without an intuitive sense of what gives them point. This, too, gives rise to an obsessive failure to comprehend one's values.

6.5.11 Another point of interest (not, necessarily, of merit) in Sartre's picture of the emotions is the way in which it finds a central place in emotion for bodily and psychic feelings. They are the incantatory, dramatizing, sympathetic magical part of the sorcerer's way with the world. Thus they are aspects of the *cognitive* evolution of emotional episodes. Here again Sartre's deeply original treatment strikes us with the shock of discovery; our ramifying grasp of the implications of his examples convinces us that he is appallingly right about some cases. But the power of his treatment lies, I think, in its illumination of essentially special cases; his examples are of secondary cases of emotion, important for ways in which emotional integrity may become corrupted.

6.6   A unity in opposites: two corruptions of emotion

6.6.1 I want to discuss two sorts of emotional failures—weaknesses or corruptions—which persons may suffer. The first sort is apt to strike us as an emotional weakness or lack, though I will argue that it is just as much a failure or corruption of reason. The second sort is apt to strike us as a lack of or a weakness in reasoning, though I will argue that it is just as much a lack of or a weakness in desire and emotion. The first failure is cynicism, the second sentimentality. As others have done, I will conclude that these apparently quite different corruptions of emotional life are intimately related.

6.6.2 A stereotype of the cynic is of someone who dismisses the values of emotions like love, friendship, grief, and other warm sympathies by appeals to realism, clear hard-headed observation, objectivity, and so on. His claims to cold detachment are typically accompanied by sneering, deriding attacks on the emotions and values of others as soft-headed sentimentality. It is hardly surprising that he should be seen as only half a person, as guided by reasoning and information but diminished by lack of, absence of, emotion.

6.6.3 This picture of the cynic can hardly be an adequate one. Cynicism is a style of behaviour, a kind of activity, so it must be sustained by desire and emotion. Indeed, cynics are dominated by passions, as their often hateful derision of others so strongly suggests. Which passions dominate may vary. But people who are ruled by ambition for power, for wealth, for prestige may readily have the coldness of cynicism. As Hume point out, it is certain desires and emotions which are cold and which oppose the warmer, often shorter-lived, more sociable emotions. Outside the structure of a dialectical process, reason cannot oppose emotions; thought may show passion what its values are and how they may be realized; it may show how and where different desires and emotions conflict in values. Reason, therefore, cannot be cold, cannot chill a warm emotion. Only another emotion can oppose an emotion. Someone may find the bitterness which feeds cynicism in some lasting disappointment, long resented. (There is, alas, no Santa Claus!) Beside cold ambition there may well be cold fear of the claims of warmer emotions. Sociable values are precarious; wounded affection leads to sour cynicism. But, whether through ambition or fear, cynicism is a rejection of the claims of sociable emotions, a rejection powered by some other emotion.

6.6.4 But cynicism is equally a failure of *reason*. How can that be so? The cynic ignores evidence that the values of the warmer human emotions *are* values for him as much as for the rest of us. Cynicism is a pretence, an avoidance of clear, straightforward facts about us all. The cynic, in defiance of evidence and argument, denies what is plainly of value to him in order not to admit, in fear, the risks and labour that other emotions require of him. Here one emotion, fear, defeats another. The cynic repudiates real values with which his fears conflict. Either because the labour involved in admitting the claim is inconvenient for his ambitions, or because he simply fears to admit their incalculable claims, he persuades himself that he disbelieves what can scarcely escape his notice. Cynicism, for all its pride in rationality, is rationally shallow, self-delusive, subjective, and deliberately ignorant. The rationality of cynicism is not sustained by the proper rational emotions, by love of truth and seriousness about its values, but by fear, envy, or spite. The values of these passions are not truth, integrity, or pride in one's own human abilities. They value mere injury to others as an assertion of self.

6.6.5 If reason has no temperature, what about objectivity and detachment? Are these not, by definition, cool if not cold? Don't we find here qualities that oppose reason to emotion? No. To be objective is to be unswayed in what you believe by your hopes and fears. It sets truth above the value of other hopes and fears; truth is the value of a certain kind of love, a passion which sustains the exercise of a certain deep human capacity. The subjective thinker flatters hopes and fears by indulging in beliefs which represent the world cosily, or magically rather than correctly. But objectivity cannot be just a state of belief if it requires sustained effort and work to resist the distortions from our hopes and fears. And surely it does require a kind of passion or desire if objectivity is a *sustained* state or activity. It is sustained by some emotion (Stocker 1980). So what opposes the hopes and fears which sway the subjective thinker is not reason itself, strictly, *but this emotion, whatever it is.* I have called it love of truth for want of a more luminous name. Love of truth fills a unique place, for it is an indispensable part of the care and labour of any value and emotion. Every emotion, if we really pursue its value, joins hands with the general love of truth, for each emotion has an interest, so to speak, in its value's being really, not just apparently, promoted and protected. The emotions have no less a stake in objectivity than reason itself has. Thus objectivity is the very reverse of unemotional (see Deutscher 1983, *passim*). It is part of any passion which retains its integrity, which really motivates pursuit of its value and does not fall away into forms of pretended pursuit issuing in the kinds of emotional corruption which we call sentimentality. It is time to talk about that.

6.6.6 The sentimental person appears to be guilty of failures of *reason*, to be unreasonably full of feelings, to gush injudiciously, to take an irrational pride in those agitations of the mind which are only one aspect of our emotions. Thus sentimentality appears to be the very opposite of cynicism. Where the latter seems to us an emotional lack, the former strikes us as an intellectual one. However, sentimentality really is a form of emotional lack just as much as it is a weakness of reasoning. Sentimentality turns out to be rather close to cynicism.

6.6.7 Sentimentalists seem not much concerned with the accuracy, probability, and detailed consistency of the belief or beliefs on which their emotions are founded. More especially, they do not think of care about the nature of the field of the emotions; they neglect the skills, planning, and labour needed to make real, to embody, the value of their emotions. They focus rather on the psychic and bodily feelings that accompany, albeit essentially, emotional life.

6.6.8 Sentimental people are unwilling to pay the labour price of their emotions (Tanner 1977). I want to make clearer sense of this idea. I suggest that the sentimentalist is unwilling to meet the real claims of his emotions; that is, he is unwilling to do the field-work, to perform the labours of love which fidelity to his emotions and the integrity of his personality would demand. Instead, the sentimentalist is content to fob off claims on his emotions, to pretend that values can be realized in some facile way which, in fact, realizes only debased or false forms of the values. He pretends that he can meet the claims *just* through nourishing the feelings and allowing the non-adaptive behaviour characteristic of the emotion.

In this, he is strikingly like the cynic who is also unwilling to admit real claims. But whereas the cynic repudiates the *values* of the more demanding emotions under cover of debased rationalizations, the sentimentalist's cover lies in repudiating the *beliefs and reasoning*, especially the careful, laborious, detailed reasoning and understanding which would direct the processes in the field which could realize the values. He resists a focus on what the value really is. Thus he accepts debased or false forms of the values and, inevitably therefore, of the feelings of emotion. This repudiates the values and the feelings of emotion just as surely, if less explicitly, as the cynic does.

6.6.9 This, I hope it is clear, does not spring *just* from a lack of reasoning. It is a lack of proper values and proper emotions. It is more like a failure of will, though that idea is problematic. By adopting this facile, evasive attitude to facts about the claims of emotion, sentimentalists are content to pass off mere agitations, mere verbal gushings, as genuine realizations of the emotional values to which they pretend. This is emotional corruption quite as much as it is a rational failure, since it prefers to debase the values of some of the most worthy and exalted of human passions—on which the sentimentalist would like to pride himself—rather than to meet the real claims these passions make. The deeper emotions of the sentimentalist may centre mainly around self-esteem. He wants the personal kudos which attaches to emotional wealth and generosity, but does not wish to undertake the labours which are an inseparable aspect of living a rich emotional life.

6.7 Negative emotions: the case of grief

6.7.1 I have been arguing, with regard to emotions on which we place a value, that they are a person's struggle with its human response to some state—usually some change in state—of its value-(desire-) affairs. A good way to illustrate this is to take the example of some common emotion which is at least *apparently* maladaptive or non-adaptive in the actions and activities that express it, and look for some explanation of why this emotion seems to us to dignify and enrich our lives.

6.7.2 Grief at the death of a beloved person seems to be an appropriate case to consider. We respect grief, yet we find it issues in no obvious benefit either to the mourner or to the dead; it is entirely backward-looking; it may be as intense and obsessive as any passion; it may go on for a long time (two years is a standard period during which to grieve). Grief is about familiar and simple ideas, yet the beliefs and preoccupations that accompany it may often be so irrational that grieving persons may fear for their own sanity.

6.7.3 Grieving seems to be work, a task of adjustment. It is not usually the task of finding new values, and a new person; that comes as grief is ending. It is a hard-won acceptance that a value is lost, that one's beloved is irrecoverably gone, and that a multitude of rewarding ties, habits, activities, and delights have ended for ever. The work of grief somehow processes information. It is epistemic. Since the information, so far as it is statable, can be conveyed in just a few short sentences, the mourner may wonder at himself as a pitifully slow learner. Those who grieve wish to talk, to dwell on the fact of bereavement, of incidents connected with the death and the illness, with the past relationship, but what they say tends to be repetitive, a recounting rather than a discovery or even rediscovery of past incidents. Unlike curiosity, which is avid always for new information, grief turns round and round the same few statable ideas. It shows signs of a strong resistance to the obvious fact of loss and the obvious need for the loss to be replaced.

6.7.4 All this seems to mean that some of the information we must process as human animals is not readily given in sentential, syntactic form. Grief is but one of the ways in which mastery of language gives us no evolutionary advantage over other species; some of them also grieve, or, if this is too bold, regularly go through a similar period of non-adaptive activity when a partner or a member of the group is lost. Somehow, then, grieving is adaptive after all, and the tears, the daily episodes of psychic anguish, the despairing rituals of return to familiar places and repetition of familiar routines meet some partly epistemic need. I guess that there is something in the lives of animals analogous to a momentum in that some of their desires are knit, by learning, into patterns of action and satisfaction and that these patterns persist strongly. Grief, and kindred retrospective emotions, accompany a possibly long process of halting the momentum which old patterns have, even though they have now obviously lost their point.

6.7.5 Grief, like depressive illness, attracts compassion: but we value grief and respect it deeply as we do not value or esteem depression. So we seem to recognize, here, how the abstract description of what it is to have values and pursue them comes dangerously close to an empty formalism (as described in 1.4), without some picture of how the structures of the state and the task of being a person come to be embodied in a concrete, person-contingent, and obdurate reality of flesh and blood (or whatever else it may be). *A priori*, it might seem that a person could just accept the fact of death and irrecoverable loss, and turn to a new life and new values. But the problem is not like that of accepting new sentential information. Grief is valued because of facts on which the abstract picture of personhood sheds no light. Conversely, understanding the concept of a person gives no hint why we may be chilled at the absence of grief in one who appeared so attached to another who has just died. Grief can do no obvious service to the dead. It pays its due to the deep and complex array of threads that tie one to a beloved. It is a *human* debt, paid because we are, quite contingently to personhood, creatures who need a time for recovery from the tearing-away of those manifold connections. But it is also personal, in the sense that many of these inarticulately forged connections and judgements constitute the value placed on the person for whom one grieves and were a part, perhaps quite dimly perceived, of the process of coming to value her.

6.7.6 In this way the philosophy of personhood, self-excellence, and the life of pursuing values is *heartless*, for what can be said about all this is mostly abstract (in the style of 1.4) and not contingent on the way the state and the tasks of being a person happen to have become concrete in us. Values and valuing are in no way conceptually tied to vision, hearing, pain, sexuality, and the slow processes of forging and breaking of what are personal ties. Yet there can be no valuing or values without such contingent concrete processes which are fields for value. A very great deal of what makes up the content of a life of value must be contingent relative to the concepts of value and valuing. It is a properly philosophical matter to make this observation, however, and to illustrate it.

6.7.7 What is more relevant for my purpose than these comments on causes of irrational persistence is the quality of the information which seems to be processed and the way in which personal, cultured, rationally sophisticated attitudes and values are tied to it and tied to psychic feelings. Perhaps what I shall say about this is more by way of identifying a kind of problem than of solving it. There are perhaps not very surprising facts such as the shock and acute pain of witnessing a loved person's death, despite one's knowing for some months, perhaps, that it is inevitable and despite one's having seen people die before. It may be that no amount of conscious, fully believed, verbal expectation prepares one for those sights and sounds themselves. Nor need a death be particularly violent or painful for this acute pity and sorrow to ensue. The wish to communicate in grief, together with a obsessive repetitive content, suggests strongly the need to assimilate and to get right something which is not articulated and is probably inarticulable. In grief, anger and fear without proper objects (excepting anger at what a place the world can be and fear at one's inability to control it) are common; so is a sense of irrationality because one persists in attitudes and even quasi-beliefs that seem inappropriate—for instance, that the lost person somehow knows of the sufferer's grief, that rituals (tending a grave, hanging a picture, gazing at it, listening to a recorded voice, treasuring an object) are a service to the dead. All this material is something to which the mourner has limited access and on which he may dwell obsessively since he has no verbal means to assimilate what he attends to so closely. I conjecture, then, that consciousness, self-consciousness, the conceptualizing of value, and the desires and emotions that accompany them admit much less of verbal articulation than the abstract account given without regard to human embodiment may suggest.

Authentic and Objective Values

7.1 The desires of persons in cultures

7.1.1 The action-concepts that define personhood have a cultural setting and reference. At least six factors make this sure. First, any explanation I give to myself for why I acted as I did will offer to justify the action. I understand what I did or said (or what I thought) as what anyone ought to have thought, said, or done, rationally, in those circumstances, however unique and peculiar they were. This is both a common and a conceptually necessary part of how we explain the deeds of others too (2.4). These perceptions of reasonableness refer us to a cultural background. In this way each of us is an agent for others in seeing our own and others' movements as actions, to be understood, in this primary way, as actions for Everyman. In this way, our understanding of agency is a universal one.

7.1.2 Next, and more simply, our culture provides the concepts under which we intend and explain our actions. Further, it provides the conventions, usages, institutions, and forms which make real and concrete the values and meanings of our actions. For example, I can steal only if there is an institution of property; I can move a motion of censure only under procedural rules of a committee in some body of which I am a member; I can pay you a compliment only if we share cultural views of what is creditable and an understanding of the form compliments may take. Fourth, to understand myself as a person, I need more than a grasp of my own oddities and of what our species is like. I have to understand what we persons are, all together, as a cultured society which moulds me and to which I contribute. Next, the mirror of interpersonal response from others teaches me what the impact and meaning of my action is. But its impact on others will depend on the cultural life we share, or fail to share. Sixth and last, it is only in (certain kinds of) social life that we can rely on getting the bare necessities of life. Only then can we turn the main focus of our desires away from the satisfaction of appetites and needs, and towards more clearly personal concerns. So what preoccupies persons depends on the culture in which they live.

7.1.3 Let us look back at the non-exclusive classification of desires set out in 4.3.5–9 to see which of them is likely to be most central to the lives of persons. I mentioned appetites first; physical pleasures and tastes second; then more conceptual but still largely passive observings, watchings, listenings; and finally two sorts of desires to change the world according to some design or concept, differing as one understands the intended change as physical or social. These make up four main related, overlapping classes of desires. The last of them will interest us most, since these desires offer most to the structure of cultural meanings which make sense of the tasks and ideal of being a person.

7.1.4 Of course it is rewarding to satisfy appetites and bathe in pleasant sensations and comforts, or to eat, gaze, and listen with taste and relish. To starve the appetites or put up with discomfort or pain may be harmful. At best it would be a means to other ends. So appetite and pleasure make up some part of the good life. We easily understand actions of this kind; the agent can justify doing what gets him the best of these goods. But people think that a life of appetite and pleasure alone is without meaning in the long run; it palls and debilitates (Taylor 1977). Sexual appetite is often an exception to this rule, but only because it may involve an intricate relation with another person. Pleasures satisfy too little in us because few second-order attitudes can attach themselves to such a life. Even those that satisfy a great deal yield little scope for development and ramification into anything much like a coherent theory, or even a kind of plot or evolving pattern of life or personality. Anyone can search out more piquant forms of appetite and taste, or look for new ways of invigorating jaded or sated pleasures; but there is little in that to tell an agent what she is or is becoming as she leads a life of that sort. There is little for enquiry to mine, or for experiment to unravel. Although these gratifications are self-centred, not much in them can engage the notice of higher-order attitudes. Nothing brings them together in the span of an overarching, expanding, interlocking self-appraisal. It is only when sensuality debilitates us or distracts us from deeper enterprises that it excites a higher-order desire to curb it.

7.1.5 Earlier (6.5.2–11), I suggested two main ways in which emotions might be mistaken. There were foundational mistakes, which get the non-evaluative picture wrong, and mistakes of proportion, where agitation, or lack of it, fits ill with the scale of the value at issue. A third emotional mistake is to make some value fill too prominent a place in life, or even to make some feature a value at all. Here we need the idea of a human (or alien) nature round which the moral life of persons must gravitate. From Hume's standpoint, all emotional mistakes are foundational; there can be no error in desire. The logical fact that desires find verbal expression either in imperatives or optatives reflects this. So does the fact that indicative assertions such as 'I want . . .', have a truth-value independent of any aptness of desire; one might want almost anything at all. But it is not automatically intelligible that a person has some *value* or other in life. Even if we ponder, fancifully, the case of alien persons with desires deeply foreign to us, we still want to grasp how these desires may be transmuted and caught up into the personal life of whatever creature it might be. Among the more arbitrary, brute, natural desires are the appetites. We have seen how one of ours, sexual passion (surely bizarre to an alien) may be transformed dialectically and caught up into fully personal life. This makes sense of the role which a lover may play in a person's values. We could hope to make an alien person understand sexually based attachments to other persons. But we cannot make intelligible (even to ourselves) far-reaching values based on the need to defecate, imperative though that need may sometimes be. Even in more domestic and trifling contexts of finding out about each other, we may need to explain how our wishes have become our values. How you make a value of some desire needs an explanation, for yourself as much as for others, since it is round these that you build a personal life.

7.1.6 We can see from this how the spectator's life of perception—watching, listening, reporting, recounting—has rather meagre offerings to the ideals of personhood. The observer or spectator enlarges his perception and perhaps his understanding of the world, but does not change what he observes. At least that is so for pure observation. In such a case, though perhaps this is too pure to be real, he does nothing to objectify what he is as a person. He would have to make something happen to achieve that. He does not test what he is by pitting his will against a possibly obdurate nature, then observing what the outcome might reveal about him. Thus the spectator's role offers a thin diet for the higher-order attitudes which begin the dialectical processes that make human life personal.

7.1.7 However, looking and listening gain much from more active, conceptually directed enterprises. What you see or hear gets point from interpretations you give to it. These call on knowledge or theory which may be cast in rich and complex conceptual structures wrung from practical grappling with a puzzling, obdurate world. If we let a wide range of observing actions count as watching, then there is value for spectators just in seeing, noticing, and understanding a rich, varied, subtle, delicate, powerful world, astonishing in the small scale, awesome in the large; there is a value simply in the existence of what is understood to be thus marvellously so (see 7.3.1–4).

7.1.8 So we usually find that the first-order desires which power agency in the full sense are those which offer most to the ideals and tasks of being a person. That means either wanting to bend the world to one's plans for it, or to interact with one's fellows with the intention of giving or getting information and help so as to change them or ourselves in some further, partly foreseen way. Making, doing, building, repairing, modelling, and reconstructing, on the one hand, and arguing, telling, bargaining, exhorting, joking, and gossiping, on the other, form *projects* or *projective action or activity*. It is in these we can make our values real, concrete, public, observable, and criticizable. Then we can discover what we are, not just in discrete and disconnected actions, but according to a series of discoveries which link our higher-order attitudes with one another; we become engaged with a systematic world which imposes a network of physical and cultural laws or meanings on our value-objects and relates these objects to each other in ways independent of our subjective wishes and hopes about things. The meanings and justifications which agents give for actions like these may be rich and subtle; these meanings and justifications can reach out and intertwine in something like a theory or coherent plot that makes personal life meaningful and rewarding. We need only think of all the complex theories and crafts that come together in the building of an aeroplane to see why it is that projects, quite generally, involve intention, desire, and satisfaction across a wide variety of discrete actions in a synoptic, interconnected pattern of activity. It is in projective action, especially, that we find *coherent* meaning in what we do. Although almost any of an agent's actions will be understood as justifiable by her, a central group leads these understandings into a ramified, systematic, at least quasi-theoretical grasp of how world and agency are related, thus to a richer role for higher-order attitudes than other actions have.

7.1.9 But projective action in the social world takes pride of place, as Hegel's dialectic of master and slave exemplifies so well (Hegel, ed. 1977: 111–19). Actions and activities aimed at one's friends, lovers, enemies, acquaintances, fellow workers, at institutions, corporations, and clubs, are intended under descriptions which engage the same stratum of concepts under which others will understand the actions and in which they frame responses to them. But, more importantly, there are so many varied, complex, and subtle rewards in interpersonal activity and so much to yield story and theory in it; there is so much to engage widening and deepening motives and beliefs and to lead anyone towards longer, more synoptic views of what they are and do, that these aspects of agency must fill the central place in the subprojects of our broad open project to take on the tasks and ideals of being a person. I need to relate these structures to the basic natural motive (4.2.12–15) which turns all the higher animals towards behaviour that springs from curiosity and play. It must also be made clear how these styles of action become cultural and universal in character.

7.1.10 Let me repeat that though the structure of higher-order self-attitudes leads them to global concerns with the kind of person one is or the kind of life one leads, it allows and encourages regard for others among first-order desires and values. Indeed higher-order, self-regarding desires may demand for their satisfaction an almost completely other-regarding satisfaction in discrete, local, practical, and direct acts and activities. I have been using friendship as an example to represent this, where the wish to be a friendly person is gratified by the satisfaction of desires and the realizing of values about the welfare of others. To be an object for yourself at some level of your desires and values is no bar to regarding others as ends in themselves at some other level, nor at the same level. Perhaps it is never quite safe to indulge in self-satisfaction with one's own unselfishness and objectivity, but though it may sometimes be a spurious feeling, it need not be an inconsistent or an unjustified one.

7.2 The authenticity of subjective values

7.2.1 To be authentic is to be true to what you are. An authentic person has to keep true to this while excelling what she is in pursuing her values; these must be authentic too. It sounds like a paradox to try both to be what you are, yet excel it. But I made it a prominent fact about a person that its higher-order desires play a deep practical role in its actions. There will be a basic conflict in the motives of any such being; the paradox merely reflects the conflict. Authentic values get produced from the conflict among desires described at some length already. The paradox is an aspect of a dialectical growth. What we need is a clearer sight of what authenticity must keep faith with.

7.2.2 Being true to what you are in a successful pursuit of self-excellence comes to the same as being free in your nature. This kind of success comes in degrees, if at all. It is not simply a stable state of any normal human being, as formal freedom is. So authenticity, like freedom, is a state one has to some degree. The end-product of an authentic quest for excellence requires some approach to consistency among desires of various orders—a near resolution, that is, of some part of the dialectical process by which we make ourselves free in our natures. But it will be more useful to look at the struggle than at its resolution; lively, enquiring, and observant people have an evolving, changing picture of what they are and of what meanings their culture gives to their doings; the dialectical processes themselves are subject to changes in direction, so that they may begin again where there seemed to have been a satisfactory resolution.

7.2.3 Authenticity also has a cultural dimension. This should come as no surprise, since it was clear in Chapter 1 that culture is natural for human beings and that we are naturally equipped for it. Neither the natural nor the cultural dimension of authenticity is altogether obvious. The best way to begin to make them clear is to focus on rather familiar ways in which people can find themselves caught in inauthentic subprojects within a self-sustaining broad open project to pursue the ideals of being a person. But the values at issue in this section will be subjective ones. Only when we can find some basis for criticizing a culture can we say what it is for values to be correct and objective. That will depend on the ideas we are at work on now.

7.2.4 Let us go back to the somewhat problematic idea of truth to a nature for a more general perspective on authentic value. We divided desires up into four broad, overlapping classes, which may not be exhaustive. In 7.1.6–10 we saw that it is the fourth of these classes which gives us the most numerous, the most systematic and intelligible, and therefore the most central to personhood, of human desires; that is, those most likely to be dialectically transformed into values and to define the idea of the kind of person an agent may want to be. In the light of those arguments, we should expect that the nature to which authentic subjective values must be true is that which lies beneath the desires to change the world according to explicit intentions and plans—and thereby to change oneself as well. However, one first thinks of what is natural to our species in terms of human appetites and pleasurable sensations. Presumably, this is because there seems to be a rather direct link from stimulus to satisfaction, one untainted by conceptual and therefore cultural colour. But for this very reason there is little in desires in these two classes to engage with the idea of authenticity except when the desires bring other complexities in their train, as sexual desire does. Alternatively, of course, other complexities may catch up appetites and sensational pleasures in their train, as the pleasure of hearing harmonies is caught up into all the depths and subtleties of music. But there is little in the appetites and pleasures of sense, just by themselves, to raise interesting problems of truth-to-nature. They are most likely to trouble us in pursuing our ideals when they obstruct or debilitate the processes of alienation and transformation. But, because they are not deeply intelligible and meaningful activities, there is little to make us worry whether we are true to ourselves in satisfying them.

7.2.5 For the spectator or observer, it is the authenticity of reports and judgements that may be at issue. This begins as simple fidelity to what is seen and heard, but questions of interpretation make it complex in familiar ways. There is a great deal that might be said about fidelity to what bare perception reveals, but since most of it is well said elsewhere and not central to the present crop of issues, I will ignore it. In so far as the spectator is watchful, precise, intense in her scrutiny, and concerned about the truth of her judgement, her actions begin to fall within the fourth class, and the authenticity of her values raises questions better looked at from that perspective.

7.2.6 So it is on the making and changing, the constructing and modifying according to plans, explicit intentions, and articulate conceptions, that the emphasis will fall in our concern with the authenticity of values. Yet it is among such actions that the relevance of what is a natural human desire is least clear. I said before that because these actions and their desires and values have complex meanings through their relations with other actions of the same class, they are inclined to fall under the projective actions of the broad open project towards being a certain kind of person. So how these actions succeed or fail in being true to a nature is not obvious, just because their satisfactions fit into complex, synoptic, highly acculturated, universalized projects. We need some criteria for their success or failure in authenticity.

7.2.7 Let us go back to that basic natural motive which we called the central self-sustaining open project to follow the tasks and ideals of being a person (4.2.12–15). I argued that this is a properly natural motive, widely shared among primates and higher mammals, which has no homeostatic function, but rather results in permanent changes to the organism's neural and other systems. These changes yield an array of skills and strengths which raise the probability of the animal's survival till it can pass on its genes. This means that it is an instinct to acquire general capacities to implement four basic animal drives: feeding, aggression, escape, and reproduction. For social animals, these acquired capacities are enmeshed with activities which bind groups together in ways which make the survival of the group and its members more likely. But think of persons in a reasonably stable society in which the biological necessities of life—food, shelter, sexual partners, freedom from predators—may be taken pretty much for granted. This agreeable state of affairs is likely to lead to the sort of division of labour which ensures that most people do not provide for their own necessities directly. They are produced by a work-force within the culture. Now the burgeoning skills and strengths, driven by that basic motive, find their employment in cultural pursuits of one sort or another. What makes them properly capacities is no longer the bare causal outcome of survival, but some significant role they have within the culture.

7.2.8 But what does this say about which desires are natural and which values authentic? First, subprojects, activities, and actions are rewarding if they expand and exercise a person's capacities for life within the culture. That is not to say that the expansion and exercise of some capacities cannot become stultifying and debilitating, as they do in crushing labour under acute poverty and hardship, or in the abysmally dreary, tightly confined, and repetitive grind of production-lines in modern industry. But for the most part, the free play in which one exercises and expands one's capacities to make, control, invent, and shape the world and events around one is the most rewarding aspect of human life. Though in our lives these activities are usually quite highly cultivated, they remain a natural reward as well as a civilized one. I am suggesting that the nature to which our most absorbing, complex, and highly acculturated actions, satisfactions, and values must be true is a set of natural *capacities*.

7.2.9 Let me offer some rough examples to make this clearer. Someone who is stone-deaf has no legitimate, authentic interest in hearing music. Maybe someone who is tone-deaf can set no true value on music either (though things turn out less simple than this suggests). A little more realistic and interesting is the inauthenticity of someone's protestation that he sets a high value on painting, yet who has no native taste on which to build the skills and sensitivities which may make an interest in painting rewarding. He cannot see the diversity and nuance of representation, has little imagination about (or recognition of) good design and form, and, perhaps most important of all, he lacks the natural gifts to see how these values can connect with the values at issue in what is represented. These natural talents, or some like them—for many will quarrel with this simplistic perspective on how painting can engage our capacities and desires—form the basis on which someone may authentically find a value in painting. That is to say, a value is authentic for a person if pursuit of it is based on capacities which he naturally, genuinely has.

7.2.10 Let us turn, now, to communal desires and actions, which are the ones that engage us most with personal tasks. Clearly the affections, the desires and satisfactions someone may find in a relationship with another person can be inauthentic. We saw already at least the structure of what this means. An attempted friendship or a love affair may be inauthentic, even though someone seeks values in it. If one lacks the kind of imagination, empathy, tact, sense of humour, and range of interests that might be common; or if the other lacks these skills in the approach to an intimacy with the first, then the relationship cannot have the value either would place on it. There is a new dimension in this appeal to projects among persons; first, there is a range of subtleties and complexities which material makings and buildings lack. But a major factor is that a value or a project does not count as authentic unless it embeds itself somehow in the culture and, at the least, does not erode in it. This embedding, in its turn, reinforces and reflects us, enabling most of our projects, activities, and discrete acts to find their meanings and purported justification. We depend on some culture for our very existence as persons; so it makes sense to see projects incoherent with the culture as, on the face of it, inauthentic.

7.2.11 Perhaps the most obvious and common way to miss being authentic is to be pretentious—pretentiously sentimental or cynical, for instance. But more often people pretend to have abilities, tastes, satisfactions, and capacities which they lack. Or sometimes they evade hard issues by a false modesty or self-deprecation. They assume a fake human or cultural status: on the human side, the status of sensitivities of taste or eye, of skills and strengths, or of sexual prowess; on the cultural side, they pretend to an inflated sophistication in emotional sensitivity, or to intellectual prowess of some kind. Again, they may take a false pride in the interest and status which belong to those they are somehow involved with. These familiar examples show clearly enough that our ordinary understanding of pretentious inauthenticity does include both human and cultural dimensions.

7.2.12 In several other familiar faults of character we fail to be authentic, too. Some of these faults are natural and some cultural, but they are alike in all being cognitive. The first is one kind of self-centredness: the fault is to be subjective in a wrong way. This leads someone to put his own desires or beliefs ahead of anyone else's, as if he thought that just their being *his* gave them some status, or special right to be satisfied or asserted. He fails to universalize objective judgements in the way Hare (e.g. 1963: ch. 2) has made us well aware that we may fail to universalize moral ones. But this failure does not occur just in moral judgements; nor is it, I think, a simply cognitive failure. It is really a failure to accept the basic lesson of all personal culture, that there is no thinking apart from general standards which relate what I do think to what anyone ought to think. There is, equally, no understanding our own actions apart from general standards which relate what I do to what anyone ought to do. This self-centredness turns a blind eye to this fundamental lesson. But unless they learn some form of it, humans do not even begin to become persons, for the lesson lies at the root of all conceptual thought. So it is hardly muddle or intellectual dullness that lies behind such a fault, but rather a human failure of will or desire. The fault cherishes those childish fantasies of omnipotence, of being at the centre of all that matters; it leads one to try to be more than anyone coherently can be. For the rules of the ethics of belief, desire, and action are both invoked in one's act of assertion and revoked in the absurd status he would give to what he asserts. He attempts here to be what he is not and never could be. It is, therefore, a kind of inauthenticity, though perhaps not often so described. To set this in a clearer light, contrast this spurious subjectivity with another form of selfishness. I may simply decide to get what I want, at whatever cost to your desires, without at all thinking that my desires being mine somehow justifies this policy. That is a deliberate moral evil rather than a corrupt failure, and there need be nothing inauthentic about it. What I have been calling self-centredness is more a form of Sartrean bad faith than proper selfishness. It is not as aware of itself as selfishness is. By no means all immorality is failure in being a person, though what I here call corruption is. Selfishness is success in being a bad person, and that is a kind of person one can, coherently, want to be.

7.2.13 In more obvious ways, the values I aspire to may be bogus or debased in my culture. I may want the false honour of macho aggression or the courage of mere foolish bravado. What I do in pursuit of the values allied to these fake virtues may be true to my natural desires and emotional capacities (and incapacities): my aggression and bravado satisfy my wish to be another John Wayne, and that takes place within a dialectical process which issues in these disappointing forms of value. There really is a kind of person that I am trying to be in acting in these ways—a painfully familiar kind, indeed. But these values may (or may not) be regarded (rightly or wrongly) in the broader culture as warped forms of other values, more refined and more tightly knit into the main structure of values current in the culture. If, therefore, bravado cannot match the deeper-reaching values of courage, but only mimic simplified or culturally shallow forms of them, then it counts as an inauthentic virtue and the value of its deeds fake and false. But here 'deep', 'spurious', and 'shallow' refer to what is current in the culture available to the person, not yet to judgements of correctness and objectivity. The authentic values of a culture are just those which are more articulate, more coherently justifiable by meanings and values which culture members understand. This leaves room for reformers and innovators to break, extend, or renew the possibly quite local and passing norms which define these depths and shallows.

7.2.14 These claims need to be hedged in two ways. Some people are too dim or too culturally deprived to understand the more complex of their culture's ideals of value or virtue. We can hardly call someone a fake because he is not able to grasp authentic courage, or has no chance to see what it might rise to. Nor should we damn him if the fault lies in the limitations of his culture. Any culture has its limitations. Ours has some, obviously. In an earlier age—or perhaps elsewhere now—honour was won and made a concrete value by setting one's personal ideal above one's animate life in duels to the death over points of honesty and decorum (Hegel, ed. 1977: 111–19). To give someone the lie used to set in action cultural processes which demanded duel or disgrace. A challenge to the *duello* now, however, would arouse an astonished contempt and amusement, rather than a conviction that the challenger's integrity and courage was worthy and formidable and one's own moral standing in jeopardy until the challenge was met. Simply, the fellow would be a bit of an ass. So we find a degree of relativity to culture and to an agent's induction into it. That relativity is an element in the authenticity of subjective value.

7.2.15 Second, though we must *relate* what we think, speak, and do to what anyone ought to think, speak, and do, this does not imply that we must *conform* to what our culture recognizes as proper realizations of adequate value. We may reform or rebel; we may invent new forms in which to realize our values without repudiating old ones. But these are departures from cultural norms, not just in the trivial sense of differing from them, but also in that the norms are starting-points and, perhaps landfalls in dialectical voyages of value-discovery. In short, reformer, rebel, and inventor begin in an ethical tradition of which they are the more or less reluctant inheritors. Even their most radical and visionary re-appraisals of value, if authentic, refer to the cultural institutions, conventions, and usages which, hitherto, have given meaning to ideals of personhood in that society.

7.2.16 Our need for a cultural understanding of open projects to meet the tasks and ideals of being a person overlaps with a need for us as persons to understand ourselves in increasingly general or universal ways. Though this springs from culture, it can lead us to alienate and try to surmount what we see as local in our culture. There is a dialectical movement, or at least a pair of opposing pressures, to and from the more universal and abstract, in the way we take part in our culture. When someone first harbours a second-order desire he undertakes an open-ended set of tasks and starts a process with no obvious conclusion. If he wants to excel what he is in this first target-desire and -satisfaction, why not in others? The perfectly reasonable push towards consistency and completeness means appraising all his desires and attitudes. Thus, too, a person wishes not to be confined by a local culture and its limited array of models and institutions. I include in this what may count as local traditions in such a highly varied and eclectic culture as our own, which probably has no single coherent identity in terms of the institutions and traditions which find some place in it. Even if we take nothing from other local cultures, at least we compare them with our own and reappraise it to strengthen our understanding of what our culture can offer anyone. Just as a person may want to learn another language to see how the same thoughts may be rephrased in it, and not be tied to a single linguistic viewpoint, so we wish not to be limited by a single cultural perspective on the structure of a person's tasks and ideals. In as far as we come to see our culture as merely local, there is a wish to go beyond at least the understanding of the usages it offers us. This may spark trends, which occur from time to time in cultures, to return to nature and cast off cultural conventions as cramping the structure which a person's life might take. Global self-criticism becomes an intelligible aim as soon as you begin it locally; it is arbitrary to confine it to some one or some group of desires or other attitudes, or to some one or group of cultural practices.

7.2.17 There is a push to see yourself in universal terms from another direction too. An agent sees her actions, if she understands them at all, as those which anyone ought rationally to perform. However unique and idiosyncratic may be the *type* of person she is, she sees herself, in understanding what she does, as one person among others, an instance of agenthood just as they are, and open to the same forms of appraisal and understanding as they. Whether or not she *thinks* herself reasonable, she actually subjects her intentions to a practice of reasoning according to her lights, just so long as she can make sense of her actions. This implies that, in practice, she treats herself as sharing rationality and personhood with all agents, however different, however strange, deviant, and other than herself in sex, race, age, culture they may be.

7.2.18 A related push towards universal styles of doing things, glimpsed in 3.2.5, makes us abstract from the way things happen to turn out for us when we follow some interest or exercise a skill. This begins within some culture or subculture, such as mathematics. What is universal belongs to the nature of the pursuit, skill, or interest. Those who practise an art or a science strive to make a discipline of it, and look past the idiosyncratic ways of even the more deft or inventive individuals towards norms and usages set by the nature of what is being pursued. Even the most novel and unique contributor defers to the spirit of the subject and to the forms in which it can be practised and presented. The subject is moulded into specific forms so that a culture can better assimilate and appropriate it. If we think of this in terms of alienation, as Lakatos (see 3.2.5) suggests, then we might see the discipline as the kind of structure which places the universal principles of our information-processing (usually in language) into some fruitful relation with the processes by which the universals dominate the subject matter (perhaps by means of causal laws). It will be a relation like resonance or harmony, though it would be unlucky if this suggested some sort of direct isomorphism between them. But the inspiration of a tradition, or of an elegant heuristic for a discipline—even a heuristic to change the discipline—is felt by many who find a skill or study absorbing. This is seen as a sweep and structure of the ideas themselves, felt even by the more revolutionary contributors, who may have a vivid sensitivity for their dynamics and architecture. Here again something produced by the culture may transcend what is local and contingent to it. Something of the same universalizing or alienating of the meanings of less theoretical projects can be found in sensitivity to the nature of materials one works in, to the workings of machinery, to the art of water-colour, or the genius of a game such as chess. Yet actions acquire rich meanings only in the light of some particular cultural forms: conventions of politeness, usages of friendship or insult, models of love. Just so, a thought can be expressed in many meaningful sentences, but each belongs always to some particular language.

7.2.19   But universalizing our desires and values must not lead to their becoming merely abstract and empty. Universals such as love, friendship, or parenthood are real only in their instances, and their values can be made real and concrete only in particular words, deeds, and looks and gestures that make up human relationships. These must be wrought, built, wrung from concrete things and processes which may be inimical to them in some ways, but which are all that is accessible to us in the local field of value. The value can thus be appropriated only through these events and processes (sayings and doings, and perhaps some objects) among individual friends and lovers, parents and children. True, I value someone I love because of qualities she has. But I do not, in the same way, love anyone with similar qualities, but only her who exemplified them in those very words, there and then, and by saying them to me, and not just to someone like me on much the same occasion. It is the particulars we value, as well as the universal; we are tied to the very objects and events which involve us, just because they are those particular ones we make, tend, nurture, and harvest. If this seems irrational, that is because we are used to seeing reasons only in terms of properties and not uniquenesses. Reasons in any theory of things must always be general and universal, so that any rationally important difference is a qualitative one. But differences purely of place and time are differences in concrete practice; when unique persons pursue their values, particularities can make value differences. This connects with two themes raised before: first is the fact that the demands of extension in time and place engage one in *being something* personal on social occasions whether one likes it or not; second is the fact that we cannot exhaust practice in principles to which we can then bind practice. This is true in the practice of ethics as well as reason: in what it is good to think and say and in what it is good to do. Sartre found the central case of bad faith in the wish to escape responsibility by seeing oneself as determined, as having one's possibilities of action exhausted by a nature or a role—being a writer, philosopher, or the child of a broken home. There is a similar dodging of responsibility in practice by taking some explicit principles as exhausting practical know-how in reason and in ethics. Thus expressiveness and particularity are linked in that satisfaction rather than desire constitutes the character of our actions. It is mainly the *backward* look that finds meaning in the *particular* action seen. So particular occasions and the individuals involved in them become valuable, and not just the qualities that they exemplify. Thus it can be that only he, not another like him in every property, has a particular value in her life (Falk 1963).

7.2.20 Like a human, a culture may be wanton—without second-order attitudes towards itself. An authentic culture has analogues of second-order desire, for instance, in the aims of its reformers and rebels. More modestly, but perhaps more significantly, it may have more steadily gazing and reflective subcultures which appraise the containing culture, develop theories about how it is working and about how it should work; perhaps a subculture forges a disciplined practice for culture at large; it may invent and test ways of probing the flexibility and finding the bounds of culture at its present stage; it may develop its own systems of self-appraisal, its own ways of alienating and regaining cultural practices. I have in mind here not only, or even mainly, the social sciences, but also the arts of the novel and of the drama, the craft of journalism and, more generally if less explicitly, music and visual arts. The power of these to suggest and explore patterns of individual and social life is, I suggest, of the first importance. It was argued earlier that the concepts of action-theory do not lend themselves to the expression of true law-like generalizations, nor is there plain reason, *a priori*, to expect statistical and probabilistic generalizations cast in those concepts to reveal deeper cultural truths to us, though they may do so. So the power of the novelist, the composer, and the performer to provide an understanding by representation and expression is indispensable.

7.2.21 At any rate, a culture is authentic only if it is not wanton, so authentic values require a culture which contains a critical subculture, and has the sort of institutions which allow the culture to evolve in the light of these re-evaluations, and which disseminates them to culture members. Thus authentic values are related to the natures of the persons who hold them, in that labour to realize these values (though its cost in human effort may be high) aims to satisfy the transformed *human* desires; but they are also related to the culture which offers some meaning, recognition, and justification to these pursuing actions.

7.2.22 In sum, then, a subjective value is authentic, first, if it is true to the person's nature; second, if the value is adequate to the forms of it which the person's culture contains; third, if the valuer attempts both to see himself and his values in universal terms, his deeds as those which anyone rationally must or may do, yet also to find values in their concrete individual realizations; and, fourth, if the culture contains some means of evaluating itself and is not wanton.

7.3   Culture and objective values

7.3.1 We have just looked at the authenticity of subjective value. But can values be objective, and, if they can, how can they? Not even subjective values are authentic just on the say-so of *individual* subjects; that is because the subject may but slenderly know himself, because individual persons owe their personhood to the culture, and because much that is specific to their view of their lives is made up by the conventions and usages of their culture. They are not arbiters of whether they have the natural capacities which fit them to pursue certain values. We shall not even say that their picture of the sort of person they aim to be encapsulates authentic subjective values: their ideals may be quite spurious in ways just shown. But we need a further step to find criteria for saying that values are objectively correct, even though I will not aim to show that they are absolute. They remain relative to culture. That is because cultures, though objectively correct or incorrect, may nevertheless be correct or incorrect in more than one way.

7.3.2 Before I try to deal with culture, though, a couple of remarks about how values can be objective are needed. There are at least two senses in which they may be independent of us. First, there is a weaker sense in which objects are valuable and the value is in them, not in us. Being valuable is like being poisonous in that although it may be a matter of how a substance affects us, or creatures like us, the poison is objectively in poisonous things, not in us. Similarly, though objects may be valuable just in that they have effects on us, or those like us, the values are in the objects, not in us and our reactions. Certainly, poison is in me only if I ingest something poisonous. So it is the drink that is poisonous—the poison is in it—even though that is a matter of what it will do to me, or you, or anyone, if we drink it. Just so, when something is valuable, then if we pursue it and make it real and concrete, there will be some personal and cultural outcomes. It will do something (possibly very general and indirect) for us; and it, or our pursuit of it, will enlarge and exercise our capacities.

7.3.3   But there is a stronger sense of independence or a distance between value and valuer. If I value something I need not want to have it or even make use of it; I may take satisfaction simply in knowing it exists and flourishes, just because of what it is. I admire its complexity, proportion, balance, fecundity, organic unity, or beauty. Of course the existence of the valued state of affairs satisfies the desire contained in the valuing. That merely repeats the fact that I value it, and does nothing to explain it. It need not be because it pleases me, is of some use to me or others, that I admire its harmony or strength; it may be the reverse—it pleases me because I value its being harmonious and strong. If that is so, then the value is not in the thing simply in the way that poisonousness is in things—a power in them to do something to or for me. Like the challenge of Mt Everest, the value lies just in that it is there; no one need take, use, climb the thing for our (transformed) desire to be satisfied and the value made real.

7.3.4   Things valued in this strongly objective way still tend to feed back into our cultural lives, though perhaps quite indirectly. Even in the value we set on keeping human hands entirely off parts of the natural environment, for instance—the value of wild rivers, rain forests, deserts, reefs—there is something in it, usually, for us. (Let me assume, for a moment, that these values are correct.) The loss of a natural species from an exploited environment is a loss to us, however unlikely it is that we would come across one of its members. It says something about us—it is *meaningful*—that we lacked the decorum, restraint, and good judgement to see and leave inviolate bushland and marsh. It is a value for persons simply to know of, without ever appropriating or even disturbing, some delicate yet long-lived ecosystem. This decorum links us to other more useful virtues and values—to temperance in what we consume, to the wisdom to recognize elegance and worth beyond our own concerns, to benevolence, perhaps even to courage in accepting that we must forgo some things we may urgently want that other species may live. We flourish just because these things, quite alien to us, flourish. To allow this, though, is not to concede that we can value things only as we think they may have value *for us*. We can value things for properties they have which make them relevantly like things which enrich our own cultural lives, even if those instances of the properties have no utility for us. (I expand this theme in 8.3.7–8.)

7.3.5 I take a very broad view of the idea of a culture. The wish to transcend local culture licenses this permissive, uncritical view. Culture embraces both the high and the low; leisure and sport, sciences and arts, pastimes and hobbies and, most significantly, labour and work. Cultures have subcultures which are more or less cohesive, though the whole which embraces them might not be. Labour and work include all of a society's modes of production of concrete life, including, for example, its concrete ways of making music. To speak of a society as a culture is not to praise it. It is simply to see it as a collection of varied, not necessarily coherent, ways of working towards personhood, of alienating and transforming desires and other attitudes which the society has. The Nazis, the Aztecs, the Vandals, and the Goths were all cultured. A culture can go badly wrong, and often does.

7.3.6 Nevertheless, it is quite clear how cultures can go right once we see what it is that they have to be right about. This can now be fairly succinctly described. A culture is a kind of theory, in a broad sense of theory, about how to alienate and regain one's nature, about the meanings and (rational) justifications which actions can have, about what models for kinds of persons are intelligible, in what ways and through which institutions and conventions of the culture they may be followed. But a good culture will be authentic, and a bad one not. Authenticity in cultures is like authenticity for their individual members. Their usages and institutions must foster the development of the capacities which are expanded and used in the open projects that make up a meaningful personal life. It is not enough for objectivity that it be thought to do so. Just so, but more obviously, its ways of slaking appetites must really slake them, and its mannered ways in seeking pleasant sensations must, in fact, thrill one agreeably. More obviously still, a wide range of foods and styles of preparing and consuming them are possible; some of them are, objectively, more satisfying and nourishing than others. In the most subtle and complex aspects of cultural life, where personhood is most deeply and meaningfully engaged—that is, in desires and actions to change the physical and social worlds by articulate intention—the elements of the culture must really invigorate and sustain its members' capacities.

7.3.7 A culture is like an engineering programme: there may be different but equally effective ways of creating the good which the engineer is asked to deliver. Well-built bridges may vary in quite fundamental design features; there is no one best way of building them. The setting in which a bridge is to operate and the kind of traffic it is to bear may well eliminate some styles as effective or elegant solutions to the local problem, but nothing guarantees that there must be a unique solution. A culture, then, is an engineering programme aimed at producing persons. So it must set up its institutions, usages, and conventions so that they really deliver their goods. Obviously, they must reward the natural appetites and desires for pleasant sensations in their alienated and sublimed forms. But, crucially, they must expand and strengthen the capacities of persons in the culture, especially their capacities to take part in a communal, cultural life.

7.3.8 A culture is a kind of broad open social project towards continuing its own vigorous and expanding life. There is a kind of benign circle here, relating individual to cultural nourishment and growth. Cultures bootstrap. We individuals have a natural, though diffuse, instinct towards (something like) creative play which rewards players simply in that the growth and exercise of their generalized strengths and skills in some specific, concrete activity is interesting and fun. There is no independently identifiable sensation of pleasure or satisfaction which is a correlative reward for active play—the fun is not separable, even in thought, from the playing, and is for this reason to be regarded as an end in itself. One of the directions in which human animals are moved by this impulse to enlarge capacities is the cultural one of language-learning and conceptually directed play. We are drilled in conceptual thinking, which permits infinite flexibility in what is thinkable but calls for rigid conformity in usage; we use others as models for our performances in this. Both these aspects of it lead to our forming higher-order attitudes as we gain our skills. The basic natural motive is moulded more and more to a deeper, subtler, more synoptic open project towards being a particular style of person. This open project is the self-sustaining desire to get better and better at building and shaping the world, other persons, and, ultimately, oneself. One shapes natural capacities in projective activities which both draw on and nourish cultural institutions and opportunities; these, in turn, expand and exercise these very same natural abilities in individuals.

7.3.9 An analogy with sports and games may shed some light here. Some sports and games are better than others in expanding the general physical capacities (strength, alertness, precision of movement, speed of response, or inventiveness in tactics), of those who play them. Games give a specific focus, within a set of rules and conventions, to a generalized impulse to activity. The rules and conventions give structure and meaning to play. To play the game or take up the sport is to exercise and expand one's skills; it is also to acquire new ones like those one has already, but more complex, precise, or structured. We play games with and for others and for ourselves, either in co-operation (as in mountaineering) or competition with them; we can play to represent country, district, club—to represent others, that is—or play for their amusement as spectators. The game or sport is a good one if it really does strengthen, sharpen, and expand our capacities in playing it. If our playing can solidify or even extend what constitutes the standards of excellence in the game, then we can explore and strengthen both the game and ourselves. A good game is an engineering programme to produce skills, endurance, strength, quick wits, and courage; all of these both make the game what it is, and are used in its service.

7.3.10 Anyone plays for various direct, terminating ends: to win, to excel others or herself, to reach the summit, to cover the ground, to drink in the view, or whatever the gratification, on some occasion, of playing her sport or game may be. However, the occasional end of games and sports, what one plays *for*, may be the same in good as in bad or indifferent games. Winning at chess is much like winning at noughts and crosses; this makes it clear that the formal goals of a game are seldom what make the game a good one. Winning is just the formal cultural recognition that one has played well on an occasion; arriving at the view is also the occasion which caps this day's trek in the bush. These ends are what a player gets to show herself that she did make her values concrete in playing. But she plays to win only as the end of a discrete *sub*project within a general broad open project to play well. At least as far as the overall project to play sport is concerned, it isn't the winning and losing that counts, but the way you play the game. The end of

the project lies in the playing itself, the deployment and development of its skills and strengths; it is an end in itself. However, we
want to win only what is worth winning; that is, what is worth
playing. Thus what makes a game good is that it really does enlarge
the capacities which you need to play it well. It will be a better sport
the more authentically it challenges those abilities, the more diverse
and open-ended the abilities themselves are, and the more it relates
them together and makes them complement each other in the sport.
In sum, a sport may offer satisfactions in terms of sub-goals like
winning or summit-reaching, though these fall within an open
project, a continual, non-terminating desire for which the development and exercise of the capacities (which constitutes action under
the desire) is its own end.

7.3.11 These analogies with sports and engineering programmes
might seem too optimistic, for how can there be knowledge that a
culture meets the sort of aims I have specified (Williams 1985: ch.
8)? Enough has been said (mainly in Chapter 2) to make it clear
that there will be no scientific knowledge that answers the questions
as framed. That does not close the issue; knowing that *modus
ponens* is valid is not scientific knowledge either. Not that logic
offers us a model for the kind of truth or knowledge that I want. If
there is an analogy with reason here, it applies where rational
practice stretches doctrine and frets at the boundaries doctrine
draws. Perhaps a better analogy lies in our knowledge of the
following sort of facts, which are not quite aesthetic ones. Surely we
know that Shakespeare and Bach each found cultural institutions
into which their natural capacities could grow and be enlarged and
fortified. They used their native gifts to explore, extend, and
strengthen what was possible in the poetry and music of their times
as forms of expression. The institutions expanded them, and they
enriched and enlarged the institutions. What I am presupposing is
some such knowledge as this, and, difficult of access though it may
be, I see no clear case for regarding it as unknowable in principle.
To be sure, such matters cannot be settled in so short a space. After
all, one can mount a sceptical case even for the implausible view
that no saying is determinately translatable into another idiolect. I
persist with a conjecture that a verdict on objectivity, as I have
described it, is not beyond our reach in principle. I hope the reader
will view this guess with an indulgent eye. Even granted that
indulgence, it is no easy matter to decide which values are objective

and correct according to these criteria. I make some assumptions about this in the next chapter which seem to me plausible ones. But their use is illustrative, and showing that they are correct would require a long, rather empirical study which could yield only tentative results in the first instance.

7.3.12 I have classified values in three ways. A value is, first of all, the product of *valuing*, the dialectical process of self-transformation described in the first six chapters. But unless we can go beyond that description, the value is merely subjective. We find something richer if the value is authentic, as summarized in 7.2.22. But this merely relates it to the contingencies of individual persons and their cultures, even though the relation of the valuing to an individual's nature and ambient culture was specified in some detail. We need also, criteria that go beyond the accidents and idiosyncrasies of individuals and the vagaries of development of their sustaining groups to relate the natures and the cultures together in ways not wholly dependent on incidental desires and social quirks. Individual natures and sustaining cultures must be mutually supportive in the ways described. Let us now reflect on what can be said as to what makes someone's life good according to this account of what can be rightly valued.

8

The Meaning and the Goodness of Life

8.1 Culture and the meaning of projects

8.1.1 What can cultures do for persons and their values? First, and most obviously, they provide the corporate skills and means whereby persons may maximize *utilities*. I mean by this that in a culture persons are better fed, clothed, housed, transported, and sheltered. Utilities are *products* of some sort, not processes (unless we stretch 'utility' so wide as to pull the content out of it). The production of utilities is *work*. No one works for the joys of working as a formal end but because work is useful. It is *right* to work, but it need not be good. Work may be rewarding in itself, though the problems and advantages of the division of labour make it not often enough so in industrialized economies. But the values that make life significant and good lie beyond utilities. Persons do not live by utilities alone. It is not in utilities or other products that the ends of the virtues characteristically lie, or that we find the deeper rewards of life.

8.1.2 A culture provides a person with a set of *meanings* for actions at large, including projective actions. Obviously, it provides the concepts with which to think about actions and under which to formulate them as projects and projective activities. But it also provides the interpersonal mirror in which our actions and projects, as interpreted by the encultured responses of others, are given back to us with the meanings we intended for them; they are made objective, enriched by the acceptances, rejections, laughter, and other reinterpretations and responses framed from the beliefs, desires, and emotions of other persons. These are local meanings of actions.

8.1.3 There are social arrangements which enrich these meanings. There are traditions, institutions such as property and politeness, social roles in work or government administration, and more familiar usages and expectations of commitment and action. These form the soil in which our particular projects grow. They provide background sources for the plots of the idiosyncratic dramas of our emotions or desires—in love, loyalty, or vengeance (MacIntyre 1985: e.g. 27–31). Further, there are the communal enterprises in which meanings are explicitly sought and articulated for personal action. There are philosophies, religions, and groups which celebrate in more or less mystical fashion the broader significance of things and deeds. There are societies to promote and make meaningful a variety of interests, in the arts and the sciences, in the values of liberty, fellowship, of prevention of cruelty to animals or of the despoliation of nature, and the like. There are political, educational, and sporting societies in any of which what you do and say takes on a meaning because of the traditions and the institutions of the groups and the interests they represent.

8.1.4 How can we give meaning to actions? What obviously applies to the special case of saying-actions applies to actions in general. I can understand my own saying only in the light of those features of it which have a sense in the language, and inasmuch as I can relate it to what anyone ought to say (or think). Just so, I can intend projective action only by intending it under some concepts which have been culturally formed; I can understand it only by relating it to what anyone ought (rationally) to do. Others may see it as irrational and even as mechanical, but I cannot. So much follows from what has been said before. Just as what I say can be new and creative despite the need to conform to linguistic usage in saying it, so my action can contribute novel meanings to my cultural circle even though, if I am to do that, I must know how actions, projects, and lives are understood in it. That knowledge obviously looms large in action which contributes to some highly universalized and cultivated activity such as doing mathematics. But I want here to focus rather on meanings which are both less culturally formal and very much more common. The meaning of these actions lies as often in the actions themselves as in products they may give rise to. Greetings, the confrontation at the office, the gestures of sympathy and support, or standing up to be counted have a meaning in being just the significant processes that they are. So are longer-term, but still confined, activities like living together, being good neighbours, loyal friends, staunch supporters. These are intended as value-actions, for we do alienate the natural human animal tendencies to be distracted, self-concerned, vacillating, and to take short views of things. On the domestic scale, we take and give meanings to and from others. It is in the concrete and particular sayings, touches, glances, tones of voice, that we assert our practical meanings, that we accept, repudiate, or comment upon the deeds, the projects, and kinds of person that others present to us. Here again what matters is these processes, not the product. It is these doings themselves that count for most people on most occasions. Their significance need not lie in any products they may give rise to.

8.1.5 This may give the false impression that I want to give pride of place in the good life and among our values and rewards to pastimes, interests, pursuits, and even hobbies. I have no wish to sniff at any of these, but they are too peripheral to personal life to play any such role. They draw upon too narrow a range of the capacities which are at the core of being a person and which make for meaningful projective action. They engage too shallow and transitory a set of values and virtues, save in so far as they are ways of loving, parenting, befriending, expressing solidarity, declaring allegiances and commitments. Though this is possible, we expect to find these expressed in activities not usually regarded as pastimes and interests.

8.1.6 But it is no reason for dismissing pastimes and hobbies from the core of the good life that they usually have no products. If we thought products make for the central rewards in the good life, then it might seem legitimate to stretch the idea of a utility to cover all that Utilitarians do cover by it. But that is a wrong tack. The rewards of action do not lie more regularly in the consequences of action than in action itself, provided that we allow ourselves to count activities, broad open projects, and lives among actions. Why on earth should it be the case that the products of action are valuable, but never action itself? Lastly, many of the more trifling pastimes and hobbies do have products: a full stamp album, or a ship in a bottle. But the meaning of these is limited. So is the reward.

8.1.7 I want to go on to show that we can give meaning to actions in such a way that these meanings are the values and the rewards of action quite generally. It will be a fundamental value for us that our actions be meaningful and their meaning what we intend by them. This will matter most, of course, for projective actions which fall within a broad open project of pursuing the tasks and ideals of being a person. A good model for this is the meaning and reward of performing art. Even in productive arts or crafts, however, the painted canvas, the poem, or the garden hardly amounts to a genuine utility. True, they may please people who see them or read them; but if it is a question of sensations of pleasure, then good surf, good food, or good sex may please them still more acutely. They have no clear *utility* outside their capacity to please, and that they please us hardly explains their value for us. It is the meanings that matter, not the pleasures. They please us because of the meanings that they have for us. They may have strongly intrinsic value as a majestic rain forest has, which pleases because it is valuable in its fecundity, diversity, and harmony. My bush garden may reward me, but perhaps just as something around which a highly local culture eddies and pauses. The rewards in that perturbation and hesitation are that it tells us what we are in fostering it or simply in leaving it inviolate—just in being spectators for whom it has this meaning: that watching it celebrates a vital and multiform vegetable life. It tells something about what all the persons are who rotate and pause round it, and they may tell this to each other. That enhances the cultural perception of what is good in being, just by itself, delicate, intricate, harmonious, colourful, and diverse. The rewards of artistic and quasi-artistic products may lie simply in their feeding back into the culture richer meanings of the projective activity which produced them.

8.1.8 But I promised to focus on the performing artist. A performer's pursuit of value may well take her into fields where the harvests are rich even though the values may be transient and momentary; this does not mean that they are lost or debased. The performance, though it ends, does not cease to have its value. It is not like the smashing of a sculpture, because the value lies in the process—a product only in the sense of a process produced—not in an end beyond it in time. Of course the performance may well be the end of other processes, those of training and rehearsal in which the performer is an object for herself, though perhaps not dialectically or in terms, mainly, of higher-order attitudes (though these will often play a significant role). However, the point is that the value of such a project is to be found in transient episodes which, highly articulated and structured though they may be, are not aimed at an end-product, a culmination in value which comes to pass when they are finished. Of course, some relevant values will exist only then: an instructed audience, a rewarded performer.

8.1.9 But these are values only of the consequences of the performance, even though the consequences are logically parasites on it. The consequential values are like the pleasure of golf—not a state of one's feelings which might be induced by some means other than playing golf (or creating the perfect illusion of doing so); just so, the enlarged state of mind of an audience is logically parasitic on the concrete unfolding of the performance. They are not the values of the performance itself. The value of the performance is objective and real in that the world really did contain this playing of a given quartet, that staging of a given play, and that the audience then followed and grasped the meaning of the music or the play. A performance is a structured event; it has beginning, middle, and it needs an end, but the performer's work does not find its value only in the completion of the performance. The value lies in the activity itself, which issues in no product. This shows that the radical impermanence of value-objects need be no bar to our sense of their richness. That performances are simply not in the category of continuants, and are pure events, takes nothing from the value they may have.

8.1.10 That values are objective implies that a person can be wrong in what he values, that his values can be mistaken. To the extent that he values things wrongly he suffers, whether or not he thinks he suffers. Of course, it may be unlikely that he is totally mistaken; his values may be no worse than somewhat awry, and his suffering correspondingly baddish. None the less he suffers. This brings us sharply up against the intuition that what you don't know can't hurt you. But it surely can, as Nagel (1979) and Nozick (1981) have also argued. The bloody culture of the Aztecs, with its crushing round of human sacrifice, is an obvious case in point. Even the most willing victims suffered, for they suffered a painful death; that they died in the belief that they served the god and were made holy detracts little from this loss, since the belief was delusive. It was delusive belief which gave merely delusive meaning to the rituals which dominated the life of the Aztecs; these reinforced nothing but their fears and their sense of themselves as impotent to take their affairs into their own hands and away from the gods; it fixed them in patterns of fruitless toil and ritual and thrust death and negation into the forefront of consciousness. Anyone's actions mean whatever they mean objectively, just as surely as what he says means something objectively, even though he says it in a language which is both local and quickly changing. If there was a happy Aztec, he nevertheless objectively suffered and *lost*. The Nazis suffered too, whatever their convictions about the matter and however much they enjoyed what they did. By refusing to treat Jews as persons they lost a sense of what they were doing and what sort of persons they made of themselves in the doing of it. They must have seen this reflected in the social mirror of Jewish suffering had they admitted that as a response of persons. As it was, most of them did not know what they had become, for they ceased to look at what might have shown it to them. For those who did look, and who embraced evil more knowingly, they lost a culture which was rich and varied in its meanings, in its styles of life, in what was there to be learned from whether by contrast or imitation. They trapped themselves in the narrow bounds of violence and mere aggression rather than the flexible complexities and wide range of meanings and rewards which might otherwise have been theirs. No Nazi led the good life, which is the life of aspirations and achievements apt for persons, and which fulfils our nature. (I return to this theme in 8.3.)

8.2 The virtues

8.2.1 The virtues are capacities (Campbell 1986), not performances or value-objects of any subproject within a broader one. But once we rise to the perspective of the broad open projects within which we choose our discrete actions according to our first-order desires and values, we can see that the virtues are values for those projects. To list the virtues describes for us the main features of a kind of person and a style of life. The list is a skeletal theory about the best kind of person and the best style of life. It is the best skeletal theory we have, and it is general enough to put us on the most rewarding track. We must not expect it to enlarge into a proper theory of a law-like sort; the skeleton can be fleshed out concretely in many ways. Since virtues are capacities and styles, it is not a true moral theory, even as a skeleton. It does not tell us what we ought to *do*. It is about what we need if we are to excel ourselves; it is about how to make something of ourselves. A properly directed open project to follow the ideals of being a person exercises these capacities, makes them virtues because of the role they play in the pursuit of authentic value. They are the main traits of character needed for the good life in an authentic culture. They are not directed at discrete, terminating ends, but at the continuing, self-perpetuating end of person- and culture-making. The virtues are subtle traits of character; even the apparently simple virtue of courage is complex. Courage must weigh the first-order values at issue, balance the risks against them, and act (or labour) accordingly. Thus it is a highly considered trait, characterizing a kind of person one wants to want to be. This makes the virtues out to be second-order values. Making yourself courageous or wise satisfies a scrutinized, transformed desire to be a certain kind of person.

8.2.2 There are no subjective virtues. Virtues have to do with objective and authentic value, so there was no saying what they are till objective and authentic values were explained. Virtues are not acts but styles of acting. A virtue is not an act or activity; one cannot *do* a virtue. It is a *way* of doing anything one does. What do the virtues do for us as we labour to make our values concrete? We use them in seeing clearly what we really want in our perspective on fields of value and in effectively cultivating them. A virtuous person knows the balance of her values, perceives what labours each merits, does not neglect the value of *manners* of doing things through a fixation on utilities and products, expends labour generously, and is steadfast in forbidding desires to lead her from the paths of value. She does not lose sight of other values which are not in the tighter focus of her attention. Thus virtues are capacities which we may have but which we exercise and expand as we gain the value-objects which make sense of what we do.

8.2.3 It is often said that virtue is its own reward: if these ideas are right, so it is. Virtue is clearly an end in itself, for the rewards of open projects lie in their own vital and skilful continuing and not in the terminating ends of actions and projects that fall within them. Terminating ends reward us, of course; but for strong, contrastive evaluators, who are free in their natures, the goal is to be a kind of person, and the activity which gains it is a self-sustaining, broad open project. It does not follow that to be virtuous is the only reward, or the only global one, in personal life. Nor is it true. But we have captured a nice intuition about the life of virtue.

8.2.4 Virtue is tied to excellence. For persons to excel their own humanity in the direction of personal ideals takes virtue. If excellence is, first, *self*-excelling, then virtue is the same for all; it is not the prerogative of special elites of wealth or birth or social position or even of abilities. This agrees with quite ancient intuitions about our equality in rights and in our intrinsic worth. It also agrees with a present body of amiable and fashionable feeling. People get widely differing luck in the raw materials to build their lives from: there is the genetic lottery of which sex or race we have, which skills and capacities we find ourselves born with, and which powers to develop new ones we might find; there is good or bad luck about where we are born and into what social and economic class we fall. But all face a problem, which they accept once they take on the tasks and ideals of personhood: how are they to tailor themselves to their predicament, good or bad? Predicaments differ, but the problems of satisfying our contrastive desires are structurally much the same in all of them. The general capacities we need to solve them are much the same too. That is, the virtues play much the same roles in the personal life of each of us.

8.2.5 Persons are to be regarded as ends in themselves, no matter who they are. That, too, gives them an equality, since it forbids our valuing them in terms of other ends that they may fulfil more or less well. But is this merely an agreeable piety? Persons are objects of value for each other in various ways; in some of these they are ends in themselves. Those you truly love are ends in themselves for you. You want their welfare for their sakes and not because they minister to ends of yours. But it is not in any such way as this that every person can be regarded as an end in himself for each of us. Hardy loves, admires, and reveres Nelson, not just because of his abilities to provide things Hardy wants, but because Hardy loves this person, the whole person, that Nelson is. For Hardy, Nelson is an end in himself. But Wellesley is not in *that* way an end for Hardy, for that depends on particular, concrete foundations of respect and love. Still, Hardy, taking the ideals of personhood seriously, recognizes Wellesley as an end in himself according to a general principle. The principle is that since Wellesley is a maker and pursuer of value, he is himself of value. Nor do his station in life and his special capacities for doing things count as to how valuable an end he may be in himself. The first-order values which Wellesley forms for himself spring both from a unique predicament in which he begins life and from idiosyncrasies of his nature. They may find a place in the culture and be appropriated by it in ways which need not be much like those Hardy is most eager to see realized. Each of us forges her own values, changes and is changed by her culture, in her own ways. A verdict on the global success of another will not be accessible to us in our limited perspectives till well after the event, if ever.

8.2.6 But the epistemic point is not the main one. Another's values enrich the meanings of our actions—for good or ill—the more so if they are other than our own. To take your own values as the only dimensions of meaning is an attempt to be what you cannot be. It is like taking your opinions as having a special status and entitlement to truth just in being yours. So another's valuing need not be *instrumental* in realizing our values. Denying others as ends in themselves is like stifling other voices: they need to be heard, if anything is to make sense. What another says may be disagreeable and even hateful to me. But he is one of a multitude of speakers; and without a multitude there are no conventions and institutions of language and my sounds would mean nothing. So for the enterprises of speaking, he is an end in himself. So it is with the broader canvas of actions and their meanings. We stand to gain in authenticity, if only by hardening, sharpening, and diversifying meanings, from the dialectical drama of another's life.

8.2.7 None the less, there remains a sense, both clear and important, in which we do not start life as equal in virtue and in which virtue is not the same for all. I do not mean that some of us are wicked, some of us angelic, and others no better than we should be. That does not show that virtue may be different for different people. But some just are natively better equipped to cultivate and harvest values than others—they are cleverer, stronger, better taught, luckier in the stability and resilience of their emotional character. With these abilities go corresponding responsibilities—I make that as an unargued claim about the morals of 'ought's and 'may's. They form an élite, if you wish, perhaps even an élite with special rights so long as these are matched with special responsibilities and duties. What these persons have is not greater virtue than others, but greater special capacities which are of use in making value-objects real and concrete. We might call this *élite* excellence.

8.2.8 It is not yet clear whether the sort of action which pursues virtue in élite excellence is meaningful in the same way as is its pursuit at the level of self-excellence. I believe that we would want to make a difference here between kinds or grades of the meaningfulness of action. In one sense each faces the same dialectical task, if he chases ideals, of alienating the desires he has in favour of forms of them which are authentic and objective values. The meaning of his second-order acts, and so of his pursuit of virtue, depends on this common structural feature. But those who remarkably excel *others* in what they do perform meaningful actions against a different background. Élite excellence has meaning in that excellent actions set for all of us meaningful goals and tasks which were not clear to us before. I cannot run very fast; as a jogger, I know my place. I learn a seemly modesty from knowing that some can run a four-minute mile, and I see by their example what persistence and the study of techniques—the universals of running—have done for those who pursue them. More modestly, those who excel me do not put me down, though they set me examples to aspire to, and give concrete meanings to what is humanly possible. Perhaps it seems unfair that some people's lives are more meaningful than others in this way. It is, anyway, quite obviously *true* that they are, though this may be rare—just think of Bach, Kant, Einstein, Rembrandt. These finer spirits forge new meanings for all who listen or look, and even new dimensions of what music, reason, natural insight, and representation are. That is given to few of us.

8.3   Meanings and rewards in personal lives

8.3.1 The good life is a life of right meanings; a life of truth. What does that mean? Part of my answer is given already. Our actions, like their values, can be authentic or not and objective or not. The meaning of a person's action relates it to what anyone ought (rationally) to do. This relation may go wrong in several ways. Obviously, one can get relevant facts wrong. Someone's view of what anyone ought rationally to do may be inauthentic in being imperfectly thought through. The meaning is inauthentic because false to his natural powers of reason. But it must also be sound both in conforming to culturally recognized canons of reasoning and in relating somehow to conventions, usages, and institutions about its meaning. These, in turn, must properly engage the capacities of culture members with the way of the world so as to secure the values (truth etc.) in question. In its authentic and objective meaning, an action's meaning works like the meaning of a saying in ways to be probed. Rather as what I say depends on the meaning of words I utter, so the meaning of what I do is culture-coloured and no mere matter of individual intention.

8.3.2 No inner state can be the final reward of life: not happiness, serenity, pleasure, or satisfaction—not even the belief that you are free in your nature. Unless life is significant, it is *all no good*. The significance of life lies simply in the meanings of actions. Actions do not mean just whatever we happen to wish, any more than words do. Meanings are made real, objective, and concrete, just as values are, by labour in value-fields. Just so, one must work to say what one wants clearly; I must say what anyone ought to say who wants to mean that, and getting the meanings of actions clear and intelligible is a similarly structured task. Because their perspective is so synoptic, the meaning of second- and higher-order actions looms largest for persons. Actions will be meaningful in rather different ways when they have second- rather than first-order satisfactions. Since, among grown humans, wantons are few, everyone's life is meaningful. Not everyone's life is good: that depends on *what* it means. It can mean failure, disgrace, confusion, misdirection, virtue overlooked or lost, a celebration of triviality—a disaster!; but folly or bad luck can happen only if a life can also mean achievement, honour, clarity, integrity, virtue found or the unworthy repudiated—a success! Significance is necessary, not sufficient, for reward.

8.3.3 If that is right, then by and large we do not get rewards unless we deserve them. A life is rewarded or punished if what it authentically and objectively meant is what it was intended to mean, and if the intention was to make real in it authentic and objective values. A cheat's life makes real a cheat's values. That is all he wants and that is surely all he gets, whether or not his deceit is detected. He cheats, wins his own game, and loses the real one. He may be happy, his cheat's desires satisfied, his conscience untroubled. But he is pitiful: his life's meaning is absurd, mean-minded, trivial, subjective, and he never even knows himself for what he is! I cannot establish these claims, but perhaps I can do something to make them plausible. I am most concerned to make the reader believe that meanings are what matters. Let my judgements on cheats and

Nazis take their chance! Meanings provide ample room for golden success in life. They also make room for tragic failures—being false to what you are, pursuing baseless, subjective values founded on false beliefs. There may be failures of will and failures of luck—being in the wrong culture and failing to see it or being unable to change it. Your plans may go astray, though well and judiciously laid; you may fail to understand yourself or those you put emotional capital into. It is on success or failure, not evil, that I will focus.

8.3.4 All actions, not just actions of saying, mean something, even though actions are not all communications. '*A* means something *to X*' is well formed. But *to whom* is one's life meaningful? Well, meaningful to oneself, to begin with. That is fundamental and obvious—without it no other meaning is possible. It is rewarding, too, though one hopes for more—as in talking to oneself, there are few disputes but little enlightenment and not much fun. We want our lives to have meaning for another. In theism, even the charm of immortality is no more bewitching than the thought that one's life is meaningful to another who grasps its every nuance, never forgets it, and whose attention to it rescues it from annihilation in the passage of time, in the staggering scale of the universe or in mere human history. More of this gilded charm in a moment. Even for my action to mean something for me, it must have a cultural sense as well. So one's life has meaning in the context of a cultivated univeralized understanding of personal tasks and ideals. That boils down, in one sense, just to its meaning something for a many-headed human (maybe alien) tribe, with a local culture, and a more or less ramshackle bunch of concepts about action. However, even if that is whom the meaningful life must be meant for, we aim to transcend this as if we meant life for the god, as the classical Greeks put it. Sometimes we do something like this in language, often when we write rather than speak. We aim to treat what will be locally expressed in a parochial language, somewhere, sometime, to some few readers, as if we offered it to truth itself, reaching beyond the accidentals of speaker and hearer to something timeless and universal. Unless a culture is seriously wanton, it sees, in cultured life and action, a *universal* sense. It can explain any action by linking it to Reason, which is not how humans act and think, but how they ought to act and think; meaning may be dressed in the alienated and transformed dress of a disciplined practice, the grave rituals and ceremonies of an art, a calling, a craft, of a style of celebration, a personal role. In our struggle towards the light of self-possession, self-excellence, freedom in a nature which nourishes the culture which nourishes us, we act in our deeper intentions and aspirations for universal personhood rather than for the individuals who make it real.

8.3.5 That attitude is familiar enough in our passive understanding of the cultures of others, however different, even alien, from ourselves. We look beyond the local, exotic, idiosyncratic, parochial, or bizarre for the dialectical struggle to alienate nature and regain it in a second, cultivated, nature. Our understanding is a universal one; we interpret the alien as acting as any person might. So, if we are not wanton, we shape our lives after patterns that transcend what we see in the individual instances: we give it to the god. As those who mean what they do as well as understand others' acts, though we act as individuals, we act for all. So here again local meanings may have a more global scope.

8.3.6 There are commonly delusions about how the meaning of life could lie beyond living itself. To think that life is a cheat and a disappointment unless the very principles which order the cosmos pause to take note of our doings is the snare of a sentimental inflation of self. It is trying to be what you are not—that round which the cosmos revolves. Whether or not such principles *do* take note, it is a deep mistake to see life as absurd if they do not. It is to undersell your personhood and make it absurd unless it has some import across the vaster reaches of space-time for some thing which is real in a way that transcends the cultural community of persons. The sense of the vast intergalactic spaces and the unimaginable aeons of time as empty, overwhelming, and alien; of human life as diminished, dwarfed, and futile is simply the cynicism of a self-regard that has got too big for its boots (Camus 1959; Nagel 1979). It condemns the dazzling range and sweep of human culture, the grandeur of its successes and failures, the brilliance of its varied powers to represent, to analyse, to invent new projects for itself and the world; it derides the deep tragedies of human inadequacy, its huge potential for destruction and for horrible evils; it has no awe for the scale of human pain and joy nor for personal struggle and achievement. It has no coherent view of value to set beside the personal values and meanings which are gradually evolved and painfully expressed in the dialectical conflicts of personal life. Its sentimental face has never made sense of supernatural foundations for human worth and meaning; therefore its cynical face has fostered a nihilism towards what human life can mean.

8.3.7 Yet I want to offer a brief speculation about whether an objective meaning and truth for a person's life might reach beyond the local lives of individuals and cultures. Consider Hegel's view that our lives are meaningful as part of the unfolding and expressing of Reason in the universe, so that we find, when we look at all of it, that the whole can be understood in the light of principles of rational explanation as a kind of action or assertion with meaning, purpose, reasons, and justification. We do not need these meanings and purposes to be those of a transcendental agent or person; there probably are no persons but ourselves. I will not pursue the question whether this view is true or even, as a whole, intelligible. It may well be neither, though I know of no proof that it is. I want to reflect, merely, whether in some such remote or large-scale way that reaches past countable gains for individual persons or cultures, reason, order, organic unity (Nozick 1981), or some such abstract property, makes sense as a value.

8.3.8 I think that something of the kind does make sense, and simply because order, reason, or organic unity are properties we are obliged to value in ourselves as basic to our being persons. There are some properties the wide instantiation of which it makes no sense to value—cubicity, for one. Not every property characteristic of humans is meaningful as a value—spreading replicas of the human shape far and wide, for instance. I doubt even that every property necessary for being a person is intelligibly valuable, for some of these will be so complex and so intricately knitted into the causal properties which underlie them (as the human brain underlies our thinking) as to be lost to view unless they are also close to sufficient for being a person. But let us take it that reason (being explicable by principles of rational explanation), order, and organic unity escape such entanglements. Then I claim that it is an intelligible value for us that they be widespread. Further, they make sense as ends in themselves, ends for which more obvious utilities in the lives of persons might have to give place.

8.3.9 Personal life is rewarding if its meaning has a *truth*. That is another way of saying that its actions are authentic and objective, true to self, true to culture, true to the world. Whoever leads a true life wins and whoever leads a false one loses. So the successes and failures of actions and lives are like the successes and failures of sayings and systems of sayings, such as theories. It is like knowledge. Indeed, even the three-part structures of these are alike. Knowledge should be truth to self—I say what *I* believe—but it must be true to the language too, using its concepts, exploiting its institutions of explanation, of reason and evidence, of the ethics of belief; and it must be suitably related to the whole culture of language, even while it may be forging new concepts and sweeping old usages and conventions away. Knowledge must be true to the world as well. We can sustain the metaphor of truth and an analogy between action generally and sayings in particular by likening projective activities and broad open projects to narratives, theories, etc. So true action—rightly understood and wanted by its agent—is a kind of inarticulate knowledge, a kind of know-*how*, at least as long as action goes on outrunning articulate principles for it (McGinn 1984). So there is meaning, truth, knowledge in living, and in its truth lies the value of life and its reward.

8.3.10 Is the good life happy and the bad life unhappy? If so, that is not what makes the good life good and rewarding. Truth makes it good and rewarding. It would seem plausible that the good life in the good culture is, with good luck, happy. This is scarcely an empirical claim. But, surely, the best we can do in life may leave us miserable. You can be wretched though the meaning of your life becomes you; it makes us flourish as persons and adds to our culture. Such claims ask us to agree that the rewards of life are independent of subjective satisfactions like happiness and pleasure (unless we allow one happy who does not know his happiness).

8.3.11 We ought not to look for rewards in life in terms of our inner states, for these are too open to the charge that they are delusive, insubstantial, fleeting, or so confined in relevance as to amount to little. Not even serenity and stoic calm are finally rewarding if these may be smug, or crudely uncomprehending of self or fellows. It *is* about what your life might mean or fail to mean that you are anxious, which makes you writhe with embarrassment when the meaning goes wrong—or with apprehension when you fear it may go wrong. The ardent wish for meaning, significance, sense, draws people to religion, to philosophy, or whatever else may seem to grant it. We want no inner satisfaction at the price of absurdity, no happiness in senselessness, no contentment in a wilderness of brute, meaningless being and doing. Better to buy significance at the risk of disastrous falsity. Only so do we make room for the possibility of the kind of success we want.

8.3.12 The lives of finite creatures will hold some truth and some falsity. We are all both winners and losers. But there are winners of more or less; how to do well, if not perfectly, deserves reflection. There is, first, the life of authenticity and integrity, of fidelity to self and to one's culture in the light of energetic attempts to understand them; there is also fidelity to the world, both social and physical. We keep this faith by means of an understanding which we owe both to our own vigilant and imaginative observation and to our culture's theories about the world. To be a person of integrity is to reap the rewards of a rapport with one's fellows, to enter perceptively into a communal life in which one's actions have an import for oneself and for one's fellows, as their actions have a meaning for oneself; it is to follow ideals with fidelity and to have this grasped and appropriated, used, enlarged, commented upon, and enriched by the responses of others. The epistemic hurdles to getting the life of integrity right are not easy but not impossible. We do our best. Yet the rewards may be lost because one's fellows lack an answering integrity and authenticity. Bad luck does not spare integrity. There is still ill health, the trap of poverty, and many another external sorrow to spoil the enterprise, but the rewards are accessible, at least some of them likely to be real and substantial, including those of our fellows' respect and affection based on a right understanding of what our lives mean. The life of truth is a harder target to hit: one needs knowledge, not just good faith. But the prize is richer. The values we pursue are untainted by delusive meanings about what we are individually, what we are as a natural and cultural kind, and what the consequences of our actions in the world might be. The losses of delusion about the world and its rewards were disastrous for the Aztecs and for the Nazis. They were cultures that knew not what they did. The meanings of their actions and their lives are horribly clear to us—the superstition, baseless fears, the sacrificial waste of the young and the brave in the one case; in the other, the crass mistaking of violence and oppression for capacity and power, the fear and loathing of the merely other, the fake grandiosity and élitism of mere genetic difference, the crude, brute, insensate, frantic values so hideously pursued—those are, objectively, the meanings of their lives even apart from their satanic intentions. Would we want to be happy at the cost of leading a life with such a meaning?

8.3.13 There are other ways in which a well-led life may fail to reap its proper harvest. The meaning of what you do may be missed. What you make of your life may pass unnoticed. It may be misunderstood, despite its integrity or truth. There is an obvious and useful analogy, here, with sayings. However true one's saying, one may cry it in the wilderness. But it is not nothing to see, to say and speak truly, even if you are ignored or no one understands you. Think of the fun of ironies that nobody else grasps! Still, unheard remarks lose much of this point, since talk is to and for others. Actions which fail to be *appropriated*, I shall say, are like unheard remarks. An action can be true and meaningful without its being seen to be so. Actions are appropriated by the culture just in being understood and responded to by more or less perceptive and appreciative individuals. But, as before, out of the value-field of concrete, parochial, placed, dated, idiosyncratic events and objects we can and do make real values that give a universal sense to our actions. One means what one does in a universal, ethical sense, and this is appropriated if it is so understood and matched with apt responses. The noisome particularities of the sick-room, for example, become a field for value and culture. One's actions become culturally appropriated if they may serve as examples to another.

8.3.14 As in talk there is gossip, chatter, and conversations which are serious, so actions may differ in the gravity of their meanings. Whether trivial or deep, true or false, these meanings are normally taken up by others—appropriated. There is wider or narrow scope for this taking-up, quite clearly. Gassing away over coffee to three friends differs from a serious explanation to your beloved, and this again from a public address, a lecture, or the publication of a book of poems. So there are wider and narrower scopes for appropriating action. There are *more or less* local meanings. In the nature of human affairs, at least, few of us have wide scope for our actions. Some are always in the limelight. It is not obvious that a wide appropriation of meaning is richer in its rewards than intimacy and privacy. What matters is the sense of acting universally—for personhood and within it. Unappropriated actions do not lose their meanings, any more than unheard remarks lose theirs. But one loses one main kind of reward if one's meanings are never grasped, seen, responded to, answered, or made part of the fabric of wider lives. Appropriation is not part of authenticity or objectivity, nor is it a subjectivity which says that there are no meanings that are not understood meanings. But if my meanings do not feed back into the culture and enrich its events (at least locally) then I lose a reward in life, whatever I may think about how little the notice of others counts for me. Appropriation is a kind of meaning—meaning to another.

8.3.15 This view of life's rewards denies that what you don't know can't hurt you. To use an example of Nagel's (1979: 4–7), suppose that you are always treated with great courtesy and apparent respect by a group of people who secretly hold you in derision; you never discover their contempt. You are injured though you never know it. In a different way, the great musicians Bach and Schubert both won and lost in ways unknown to them. They won because their work has proved greater than they supposed; they lost because much of their work has been lost since their deaths. Suppose all Bach's music had been lost after his death. Would this not be a tragedy, not just for us but for him? Would not the meaning of his life thereby have been diminished? Surely it would, unless we suppose that nobody's life has meaning beyond meanings he has for it, and unless meaning and value have no dimensions such as authenticity and objectivity.

8.3.16 If this is correct, there is a last form of success (and of failure) which, in the nature of the case, can be given only to rather few. That is to contribute not just the local meanings of particular actions to the sum of cultural meanings, but processes or products with quite global meanings which are widely appropriated. To these few it is given to live a life or to make things or patterns of meanings which are beacons and models for many beyond the immediate impact that each makes. For Ghandi, Einstein, Mozart, Leonardo, there is an emblematic meaning, a global assimilation by the culture of what they did or made. The meaning and global assimilation might not be of what is good—think of the way we find meaning in the life of Hitler and assimilate it as a pattern of evil. These provide us with not merely new meanings, but rich, deep suggestions for new uses of our powers, new worlds of value to conquer and old worlds to be transcended. Here assimilation is not merely by the local order, where one acts directly for and with other individuals. Some persons enrich and expand those universal, alienated meanings which form the pinnacle of high culture. That is the best kind of good life.

References

ALSTON, WILLIAM P. (1969), 'Feelings', *Philosophical Review*, 78: 3–34.

ARISTOTLE (ed. 1941), *Ethica Nicomachea*, in *The Basic Works of Aristotle*, ed. R. McKeon, Random House: New York.

ARMSTRONG, DAVID MALET (1983), *What is a Law of Nature?*, Cambridge University Press: Cambridge.

AUSTIN, J. L. (1966), 'Ifs and Cans', in Berofsky (1966), 295–322.

BEDFORD, ERROL (1957), 'Emotions', *Proceedings of the Aristotelian Society*, suppl. 57: 281–304.

BEROFSKY, BERNARD (1966), ed. *Free Will and Determinism*, Harper & Row: New York.

BRANDT, R. B. (1979), *A Theory of the Good and the Right*, Clarendon Press: Oxford.

BUTLER, JOSEPH (1895), *Works*, ed. W. E. Gladstone, Clarendon Press: Oxford.

CAMPBELL, KEITH (1986), *A Stoic Philosophy of Life*, University Press of America: Lenham, Md.

CAMPBELL, NORMAN (1957), *Foundations of Science*, Dover: New York.

CAMUS, ALBERT (trans. 1959), *The Myth of Sisyphus*, trans. Justin O'Brien, Vintage: New York.

CHURCHLAND, PATRICIA S. (1980), 'Language, Thought, and Information Processing', *Nous*, 14: 147–70.

—— and CHURCHLAND, PAUL M. (1981), 'Functionalism, Qualia and Intentionality', *Philosophical Topics*, 12/1:121–45.

CHURCHLAND, PAUL M. (1979), *Scientific Realism and the Plasticity of Mind*, Cambridge University Press: Cambridge.

—— (1981), 'Eliminative Materialism and Propositional Attitudues', *Journal of Philosophy*, 78: 67–90.

CURTISS, SUSAN (1977), *Genie: A Psycholinguistic Study of a Modern-Day Wild Child*, Academic Press: New York.

DENNETT, DANIEL C. (1978), *Brainstorms: Philosophical Essays on Mind and Psychology*, Bradford Books: Montgomery, Vt.

—— (1982), 'Beyond Belief' in Andrew Woodfield (ed.), *Thought and Object: Essays on Intentionality*, Clarendon Press: Oxford, 1–95.

—— (1984), *Elbow Room: The Varieties of Free Will Worth Wanting*, Bradford Books: Cambridge, Mass., and MIT Press: London.

DEUTSCHER, MAX (1983), *Subjecting and Objecting: An Essay in*

Objectivity, University of Queensland Press: St Lucia.

DEVITT, MICHAEL (1984), *Realism and Truth*, Princeton University Press: Princeton, NJ.

DRETSKE, FRED I. (1977), 'Laws of Nature', *Philosophy of Science*, 44: 248–68.

ELSTER, JON (1983), *Sour Grapes*, Cambridge University Press: Cambridge.

FALK, W. D. (1963), 'Morality, Self and Others', in Hector-Neri Castañeda and George Nakhnikian (eds.), *Morality and the Language of Conduct*, Wayne State University Press: Detroit, 25–67.

FEYERABEND, PAUL KARL (1975), *Against Method: Outline of an Anarchistic Theory of Knowledge*, Humanities Press: London.

FRANKFURT, HARRY (1971), 'Freedom of the Will and the Concept of a Person', *Journal of Philosophy*, 68: 5–20; repr. in Watson (1982*a*), 81–95.

FREUD, SIGMUND (trans. 1925), 'Contribution to the Psychology of Love, I: The Most Prevalent Form of Degradation in Erotic Life', auth. trans. under supervision of Joan Riviere, in *Collected Papers*, iv (International Psychoanalytical Library, 10), Hogarth Press: London, 203–16.

GALILEI, GALILEO (trans. 1967), *Dialogue Concerning the Two Chief World Systems, Ptolemaic and Copernican*, trans. Stillman Drake, University of California Press, Berkeley.

—— (trans. 1974), *Two New Sciences, including centers of gravity and force of percussion*, trans. Stillman Drake, University of Wisconsin Press, Madison.

GOLDMAN, A. (1970), *A Theory of Human Action*, Prentice Hall: Englewood Cliffs, NJ.

GRICE, H. P. (1957), 'Meanings', *Philosophical Review*, 66: 377–88.

GRIFFITHS, A. PHILLIPS (1967), ed. *Knowledge and Belief*, Oxford University Press: Oxford and New York.

HARE, R. M. (1963), *Freedom and Reason*, Clarendon Press: Oxford.

HEGEL, G. W. F. (ed. 1977), *Die Phänomenologie des Geistes*; trans. *Phenomenology of Spirit*, by A. V. Miller, with analysis of the text and foreword by J. N. Findlay, Clarendon Press: Oxford.

HILGARD, ERNEST R. and ATKINSON, RICHARD C. (1967), *Introduction to Psychology*, Harcourt Brace: New York.

HOBART, R. E. (1966), 'Free Will as Involving Determination and Inconceivable Without It', in Berofsky (1966), 63–95.

HUME, DAVID (ed. 1888), *Treatise on Human Nature*, ed. L. A. Selby-Bigge, Clarendon Press: Oxford.

ITARD, JEAN MARC GASPARD, and MALSON, LUCIEN (1972), 'The Wild Boy of Aveyron', in Malson (1972), 95–179.

JACKSON, FRANK (1985), 'Internal Conflicts in Desires and Morals', *American Philosophical Quarterly*, 22: 105–14.

JACOBS, W. W. (ed. 1975), 'The Monkey's Paw', in *Classic Ghost Stories by Charles Dickens and Others*, Dover Publications: New York: 34–44.

KAPLAN, DAVID (1968), 'Quantifying In', *Synthese*, 19: 178–214.

KENNY, ANTHONY (1963), *Action, Emotion and Will*, Routledge and Kegan Paul: London.

KIM, JAEGWON (1978), 'Supervenience and Nomological Incommensurables', *American Philosophical Quarterly*, 15: 149–56.

—— (1982), 'Psychological Supervenience', *Philosophical Studies*, 41: 51–70.

KUHN, THOMAS S. (1970), *The Structure of Scientific Revolutions*, University of Chicago Press: Chicago, Ill.

LAKATOS, IMRE (1976), *Proofs and Refutations*, Cambridge University Press: Cambridge.

LOAR, BRIAN (1981), *Mind and Meaning*, Cambridge University Press: Cambridge.

LYONS, WILLIAM (1980), *Emotion*, Cambridge University Press: Cambridge.

McGINN, COLIN (1984), 'The Concept of Knowledge', in P. A. French, T. P. Uhling, and H. K. Wettstein (eds.), *Causation and Causal Theories* (Midwest Studies in Philosophy, 9), University of Minnesota Press: Minneapolis, 519–44.

MacINTYRE, ALASDAIR (1985), *After Virtue: A Study in Moral Theory*, 2nd edn., Duckworth: London.

MacKAY, D. M. (1960), 'On the Logical Indeterminacy of a Free Choice', *Mind*, 69: 31–40.

—— (1962), 'The Use of Behavioural Language to Refer to Mechanical Processes', *British Journal for the Philosophy of Science*, 13: 89–103.

MALSON, LUCIEN (trans. 1972), *Les Enfants Sauvages* (Union Générale d'Editions: Paris, 1964), *Wolf Children and the Problem of Human Nature*, by Edmund Fawcett, Peter Ayrton, and Joan White, Monthly Review Press: New York and London.

MARX, KARL and ENGELS, FRIEDRICH (ed. 1959), *Basic Writing on Politics and Philosophy*, ed. Lewis S. Feuer, Anchor Books, Doubleday & Co.: New York.

MASTERS, WILLIAM HOWELL, and JOHNSON, VIRGINIA E. (1966), *Human Sexual Response*, Churchill: London.

MORTON, ADAM (1980), *Frames of Mind: Constraints on the Commonsense Conception of the Mind*, Clarendon Press: Oxford.

NAGEL, THOMAS (1979), *Mortal Questions*, Cambridge University Press: Cambridge.

NERLICH, GRAHAM C. (1972), 'A Scrutiny of Reference', *Canadian Journal of Philosophy*, 1: 315–26.

—— (1976), 'Quine's "Real Ground"', *Analysis*, 37: 15–19.

—— (1979), 'How to Make Things Have Happened', *Canadian Journal of Philosophy*, 9, 1–22.

NOWELL SMITH, P. H. (1966), 'Ifs and Cans', in Berofsky (1966), 322–39.

NOZICK, ROBERT (1981), *Philosophical Explanations*, Clarendon Press: Oxford.

PETTIT, PHILIP (1986*a*), 'Broad-Minded Explanation and Psychology', *Subject, Thought, and Context*, Clarendon Press: Oxford, 17–58.

—— (1986*b*) 'Social Holism and Moral Theory', *Aristotelian Society Proceedings*, 86, 1985/6.

—— (1987), 'Humeans, Anti-Humeans, and Motivation' *Mind*, 96: 530–3.

POPPER, KARL RAIMUND (1950), 'Indeterminism in Quantum Physics and Classical Physics', Part I and Part II, *British Journal for the Philosophy of Science*, 1: 117–33, 173–95.

QUINE, WILLARD VAN ORMAN (1960), *Word and Object*, The MIT Press: Cambridge, Mass.

—— (1969), 'Epistemology Naturalised', in *Ontological Relativity: and other essays*, Columbia University Press: New York: 69–90.

—— (1981), *Theories and Things*, Harvard University Press: Cambridge, Mass.

RAWLS, JOHN (1971), *A Theory Of Justice*, Belknap Press of Harvard University Press: Cambridge, Mass.

—— (1980), 'Kantian Constructivism in Moral Theory: the Dewey Lectures 1980', *Journal of Philosophy*, 77/9: 515–72.

ROSS, LEE, LEPPER, MARK R., and HUBBARD, MICHAEL (1975), 'Perseverance in Self-Perception and Social Perception: Biased Attributional Processes in the Debriefing Paradigm', *Journal of Personality and Social Psychology*, 32: 880–92.

RYLE, GILBERT (1949), *Concept of Mind*, New York: Hutchinson's University Library.

SARTRE, JEAN-PAUL (trans. 1956), *Being and Nothingness*, trans. Hazel Barnes, Philosophical Library: New York.

—— (trans. 1962), *Sketch for a Theory of Emotions*, trans. Philip Mairet, pref. by Mary Warnock, Methuen: London.

SCHLICK, MORITZ (1966), 'When is a Man Responsible?', in Berofsky (1966), 54–63.

SCRUTON, ROGER (1986), *Sexual Desire: A Philosophical Investigation*, Weidenfeld & Nicolson: London.

SELLARS, WILLFRID (1963), *Science, Perception and Reality*, Humanities Press: New York.

SIMON, A. (1957), 'Bandwagon and Underdog Effects of Election Procedures', in *Models of Man*, Wiley: New York.

SHAKESPEARE, WILLIAM (ed. 1986), *William Shakespeare: The Complete Works*, Stanley Well and Gary Taylor (eds.), Clarendon Press: Oxford.

SLOTE, MICHAEL A. (1982), 'Selective Necessity and Free Will', *Journal of Philosophy*, 74: 5–24.

SMITH, MICHAEL (1988), 'The Humean Theory of Motivation', *Mind*, 97: 36–61.

SOLOMON, ROBERT (1976), *The Passions*, Doubleday-Anchor books: New York.

STICH, STEPHEN P. (1983), *From Folk Psychology to Cognitive Science: The Case Against Belief*, The MIT Press: Cambridge, Mass.

—— (1985), 'Could Man be an Irrational Animal?: Some Notes on the Epistemology of Rationality', *Synthese*, 64/1: 115–35.

STOCKER, MICHAEL (1976) 'The Schizophrenia of Modern Ethical Theories', *Journal of Philosophy*, 73: 453–66.

—— (1979), 'Desiring the Bad: An Essay in Moral Psychology', *Journal of Philosophy*, 76: 738–53.

—— (1980), 'Intellectual Desires, Emotions, and Action', in Amelie Oksenberg Rorty (ed.), *Explaining Emotions*, University of California Press: Berkeley: 323–38.

—— (1983), 'Psychic Feelings: Their Importance and Irreducibility', *Australasian Journal of Philosophy*, 61/1: 5–26.

STORR, ANTHONY (1975), *Sexual Deviation*, repr. Penguin Books: Harmondsworth.

STRAWSON, PETER FREDERICK (1974), *Freedom And Resentment and Other Essays*, Methuen: London, repr. in Watson (1982*a*), 59–80.

TANNER, MICHAEL (1977), 'Sentimentality', *Proceedings of the Aristotelian Society*, New Series, 77: 127–47.

TAYLOR, CHARLES (1977), 'What is Human Agency?', in Theodore Mischel (ed.), *The Self: Psychological and Philosophical Issues*, Rowman & Littlefield: Totowa, NJ, 103–35.

TOOLEY, MICHAEL (1977) 'The Laws of Nature', *Canadian Journal of Philosophy*, 7: 667–98.

VAN DE VATE, D. (1971), 'The Problem of Robot Consciousness', *Philosophy and Phenomenological Research*, 32: 149–65.

WATSON, GARY (1982*a*), (ed.) *Free Will*, Oxford University Press: Oxford and New York.

—— (1982*b*), 'Free Agency', in Watson (1982*a*): 96–110.

WILLIAMS, BERNARD (1985), *Ethics and the Limits of Philosophy*, Harvard University Press: Cambridge, Mass.

WITTGENSTEIN, LUDWIG (1958), *Philosophische Untersuchungen*, trans. *Philosophical Investigations*, by G. E. M. Anscombe, Basil Blackwell: Oxford.

Index

access, conscious 2.2.4; 2.3.2, 9, 13;
 6.1.5; 6.7.7
act and activity 1.4.8; 4.3.2, 4, 17;
 4.5.5; 4.6.1
 see also action concepts; higher-
 order: actions; meanings: of
 actions
action concepts 1.4.1; 1.7.3; 1.7.14, 19,
 22; 2.1.1; 2.3.1; 2.4.5; 3.2.3;
 4.3.2–4; 7.1.1–2
 and law-like explanation 1.7.18;
 2.3.3
 see also human nature: description of
agents 1.4.7–8; 2.1.3, 6; 2.2.2, 4, 6–7,
 16; 2.3.2–4, 8, 13; 2.5.3; 4.1.1;
 4.3.9; 7.1.1
 and speakers 2.3.2–4; 2.3.9–13
agitation of the mind 6.1.3–4; 6.2.2, 6;
 6.3.1, 3–4, 6–9; 6.4.7; 6.5.1
alienation 1.4.8–11; 5.2
Alston, W. 6.2.1
anatomy 1.2.1; 1.7.16–17
anguish 4.2.6–8
appetites 4.1.4; 4.2.1–2; 4.3.6;
 5.1.2–3; 7.1.3–5; 7.2.4; 7.3.6–7
Aristotle 1.1.1; 1.6.4; 2.3.4; 4.3.10;
 4.6.8
Armstrong, D. 3.2.1
attitudes 1.4.1; 2.1; 4.6.11–12
 engaged 2.1.3–5; 2.2.1–4; 5.5.10
 objective 2.1.3–4, 6; 2.2.1, 5, 8;
 5.4.13
 see also higher-order: attitudes;
 intentional attitude
Austin, J. 1.5.1; 2.2.3
authenticity 4.2.8; 5.3.3; 7.2; 8.2.1–2;
 8.3.3, 9, 12
 cultural 7.2.20–1; 8.2.1

bad faith 1.6.7; 2.4.7; 5.3.3; 6.4.6;
 7.2.12, 19
basic natural motive 4.2.10–15; 7.1.9;
 7.2.7; 7.3.8
Bedford, E. 6.2.3

being a kind of person 1.4.8; 4.6.1,
 8–12; 4.7.2–3; 7.3.8
being in touch with 1.1.5; 3.1.2; 3.2.4;
 3.3.9; 3.4.4; 3.5.8; 4.6.7; 6.1.1
belief:
 distinct from desires 1.4.3–5; 4.1
 see also intentional attitude; sayings
bodily feelings 6.1.6; 6.2.2–3
brain, survival trait of 1.2.1, 8
Brandt, R. 1.7.13
Butler, J. 1.1.8

Campbell, K. 8.2.1
Campbell, N. 5.5.4
Camus, A. 8.3.6
capacities:
 authentic to 6.4.4; 7.2.7
 for cultural life 7.2.7–12; 7.3.6–11;
 8.1.5; 8.2
 see also virtues
Churchland, Patricia 1.2.4; 2.3.14
Churchland, Paul 1.2.4; 1.7.20–1;
 2.3.14; 2.4.5
communication, *see* persons: state of
consciousness:
 and culture 3.2
 debased 6.4
 see also access, conscious; self-
 consciousness
corruption 5.2.8; 5.3.3; 5.4.12
 see also cynicism; sentimentality;
 sexual perversion
cultural:
 life 5.1.2–4
 practices 2.2; 2.3
 relativity 1.4.13; 3.5.7; 7.2.14
 understanding 3.5.6–8
 verdict 3.2.5–6
 see also capacities
culture 1.1.4; 3.2; 3.3
 authentic, *see* authenticity: cultural
 broad sense of 1.4.11; 7.3.5
 and dialectic 1.4.11; 5.4.13
 institutions of 1.2.2; 1.6.1–2; 1.7.1,

culture *(cont.)*:
11; **2.5.5**; **3.2.2**; **3.5.2**; **7.1.1**;
7.2.12, 15, 17; **8.3.1–2**; **8.4.1**
natural for humans **1.1.4**; **1.2**
and norms **1.2.2**; **3.2.3**
and valuing **1.4.11–14**; **7.1**
Curtiss, S. **1.2.4**
cynicism **6.6.1–46**; **8.3.6**

decisions **4.4**
Dennett, D. **1.4.1–2**; **1.5.1**; **2.1.2**;
2.3.10; **3.3.4**; **4.3.13**; **4.4.1**
description **1.7**
vs. law-like explanation **1.7.14–23**
vs. prescription **1.7.1**
see also ontology
desires:
to change **4.3.8–11**; **7.1.8**
classification of **4.3**; **7.1.3–9**; **7.2.4–6**
conflict of **1.4.5–6**; **4.1.9–10**
distinct from beliefs **1.4.3–6**;
1.5.3–7; **4.1**
homeostatic **4.2**
for pleasures **4.3.7**; **7.1.4–5**; **7.2.4**
representation in **4.1.6–10**
social action **4.3.9–11**; **7.1.9**; **7.2.4**
of spectators **4.3.7**; **7.1.6–7**; **7.2.5**
strength of **4.4**
see also higher-order: desire; intentional attitude; second-order:
desires; sexual desire
determinism **1.3.7–8**; **1.6.1**, 7; **2.1.3**;
6.4.6
Hard Determinism **1.3.10**; **1.5.1**
Deutscher, M. **5.4.13**; **6.1.10**; **6.6.5**
Devitt, M. **2.2.14**
dialectic **1.1.7**; **1.4**; **2.5.2**; **5**
and concept of a person **1.4**
and science **5.5**
and sexual desire **5.1–4**
see also alienation
Dretske, F. **3.2.1**
dualism **1.7.1–3**, 12; **5.5.10**

élite excellence **8.2.7–8**; **8.3.16**
Elster, J. **4.6.20**
emotions **6**
cognitive critique of **6.3.2**, 9; **6.5.1**,
11; **6.6.3–9**
corruption of **6.5**; **6.6**
and desires **6.1.8–10**
foundation of **6.3.2**
intended **6.1.2**, 4; **6.2.4**; **6.4**

judgement in **6.1.3–7**
and meanings **6.1.1**, 4
non-adaptive activity in **6.1.2**, 9; **6.7**
object of **6.1.4**
occasion for **6.2.6–7**
proportion in, *see* values: proportion
in
see also corruption
ends **4.3.1–4**; **4.5.5**; **4.6.3**; **7.3.10**;
8.2.3; **8.3.8**
see also persons: as ends
engineering programme **1.4.11–12**;
7.3.7, 9, 11
epicyclic monitoring **4.6.17–22**; **5.4.2**
ethics of belief **3.1.4**; **3.4**; **3.5.1**; **4.6.7**;
5.5.9–10; **7.2.12**
evaluation:
contrastive **3.1.6**; **4.6.6**, 10–14;
6.1.1; **8.2.3–4**
weak **4.6.5**
excellence **1.1.3**; **1.4.9**; **4.3.9**; **5.3.6**;
6.7.6; **7.2.1–2**; **7.3.9**; **8.2.4**, 7–8
explanation:
rational **1.4.1**; **2.1.1**; **2.3**; **2.4**; **2.5**; of
scientific practice **2.5.3–6**; *see also*
institutions of language; justification, rational
scientific **2.1.1**; **2.2.8–15**; **2.3.5**; **2.5**;
of persons **2.5.2**; *see also* ideals of
explanation
expressivism **1.2.7**; **1.3.11**; **1.6**;
4.2.6–10; **4.3.16–18**; **6.1.9**; **7.2.19**
see also being a kind of person

Falk, W. **7.2.19**
feelings, *see* bodily feelings; psychic
feelings
Feyerabend, P. **2.3.6**
folk psychology **1.7.12**, 19–23; **2.3.14**;
2.4.5; **6.1.2**
Frankfurt, H. **4.5.3–8**; **4.6.1**; **4.7.4**
free in one's nature, *see* human nature:
free in
freedom **1.3**; **1.4.9**; **1.5.6**; **2.1.3–4**;
4.5.8; **5.3.7**; **5.4.4**; **5.5.10**; **7.2.2**
formal **1.5.1–2**; **1.6.7**; **7.2.7**
Freud, S. **2.4.5**; **4.2.4**; **5.4.9**

Galilei, G. **2.2.10–11**; **2.2.13**; **3.5.6**
goals **4.3.3**; **4.5.4**, 7; **4.6.1**, 4
appraisal of self as having **4.6.4**, 14
Goldman, A. **1.3.5**

good life 1.1.1, 7, 9; 3.1.1; 4.7.2;
  7.1.4; 8.1.5–6, 10; 8.2.1; 8.3.1,
  10, 16
Grice, H. 3.1.3
grief 6.7
Griffiths, A. Phillips 2.3.10

happiness 8.3.2, 10–11
Hare, R. 1.1.8; 7.2.12
Hegel, G 1.6.3–5; 3.2.1–2, 4, 6; 3.5.3;
  4.5.1; 5.5.11; 7.1.9; 7.2.14; 8.3.7
higher-order:
  actions 4.6; 5.2.1; 5.4.1–2; 5.9.1–2;
    6.2.4; 8.2.8; 8.3.2
  attitudes 1.4.2–7; 1.5.1, 6; 4.5;
    4.6.11; 4.7; 5.1.1; 5.4.2; 7.1.4,
    10; 7.3.8
  consciousness 1.3.4–5, 8
  desire 1.4.5–7, 12; 1.5.7; 4.1.1;
    4.2.15; 4.5.2–3, 6–8; 4.6.6, 14,
    23–4; 4.7.1, 5; 5.4.3; 6.1.5; 7.2.1
  satisfaction 4.5.6–7, 9; 4.6.1, 20–3;
    4.7.1–3
Hilgard, E. 4.2.13
Hobart, R. 4.4.1
homoestatic image 4.2; 5.1.5
human metric, *see* values: inarticulate
human nature 1.4.8
  becoming a person 1.1.5–7
  and culture 1.2
  description of 1.7.16–19
  free in 1.4.7–8; 4.6.23
  and language 1.1.3, 7; 1.2.2–6
  response 6.2.6; 6.3.3; 6.7.5–6
  role in valuing 7.1.5
  see also action concepts; capacities;
    desires: classification of; express-
    ivism; person contingent traits;
    values: inarticulate
Hume, D. 1.1.8; 1.3.3; 1.5.3–6; 3.1.5;
  4.1.2–4, 6; 4.7.6; 6.3.2; 6.6.3;
  7.1.5

ideals of explanation:
  rational 2.3.4
  scientific 2.2.12, 14
ideational desire 5.1.4, 6–9; 5.4.3, 5, 9
inarticulate, *see* values: inarticulate
institutions of language 1.7.11–12, 19;
  2.2.4; 2.3.2, 4; 2.4.3, 6, 8; 3.3;
  3.4.2; 3.5.5; 8.3.9
  see also propositions
intensionality 5.1.3; 6.1.4; 6.2.3

intentional attitude 1.4.1; 3.1.3; 4.1.5
interpersonal mirror 4.2.15; 5.2.6;
  5.3.2–3, 5; 8.1.2
isolates, human 1.2.4; 2.3.14
Itard, J. 1.2.4

Jackson, F. 4.1.9
Jacobs, W. 4.3.15
jealousy 4.2.9; 6.1.10; 6.2.4; 6.5.6
judgement:
  on desires 1.5.5; 4.6.2; 4.7.6
  see also emotions: judgement in
justification, rational 2.4
  first person 2.4.1–7
  see also explanation: rational

Kaplan, D. 3.3.4
Kenny, A. 6.1.4
Kim, J. 1.7.4
Kuhn, T. 2.3.6

labour theory of value 4.4.3; 6.3
  weakness in 6.3.10
Lakatos, I. 3.2.5; 7.2.18
language, *see* action concepts; explana-
    tion: rational; human nature: and
    language; institutions of language;
    persons: as communicators
leading a kind of life, *see* being a kind
    of person
life, meaning of 8
  see also meanings: of actions
life of reason 3.1.1–2; 3.3.1; 3.4.8;
    6.5.8
life of truth 8.3.1–2, 9–16
life of valuing 1.1.7; 4.2.15; 4.6.10–12
Loar, B. 2.3.9
logic 2.3.4, 7; 3.2.6; 3.3.4; 3.4.5–6;
    4.6–11; 7.1.3.11
lust 4.2.9; 5.1.8; 5.2.2–4, 8–9; 5.3.6
Lyons, W. 6.1.3–4, 7

McGinn, C. 8.3.9
MacIntyre, A. 8.1.3
MacKay, D. 1.3.5; 2.1.2
Malson, L. 1.2.4
manifest image 2.2.1, 7–8, 12, 16; 2.3;
    2.5.6; 5.5.5, 9–10
  and cultural practice 2.2; 2.3
  magnified 2.2.9
Marx, K. 1.6.3; 3.2.2; 4.3.10–11
masochism 5.4.7
Masters, W. 5.1.5; 5.2.1

meanings 3.5; 8
  of actions 3.2.2–4; 7.1.8–9; 7.2.16–
    18; 7.3.4; 8.1.2–7; 8.3
  of life 8.3
  not products 8.1.4, 9
  and values 8.1.7–10
  see also persons: as communicators;
    sayings
morals, *see* values
moral theory:
  distinct from theory of valuing 1.1.2, 8
  gap in 1.1.8–9
Morton, A. 1.7.14
motives:
  basic natural 4.2.10–15
  obscurity of 1.6.7; 4.2.5–10
  see also desires; emotions

Nagel, T. 5.1.8; 5.2.4; 8.1.9; 8.3.6, 15
Nerlich, G. 3.3.4, 8
Nowell-Smith, P. 1.5.1
Nozick, R. 8.1.10; 8.3.7

obsession 6.5.2–10
ontology 1.7.1–3; 3.3.8
orgasm 5.1.4–5; 5.2.5–6; 5.3.8; 5.4.6

paradigm case 1.4.5–8; 4.6.24
Parolles 6.5.4
passions, *see* emotions
perception 1.1.7; 5.1.4; 5.5.3–7; 6.5.8;
  7.1.6; 7.2.5
performing artists 4.6.18–20; 8.1.8–9
person-contingent traits 1.1.7, 9;
  1.4.6–8; 5.1; 5.2; 5.5.4; 6.7.5–6
persons, personhood 1; 3; 4
  abstractness of concept 1.1.7, 9;
    1.4.6
  clash with scientific image 2.5; 5.5
  as communicators 3.1
  desires which are central to 7.1.3–10
  as ends 6.3.7; 8.2.5, 6
  inescapability of being one 4.3.17;
    5.1.9; 5.2.2–4; 7.2.19
  state of 3; 4.6
  tasks of 1.1.5, 12; 1.4.12; 3.1.1–2;
    3.2.4; 4.2.12–15; 5.1.1; 6.1.1;
    6.4.4; 6.7.6; 7.1.8–9; 7.2.16; 8.2.4
  see also being a kind of person;
    higher-order; human nature; pro-
    jects: broad open; reciprocal
    attitude
Pettit, P. 3.2.3; 4.1.2

philosophy, nature of 1.7.22–3; 5.5.10
pictures:
  of faces 1.7.15; 2.3.13
  and supervenience 1.7.6–10
play 4.2.10, 13; 7.1.9; 7.3.8–10
  see also sports
Popper, K. 1.3.5
practical life:
  modes of 2.2; 2.3
  role of language in 2.2.3–5
processes, products, and states 4.3.4;
  4.5.7; 4.6.3; 4.7.3; 8.1.1, 4, 8
projective action 7.1.8–9; 7.2.6; 8.1.2,
  4–7
projects:
  broad open 4.2.10–15; 7.2.10; 8.1.6;
    8.2.1; 8.3.9
  personhood 4.2.15; 7.1.9; 7.2.6–8;
    7.3.8; 8 .1.7; 8.2.3
  self-sustaining 4.2.11, 13–15; 4.3.4;
    8.2.3
propositions 3.3
psychic feelings 6.1.6; 6.2

Quine, W. 1.7.13; 2.3.6; 3.3.4; 4.3.13

radical choice 1.3.9; 2.1.6; 2.2.6;
  4.6.12; 7.2.15
Rawls, J. 1.1.8
reason:
  abandoning of 2.5.7–8
  life of, *see* life of reason
  as practice 3.4.4–10
reciprocal attitude 1.1.10–11; 3.1.3
reduction, *see* ontology; supervenience
reformers 7.2.13, 20
relativity, *see* cultural: relativity
representation 1.7.6–12
  see also desires: representation in;
    pictures
reward 8.1.6–7; 8.3
  virtue its own 8.2.3
Ross, L. 2.4.3
Ryle, G. 1.3.3

sadism 5.4.5–7
Satre, J. 1.3.9; 1.6.7; 4.1.8; 4.2.6, 8;
  4.6.11; 5.1.6, 8; 5.2.4; 5.3.4;
  6.1.4; 6.4; 6.5.1, 11; 7.2.12, 19
satisfaction 4.3.12–18; 4.7.1; 5.1.4–6
  see also higher-order: satisfaction;
    second-order: satisfaction
sayings 2.3.9; 8.3.9, 13
  and belief 2.3.9–11

and contents 3.5.1; 8.1.4
and desire 2.3.11–12
Schlick, M. 2.1.3–4; 2.2.5
science:
dialectic 5.5
doctrine 2.3.5
inconsistent with persons 2.5; 5.5
practice 2.3.5–8; 5.5.6–10
see also explanation: scientific
scientific image 2.2.1, 5, 7–9; 2.3.5;
2.5.3, 6; 5.5.5, 8–9
Scruton, R. 5.1.3; 5.2.1
second nature 1.4.9; 4.6.19, 23; 8.3.5
second-order:
desires 1.4.2, 6, 9; 3.1.6; 4.5.3–4,
6–9; 4.6; 4.7; 6.5.6; 7.2.16
satisfaction 4.5.6; 4.6.1; 6.5.6
values 8.2.1
volition 4.5.3–4, 8
self-appraisal 1.2.3; 1.4.7; 1.6.5;
3.1.5–6; 5.2.4–7
self-consciousness 1.1.11; 1.3
and consciousness of others 1.6.5;
4.2.12–15
knowledge 1.3.11; 4.2.6–10;
5.3.2–8; 5.4.13
see also interpersonal mirror; self-
appraisal; spontaneity
self-delusion 5.2.9–10
self-encounters 2.5
self-evaluation 1.4.9–10; 3.1.6; 4.5.5;
4.6.5–7; 5.2.7; 5.4.2
self-excelling, *see* excellence
self-reference paradoxes 1.3.4, 8
Sellars, W. 2.2.1, 7–8; 2.3.3; 2.5.1;
3.1.4; 3.4.3; 3.5.1–2
sentimentality 6.6.1–2, 6–9
sexual desire 1.1.9; 5.1–4
absorbing 5.1.9; 5.2.1, 3, 7–8; 6.5.8
dialectic of 5.2; 5
ideational, *see* ideational desire
sexual perversion 5.4
Shakespeare, W. 1.7.21; 5.2.8; 6.5.4;
7.3.11
Simon, A. 1.3.5
Slote, M. 1.5.1
Smith, M. 4.1.2
Solomon, R. 6.1.3
spontaneity 1.6.4; 4.6.17–18, 20–2;
5.4.2
sports 7.3.9–11
states, *see* processes, products, and
states

Stich, S. 1.7.20–1; 2.4.5; 3.2.6
Stocker, M. 4.1.2; 4.5.6; 6.2.1; 6.6.5
Storr, A. 5.4.6–7
Strawson, P. 2.1.2; 2.2.5
supervenience 1.7.4–13

Tanner, M. 6.6.8
Taylor, C. 1.3.9; 3.1.6; 4.6.5–7, 10;
7.1.4
thinking what one ought 2.5.6; 3.1.4;
3.4.3; 5.5.2, 9
Tooley, M. 3.2.1

understanding 3.5
universal *see* universalized understanding
universalized understanding 3.1.4;
3.2.5; 3.5.3, 5–6; 7.1.1, 9–10;
7.2.12, 16–19; 8.3.4, 5
universals 3.2.1, 5; 7.2.18
unselfconsciousness, *see* spontaneity
utilitarianism 1.1.8; 4.2.4; 8.1.1; 8.2.2;
8.3.8

values:
appropriation of 8.3.13–18
authentic 1.4.13; 7
false 1.1.2; 1.4.9; 7.2.13–14
field of 6.3.4–6
inarticulate 1.3.9; 3.4.3; 4.6.11–12,
14; 6.1.5; 6.5.9–10; 6.7.5, 7
mistakes about 6.5.5–11; 8.1.10
objective 1.4.12–14; 8.3.4–15
and practice 4.6.11–12
proportion in 6.3.2, 6; 6.5.2–6;
6.6.8–10
reason in 6.6.4
subjective 1.4.12
and transformed desires 1.4.12–14;
1.5; 4.6.17; 4.7.6; 5.3
valuing:
being in touch with 3
and higher-order values 3.1
see also ethics of belief
Van de Vate, D. 1.1.10; 2.1.2
virtues 1.1.1, 12; 1.4.14; 1.6.4; 3.1.5;
3.4.4, 10; 4.6.8; 6.5.9–10; 8.2
volitions 4.5.3–4, 8

wantonness 1.4.2; 4.5.8; 7.2.20
Watson, G. 1.5.2; 4.5.8
Williams, B. 7.3.11
Wittgenstein, L. 2.2.3; 3.1.4